LOUIS-FERDINAND CÉLINE

LOUIS-FERDINAND CÉLINE
Merlin Thomas

NEW DIRECTIONS

New Directions gratefully acknowledges Editions Gallimard, Paris for their permission to quote extracts of the French texts of the works of Louis-Ferdinand Céline and Delacorte Press/Seymour Lawrence for their permission to use excerpts from *Rigadoon* (Copyright © 1974 by Dell Publishing Co., Inc.).

Manufactured in the United States of America
First published by New Directions in 1980
Published simultaneously in Canada by George J. McLeod, Ltd., Toronto

Thomas, Merlin.
     Louis-Ferdinand Céline.
     Bibliography: p.
     Includes index.
     1.   Destouches, Louis Ferdinand, 1894-1961.
2.   Authors, French—20th century—Biography.
PQ2607.E834Z933   1980   843'.9'12 [B]   79-20591
ISBN 0-8112-0754-4

New Directions Books are published for James Laughlin
by New Directions Publishing Corporation,
80 Eighth Avenue, New York 10011

For Gianni and Cesira
in whose presence most of it was written

Contents

Acknowledgements

I owe especial thanks to Jean-Pierre Dauphin, not only for help and encouragement but above all for permission to consult and use material from his incomparable collection of archives concerning Céline. If this book is factually accurate, it is largely due to his generous assistance.

Much of this book is personal *opinion*: it seemed proper to make this clear by considerable use of the first person singular. However, I owe a great deal to the comments of friends and colleagues who have been kind enough to look at my manuscript. My thanks in this respect go to Alex de Jonge, Andrew Harvey, Jeremy Jeanes, Mark Treharne and Christopher Tyczka.

I also gratefully acknowledge help in the form of research grants from the Board of the Faculty of Modern Languages, Oxford, and from the French Ministry of Foreign Affairs.

Siracusa, 1978

Note on the Translations and Quotations

These translations are deliberately over-literal. They are intended above all as a guide to deciphering the French original, and at times they bruise normal English syntax (see below, p. 100, note 20). Inevitably much is lost, especially where a French word palpably has a double-meaning in context. An effort has been made to attain a comparable stylistic register: I know it has not always worked.

Something should perhaps be said about the use of so-called 'obscene' words (Céline had views on this—see below, p. 145). Some of these in French have entered into common parlance and have lost their sexual connotations in many—but not all—contexts. A good example is *con*. Sometimes in the passages quoted the only correct English translation is an unequivocal four-letter word. But more frequently it means little more than 'idiot'. A recent boulevard comedy in Paris was called *Le Roi des cons*: even in this permissive age one can hardly imagine seeing in lights in the West End the title *The King of Cunts*.

There are a few places where an English *equivalent* is given preceded by the sign (=) instead of a translation.

Céline's extensive use as a device of punctuation of three dots . . . means that this sign cannot be used to indicate an omission in the texts quoted. Such omissions are shown by placing three dots inside brackets—(. . .).

Biographical Note on
Louis-Ferdinand Destouches

27 May 1894	Birth of Louis-Ferdinand Destouches at Courbevoie, suburb of Paris. His father, Ferdinand Destouches, works in an insurance office: his mother, whose maiden name was Louise-Céline Guillou, runs a shop in the Passage Choiseul, specializing in old lace.
	Childhood spent in Paris. Sent for short stays in Germany and England. Leaves school with *Certificat d'études primaires*, and then has various jobs, mostly as errand-boy. Studying by himself for the *Baccalauréat* —passes Part I in 1919.
	Joins the army as a volunteer in Sept. 1912, serving in a cavalry regiment. Soon after the outbreak of war, is gravely wounded in action (Nov. 1914). Mentioned in despatches and awarded Médaille Militaire. (Before Pétain, as he liked to point out.) Invalided out of the army (75 per cent disability), spends some months (1915–16) in London, employed by the French Consulate. Jan. 1916 marries Suzanne Germaine Nebout in London. Leaves Liverpool in May for W. Africa (Cameroons), returning in May 1917.
1919	Begins medical studies at University of Rennes.
1919	Marries Edith Follet, daughter of the head of the medical school at Rennes.
1920	Birth of a daughter, Colette.
1924	Qualifies as a doctor.
1925–8	After practising briefly in Rennes, takes a job with the League of Nations in Geneva. Journeys to England, Africa, America, Canada, Cuba. Is divorced by his wife.
1928	In medical practice in Clichy, Paris.

1931–8   Doctor at the municipal clinic in Clichy. During this period beginning of his literary career. Journeys to Germany and to the Soviet Union. Serves for a time as a ship's doctor.

1938   Brief period in practice at St Germain-en-Laye.

1939   Volunteers for military service at outbreak of war, but rejected on medical grounds. Serves as doctor on a vessel in service between Marseille and Casablanca, which was torpedoed by a German submarine.

1940   Doctor at the municipal clinic in Sartrouville near Paris.

1942   Doctor in charge of the municipal clinic in another Paris suburb—Bezons.

1943   Marries Lucette Almanzor, former dancer at the Opéra-Comique.

1944–5   In Germany—Baden-Baden, Prussia, Sigmaringen.

1945   Arrives in Copenhagen just before the end of the war in Europe. Arrested (18 Dec.) by the Danish police at the request of the French Legation. His wife is released three months later, but he remains in custody until Feb. 1947, when he is released on parole. Definitive release in June 1947, on giving an undertaking not to leave Denmark without authorization. From Sept. 1947 until June 1951 lives near Körsor on the Baltic coast.

1950   Condemned in absence by a court in Paris to one year's imprisonment, a fine of 50,000 (old) francs, and the confiscation of half his assets, on charge of collaboration, etc., during the war.

1951   Amnestied by the military court of Paris. Returns to France with his wife. July, settles in Meudon just outside Paris and resumes medical practice.

1961   1 July. Death.

Bibliographical Note on Céline's Works

(The technical works on medical topics—1 and 2—were signed Louis-Ferdinand Destouches. With the publication of *Voyage au bout de la nuit* in 1932 came the adoption of the pen-name *Céline*, which was one of his mother's Christian names—thereafter universally used. There are various articles, interviews, etc., by Céline which are *not* included here.)

The bibliographical details are of the *editions referred to in the course of this book*. Where these are *not* the original editions, indication to that effect is given.

1   *La Vie et l'oeuvre de Philippe-Ignace Semmelweis* (first published 1924 as thesis for the Faculty of Medicine, Paris): Gallimard, Paris, 1952.

2   *La Quinine en thérapeutique*: Doin, Paris, 1925.

3   *Voyage au bout de la nuit* (first published Denoël et Steele, Paris, 1932): Bibliothèque de la Pléïade, Gallimard, Paris, 1963.

4   *L'Eglise* (first published Denoël et Steele, Paris, 1933): Gallimard, Paris, 1952.

5   *Mea Culpa* suivi de *Semmelweis*: Denoël et Steele, Paris, 1936.

6   *Mort à crédit* (first published Denoël et Steele, Paris, 1936): Bibliothèque de la Pléïade, Gallimard, Paris, 1963.

7   *Bagatelles pour un massacre*: Denoël et Steele, Paris, 1937.

8   *L'Ecole des cadavres*: Denoël et Steele, Paris, 1938.

9   *Les Beaux Draps*: Nouvelles Editions Françaises, Paris, 1941.

10 *Guignol's Band I* (first published Denoël et Steele, Paris, 1944): Gallimard, Paris, 1957.

11   *A l'Agité du bocal*: (first published in Paraz: *Le Gala des vaches*: *L'Elan*, Paris, 1948. Then separately P. Lanauve de Tartas, Paris, 1948); reproduced in *Cahiers de L'Herne*, 1972.

12   *Casse-pipe* (first published Chambriand, Paris, 1949): Gallimard, Paris, 1952.

13   *Féerie pour une autre fois*: Gallimard, Paris, 1952.

14   *Féerie pour une autre fois II, Normance*: Gallimard, Paris, 1954.

15   *Entretiens avec le Professeur Y*: Gallimard, Paris, 1955.

16   *D'un Château l'autre* (first published Gallimard, Paris, 1957): Bibliothèque de la Pléïade, vol. II, Gallimard, Paris, 1974.

17   *Ballets, sans musique, sans personne, sans rien*: Gallimard, Paris, 1959.

18   *Nord* (first published Gallimard, Paris, 1960): Bibliothèque de la Pléïade, vol. II, Gallimard, Paris, 1974.

19   *Guignol's Band II* (*Le Pont de Londres*): Gallimard, Paris, 1964.

20   *Rigodon* (first published Gallimard, Paris, 1969): Bibliothèque de la Pléïade, vol. II, Gallimard, Paris, 1974.

21   *Progrès*: Mercure de France, Paris, 1978.

Select Bibliography of Works on Céline

An essential document—though very uneven in interest, and full of horrible misprints—is the volume of the *Cahiers de l'Herne* (Paris, 1972) on Céline. (This is a reprint of *two* earlier *Cahiers* published in 1963 and 1965.) This volume contains reprints of minor texts by Céline that are hard to find elsewhere, a large number of letters by him to various correspondents, and a long series of articles, *témoignages* etc., by a diversity of people, many of them interesting, some of them fatuous. Anyone seriously interested in Céline needs to consult this volume.

Studies of Céline that are particularly helpful:

M. Hanrez: *Céline*: Gallimard, Paris, 1961. Outdated, with mistakes, but the first serious attempt to assess the author as a whole, and certainly helpful.

J. Morand: *Les idées politiques de Louis-Ferdinand Céline*: Pichon et R. Durnad-Auzias, Paris, 1972. Sensible and very informative.

A. Thiher: *Céline: the novel as delirium*: Rutgers University Press, New Brunswick, New Jersey, 1972. Useful and interesting account of the whole of Céline's output.

J.-P. Richard: *La Nausée de Céline*: Scolies Fata Morgana, Paris, 1973; essentially a reprint of an earlier study dating from 1962. Interesting and stimulating considerations, mainly on *Voyage au bout de la nuit*.

F. Vitoux: *Louis-Ferdinand Céline: Misère et parole*: Gallimard, Paris, 1973. Confined to *Voyage* and *Mort à crédit*. Irritating, but with some useful ideas.

P. McCarthy: *Céline: a critical biography*: Allen Lane, London, 1975.

Studies of Céline that are interesting:

N. Debrie-Panel: *Louis-Ferdinand Céline*: Bitte, Lyon, 1961. Shortish, well-written general study.

P. Vandromme: *Céline*: Editions Universitaires, Paris, 1963. Over-written in places, but interesting.

R. Poulet: *Mon ami Bardamu*: Plon, Paris, 1971. The best of the 'anecdotal' books on Céline. But not to be relied upon.

Note: Some of the most useful material on Céline is to be found in volume II of the Pléiade edition of his works (published 1974). The introduction and the notes (Henri Godard) are very informative.

Also in the Pléiade collection is the 'iconographical' *Album Céline* (Gallimard, Paris, 1977), prepared and presented by Jean-Pierre Dauphin and Jacques Boudillet. It contains a mass of information and 458 photographs.

Preface

'Céline? . . . Le seul romancier français depuis Proust.'

JEAN-PIERRE RICHARD—in conversation

('Céline? . . . The only novelist in France since Proust.')

'Céline . . . depuis Proust le plus grand événement de la littérature française.'

LUCIEN REBATET

('Céline . . . since Proust the greatest event in French literature.')

'En lui je vénérais la Pauvreté, le prestige du Martyre. Pour moi, je n'avais que mes ouvrages qui pussent me recommander, et que le relief des siens faisait paraître si peu de chose.'

MARCEL JOUHANDEAU

('In him I venerated Poverty, the prestige of Martyrdom. As for me, I only had my own works which might have recommended me, and which were made to seem so trifling by the vividness of his.')

'Pour nous la question n'est pas de savoir si la peinture de M. Céline est atroce, nous demandons si elle est vraie. Elle l'est.'

GEORGES BERNANOS

('For us the question is not to know whether M. Céline's picture is grim, we ask whether it is true. It *is*.')

'Certes, ses livres resteront, dans un futur qui dépassera l'imagination, les seules marques profondes, hagardes de l'horreur moderne.'

PHILIPPE SOLLERS

('Certainly, his books will remain, in a future which will exceed imagination, the only deep, anguished marks of the horror of our times.')

'Louis-Ferdinand Céline est entré dans la grande littérature comme d'autres pénètrent dans leur propre maison.'

LEON TROTSKY

('Louis-Ferdinand Céline has walked into great literature just as others go into their own homes.')

* * *

From the first extant text from the pen of Céline—the diary he kept as a soldier between 1912 and 1914:

'. . . si je traverse de grandes crises que la vie me réserve peut-être je serai moins malheureux qu'un autre car je veux connaître et savoir en un mot je suis orgueilleux est-ce un défaut je ne la crois et il me créera des déboires ou peut-être la Réussite.'

('. . . if I go through great crises which life holds for me perhaps I will be less unhappy than the next man because I want to know and understand in a word I'm proud is it a fault I don't think so and it will cause me misfortunes or perhaps Success.')

* * *

There are reasons why Céline (Louis-Ferdinand Destouches), who died in 1961, is less well known than he deserves. Political reasons. They will be discussed at length in these pages, but they are less important than the positive artistic reasons for considering him to be one of the very few great and original writers in twentieth-century France. Proust and Céline—way out in front of all the rest—are original creative artists whose work can change your view of life, not what Céline himself called 'hommes à *idéâs*': there have been plenty of those, headed by Gide, Valéry, Claudel, Péguy and so on down to Camus and Sartre. ('C'est bien le diable s'il ne sort pas dix Gides de l'Ecole Normale chaque année' ('It's pretty poor if ten Gides don't emerge each year from the Ecole Normale'), wrote Céline in 1948 on hearing of Gide's Nobel Prize: sad to think he was wrong about that—ten Gides a year for a while would be nice.)

I mean to try and present an argued and balanced assessment of Céline, but it seems honest to declare my underlying convictions at the outset, so that you can judge what I have to say in the light of them. I have to confess that my opinion of French twentieth-century prose as a whole is not very high. Intellectually interesting, of course, on many occasions. Well-intentioned too. But so lacking in any real emotional force and, with few exceptions, devoid of real linguistic invention. A good test is re-reading. The only twentieth-century French prose writers I can re-read for pleasure and with pleasure are Proust, Céline and Gide. In all other cases it is mere professional duty that pushes me through, though I wish I did not have to say this in the case of Camus. No one who loves literature can live long enough to read all he would like, and I am increasingly conscious that for me life is far too short to warrant the re-reading of, say, Duhamel, Romains, Giraudoux, Mauriac, Bernanos, Sartre, Anouilh or Robbe-Grillet, save in the case of absolute need. There are at least thirty French authors writing before 1900 whom I find inexhaustible; I'd rather spend my time on *them*. 'Relevant' is not really a meaningful critical term, but using it in its general sense, I would say that the *Chanson de Roland* is a great deal more relevant to human experience than anything I've read by, say, Nathalie Sarraute.

I should perhaps add that these melancholy views, which I really am neither proud of nor pleased about, do not apply to *all* twentieth-century literature: not to English until about 1930, not to what I know about German, and certainly not to Italian. Only to French.

The aim of this book is to present Louis-Ferdinand Céline in general terms as a writer. There are in existence in English, some specialized articles, at least two unpublished theses, and a fair number of reviews of various works by Céline and an excellent critical biography—Patrick McCarthy, *Céline* (Allen Lane, London, 1975). (There is also an interesting American study— Allan Thiher, *Céline: the novel as delirium*, Rutgers University Press, 1972.) The dimensions of this book are modest and it does not pretend to be more than an introduction to what is an immensely complicated subject and one which is going to require much more detailed research before anyone can hope to write a really authoritative piece about it. In France the literature on Céline is growing fast. Indeed, after quite a spate of anecdotal books by acquaintances, there are now a number of significant critical works, a substantial mass of correspondence, an ever-growing stream of learned articles, the first critical texts,[1] and

[1] Notably vol. II of the Pléïade edition.

launching of a series of *Cahiers Céline*,[2] and the founding in July
1976 of a 'Société des études céliniennes'. But there are still many
problems to be solved about his life, and little in the way of close
study has yet been done on the later works. It does not seem
likely that anyone can hope to produce anything approaching a
definitive piece on him for some years to come. This present
volume is certainly no more than an attempt to outline those
aspects of Céline's experience which are directly relevant to an
understanding of his creation and its processes, to indicate the
main features and qualities of his substantial literary output, and
to tackle the major issue of his 'political' activity from 1937 to
1945, activity which caused him to be neglected, even ostracized—
and quite understandably—until his death in 1961. This statement
of intent needs a little further development.

Who are the undoubtedly original prose-writers in French since
the Renaissance? A conservative list down to about 1930 would
perhaps run something like this: Rabelais, Calvin, Montaigne,
Pascal, La Bruyère, Voltaire, Montesquieu, Rousseau, Diderot,
Balzac, Stendhal, Flaubert, Zola, Gide and Proust. There would
be a good case, no doubt, for adding some of the following:
Descartes, La Rochefoucauld, Madame de Lafayette, Bossuet,
Marivaux, Laclos. Perhaps also Chateaubriand, Huysmans and
Péguy. Making up such a list is probably an idle pastime, but it
can lead to certain reflections of use. The writers mentioned seem
at first to be so varied as to have little in common: one can
certainly get some odd pairings amongst them—Rabelais and
Proust, Calvin and Stendhal, Voltaire and Zola, for instance. . . .
Yet there is one very simple and obvious characteristic that they
all have in common. However different their material, their ideas,
the structure of their works may have been, every one of them did
something to the French language as a means of intelligent communication. Style. Not elegance, not clarity, not the number of
dark vowels in the passage describing a forest, not the use of the
mot juste, not superabundance of imagery, not rhythmical ingenuity—at least, none of these things in isolation, and none of them
purely as tricks. No: style in the broad sense of expression of an
individual sensibility and imagination. (All this of course is so
obviously true of the great poets that it barely needs saying of
them.) When an author does evolve a satisfactory style of his own,
when he attains thereby a full control of his medium, what he has

[2] Ed. J.-P. Dauphin (Minard, Paris, vol. I, 1975, vol. II, 1976).

to say becomes, clearly, in one way infinitely more telling, and yet, in another way, matters less. It is possible to find the content and the standpoint in much of Pascal profoundly antipathetic, and also the personality and many of the attitudes of Rousseau. But if someone holding such views also finds it impossible to read either of them with pleasure and profit, the weakness is his not theirs.

There is much to be said for believing, when it comes to trying to make up one's mind about the writers of the twentieth century, that the only sure guide is style. Contemporary writers can often arouse in us an excitement and enthusiasm that is more attributable to our being willing to espouse their views on current problems than to their absolute merit or originality—and vice versa. A militant anti-clerical may find Martin du Gard's *Jean Barois* a greater work than it really is, and someone of left-wing views may find Malraux's glissade into the arms of de Gaulle so distasteful (I do, for one) as to affect his assessment of *La Condition Humaine*. This sort of thing applies with force only to writers who are close to us in time. That there is good reason to believe that Racine was to some extent both nasty and unscrupulous as a man, that Balzac's political views—if taken seriously—were alarmingly reactionary, need trouble us little or not at all as we read them now. Two points emerge from this. First, as Proust so rightly maintains in *Contre Sainte-Beuve*, the private life of an artist can never fully explain his creative processes. Secondly, that *engagement* (in its twentieth-century sense) may excite an artist's contemporaries, but will serve him ultimately in poor stead if it is his only virtue. If, however, a writer has contrived a mode of expression which is first of all *just* in relation to his subject matter, and then also positively inventive and resilient, he is still likely to be read in a hundred years' time, at which juncture no one will really care whether he voted with Giscard d'Estaing or with Marchais.

The purpose of these remarks is to underline a number of points with regard to Céline. He certainly forged a language of his own, alive, startling, and capable of denoting a great range of emotional experience: on this achievement rests a substantial part of the case in his favour. He was deeply concerned with the problems and the misery of human existence (as befits one who was a doctor in general practice, mostly in slum areas, for thirty-six years), but he had at no time any real political commitment:

Moi je n'ai jamais voté de ma vie. J'ai toujours su et compris que les cons sont la majorité, que c'est donc forcé qu'ils gagnent.

(Well, I've never voted in my life. I've always known and understood that the twats are in the majority and so they're bound to win.)

he wrote in 1937,[3] and throughout his life he remained detached from all political parties. Indeed, in the years before the war, as will be seen, he seemed intent above all on alienating the sympathies of both left and right. He was, in fact, politically very ignorant— he was not interested—and very naïve. He did, however, in his writings, make two incursions into the domain of what might be called 'politics', even if the 'political' content of the works is negligible. The first came in 1936, when he published *Mea Culpa*, a brief and pungent account of his disillusionment after a visit to the Soviet Union. The second was much more important, and was to have a profound effect on the rest of his life. In 1937 he published *Bagatelles pour un massacre* and in 1938 *L'Ecole des cadavres*, both substantial works, both inspired by his hatred of war and seeking to avert the conflict that was to begin in 1939. However, in these two pamphlets—the first of which at least, was written with a quite extraordinary polemical virtuosity—Céline attributes both the ills of France and the growing danger of war to the Jews, and sees as the only way of preventing war, an alliance between France and Nazi Germany.[4] Stated baldly in this fashion, these views would seem to make him not only into an anti-semite, but also into a pro-Nazi. However, the truth is much more complicated than that, as will be seen when this part of his life and work is examined closely below (Chapter 4, pp. 124ff.). For the moment it is enough to suggest that while no one in his right mind can condone anti-semitism—and indeed no attempt will be

---

[3] *Bagatelles pour un massacre* (Denoël et Steele, Paris, 1937), p. 31.

[4] He said of this period in a radio interview in 1957 (see Pléiade, vol. II, p. 939) 'Alors voilà, n'est-ce pas: je me suis pris pour Louis xv ou pour Louis xiv, c'est évidemment une erreur profonde. Alors que je n'avais qu'à rester ce que je suis et tout simplement me taire. *Là j'ai péché par orgueil, je l'avoue, par vanité, par bêtise.* Je n'avais qu'à me taire . . . *ce sont des problèmes qui dépassaient de beaucoup.* Je suis né à l'époque ou l'on parlait encore de l'affaire Dreyfus. Tout ça c'est une vraie bêtise dont je fais les frais.' (author's italics) ('Well you see, I suppose I took myself for Louis xv or Louis xiv and clearly I was deeply wrong. Because all I had to do was to remain what I am and keep my trap shut. *Guilty of the sin of pride is what I was, I admit, through vanity and stupidity.* I only had to keep my trap shut . . . *they were problems that were far beyond me.* I was born at a time when people were still talking about the Dreyfus affair. The whole thing was crass stupidity and I'm paying for it now.')

made to do so in this book—Céline's brand of it was very peculiar. So peculiar as to have caused Gide to think Céline was either joking or trying to discredit it.[5] It should also be said at once, and firmly, that Céline was predominantly anti-German, and that he cannot be said to have collaborated with the Germans during the Occupation. In a third pamphlet, *Les Beaux Draps*, published in 1941 (the last of his 'political' texts, and the only one published during the war) the tone has changed: anti-semitism is still discernible but very muted—the Germans are barely mentioned. The book is largely taken up with a Utopian plan for an egalitarian society. However, the three pamphlets were quite enough for him to be a marked man as far as the Resistance was concerned—and understandably too—so that it is not surprising that he got out of France in 1944, through Germany, and eventually to Denmark, where he had to remain until 1951. The three pamphlets were also enough for him to be virtually ostracized in France until his death and for his later works to be wrongly denigrated for a while. Only after his death in 1961 did things begin to change. (He had forecast this, saying that Gallimard, his publishers, would make a packet after he was dead.) Since then there have been two volumes of the Pléiade[6] series devoted to him (the second of which, published in 1974, is a major effort of scholarship . . .) and a considerable number of his works edited in paperback—always proof of a publisher's confidence.

What this study will suggest regarding the pamphlets and Céline's 'political' position in general, is that, shameful as the anti-semitic tone was, a considerable injustice was done to him by those who accused him of treachery and collaboration. The list of French writers who *did* undoubtedly collaborate and were much more positively pro-Nazi than Céline ever was, is quite interesting and contains some surprising names. It will also be maintained that Céline must be judged *as a whole*—with the pamphlets taken into account. It is wrong to pretend he never wrote them (they have not been republished) and equally wrong to write off his subsequent writings—five full-scale novels and

---

[5] Article in *La Nouvelle Revue Française* (April, 1938); reproduced in *Cahiers de l'Herne* (Paris, 1972), p. 468.

[6] The Bibliothèque de la Pléiade is a collection of what can be loosely called 'classical' texts (from the Middle Ages to the twentieth century). The volumes are excellently presented and—especially the most recently published ones—are edited with great care and skill by leading authorities. Publication in the Pléiade series is a kind of consecration.

various shorter pieces—because of the pamphlets. Both these
errors were being commonly committed by French writers until
relatively recently.

In the narrow sense of the word, Céline was never—even in the
pamphlets—an *écrivain engagé*. But on the other hand he was
always deeply preoccupied with what he was to call the only real
subject for the modern novelist—'les circonstances où le bonhomme se trouve' ('the plight of the average man').[7] He had,
throughout his life, a deep involvement with the predicament of
the poor, and amidst the seemingly destructive violence and
bitterness of his portrait of humanity there are constantly moments
of tenderness and compassion: he was, in fact, *engagé* in the only
way that makes sense for a great artist. Both the despair and the
compassion are directly connected with his life as a doctor.

Another major interest affected his writing throughout—love
of ballet. He wrote at various times (from 1937 onwards) five
ballet scenarii (published by Gallimard in 1959 under the title
Ballets sans musique, sans personne, sans rien), and there are countless
references to the beauty and grace of the art of ballet scattered
about his works. His first novel, *Voyage au bout de la nuit*, is
dedicated to the American dancer Elizabeth Craig, a first play,
L'Eglise, to the Danish dancer Karen Marie Jensen, and in 1943
he married Lucette Almanzor, a dancer at the Opéra-Comique.
The doctor in Céline causes part of his passionate love of the art
of dancing: even if his overall judgement of human behaviour is
pessimistic enough, he is deeply sensitive to the beauty of the
human body, and sees in dance the most admirable demonstration
of this, in terms of control, grace and the perfect functioning of
the physical mechanism. There is no eroticism in this: indeed
there is slight erotic content in his works (he considered what he
called the literature of 'L'Hââmour' to be the only real obscenity),
but rather a sense of fantasy, of irreality which arouses a new
mystic excitement.

However, it must not be thought that the emphasis I have been
laying on language means that the reading of Céline is uniquely
concerned with savouring stylistic ingenuity. He is a splendid
narrator and his novels are full of varied incident of a kind that
draws the reader ever onwards in a desire to know what will
happen next. Yet while this is so, the novels do not have a

[7] Recorded monologue, Festival FLD 149 (1950). Text reproduced in Pléïade,
vol. II, pp. 931–6.

traditional pattern of exposition, development of action and
conclusion: they have a very discernible structure—as I hope to
show later—but it is loose and unconstraining, designed to
accommodate apparent digression and to enable characters and
themes to appear and depart—sometimes temporarily, sometimes
for good—as they might in real life. The use in all the novels of a
first-person narrator makes this seem all the more natural.

The treatment of character and of setting is at times highly
realistic and at others highly tinged with fantasy. The narrator,
whether he be called Bardamu (*Voyage au bout de la nuit*), Ferdinand
(*Mort à crédit*, etc.) or Céline (*Féerie* onwards), does not overtly
seek the reader's complicity: indeed, he often startles and even
alienates the reader by revealing unlovely characteristics (see
below, p. 85). He is principally an *observer*, and only from time to
time are his own feelings brought into prominence, though he is
ultimately the chief focus for the reader's attention. We see him in
childhood and adolescence, as a front-line soldier in 1914, in wartime Soho in 1915, in Africa, in America, as a doctor in the slums
of Paris, in Germany during the Second World War just before
the collapse of the Nazi regime, in prison and in exile in Denmark
and finally in aggressive seclusion in the Paris suburb of Meudon.
The narrator stands in relationship to Céline himself very much
as does Proust's narrator Marcel to Proust, and while the gulf
between the two writers with regard to standpoint and pre-
occupations seems immense, there is an undoubted parallel in
narrative method, and, as I shall suggest later, even at times in
subject matter. Both writers are concerned with authenticity, both
engage on a journey of discovery, both devise a method for
understanding the motives of other people, and both remain
firmly rooted in their respective milieux. And, above all, both
seek to unmask falsehood and to establish what truth they can.
Whatever personal defects each may have had—poor Proust has
been gleefully stripped pretty naked of late, and Céline was far
from being everyone's idea of a nice man—as artists each was of
absolute integrity.

The quality of observation by Céline's narrators is of continuous interest. It extends through both characterization and
description of milieux in an entirely plausible and convincing way
for the most part. But there are also passages of what can only
be called fantasy, where a kind of delirious hallucinatory mood
takes hold of the narrator and causes him to launch into descrip-

tions that transcend the everyday reality of the rest of the narrative and stand in powerful relief against it. The 'hallucinatory' passages contain some of the most impressive feats of writing by Céline, enabling him to unleash a torrential lyricism that can range from the comic to the terrifying and which forms a highly personal and original part of his vision of our world. Such passages occur in every work from *Voyage au bout de la nuit* to *Rigodon*, and, except perhaps in *Féerie II, Normance*, they are very carefully placed and modulated so as to produce maximum effect.

Lest this should sound either daunting or pretentious to the intending reader, it must be emphasized that above all Céline does set out to grip and *entertain*—and he is often very funny indeed. While naturally concerned with what sort of a critical reception he got, he had a certain contempt for the activity of literary criticism. This, together with his view of the artist's role as entertainer, is clearly expressed in the recorded monologue of 1958, where he says:

> Le lecteur n'est pas supposé voir le travail. Lui c'est un passager. Il a payé sa place, il a acheté le livre. Il ne s'occupe pas de ce qui se passe dans les soutes, il ne s'occupe pas de ce qui se passe sur le pont, il ne sait pas comment on conduit le navire. Lui il veut jouir. La délectation. Il a le livre, il doit se délecter. Mon devoir est de le faire se délecter, et à cela je m'emploie.[8]

(The reader isn't meant to see the work that goes on. He's just a passenger. He's paid his fare, he's bought the book. He's not bothered about what's going on in the bunkers, not bothered about what's going on on the bridge, doesn't know how the ship is being sailed. Pleasure's what he wants. Enjoyment. He's got the book, he's a right to enjoy himself. My job is to make him enjoy himself, and that's just what I set out to do.)

Emphasis on the comic side of Céline is found too little in what has been written about him. (And is that not true also of the vast amount written about Proust, who is also a great comic writer?) Much of what he says is extremely funny—and not always abrasively so. There is no inconsistency in painting overall a pretty grim picture of society and yet finding therein the incongruities that trigger laughter: he does so throughout all his works, even in those of violent polemic. Without this powerful sense of humour, Céline would not have been able to give so affecting a

[8] See Pléïade, vol. II, p. 934.

picture of human suffering nor so shattering an indictment of our times.

Since it is upon Céline's remarkable contribution to narrative technique by means of a highly original use of language that his greatest claim to literary distinction rests, the chapters in this study have been arranged in what may seem a slightly unusual order. It is conventional to leave the subject of style until late on, but in the case of this author the issue is so important that it must be tackled earlier. From the start Céline showed himself to be an innovator in narrative manner, but it was not until after his first two novels—*Voyage au bout de la nuit* (1932) and *Mort à crédit* (1935)—that he began to forge what may be called his definitive and very idiosyncratic style. The chapter on language is placed after that on *Mort à crédit*, to facilitate the understanding of the later works. They are rewarding.

Louis-Ferdinand Destouches (1894–1961)
The relationship between his life and his fictional works

It is not yet possible to give a full and accurate account of the life of our author. This is partly because a great deal of research remains to be done about certain parts of it, and partly because he delighted in giving misleading information to critics and journalists who succeeded in interviewing him. The fact that all his fictional works were published under the pen-name Louis-Ferdinand *Céline* indicates his desire to make a firm separation between his actual life and the transposed version of it which we find in his novels. (Indeed, when he published his first novel, *Voyage au bout de la nuit*, in 1932, he had the vain hope that he would be able to preserve his anonymity.) The brief account of his life and personality which follows is given because all his narrative works pretend to be autobiographical (all have a first-person narrator), though none of them are in fact representations of what *really* happened to him. In no way does information about his life *explain* the creative process in Céline, but it shows the raw material upon which he worked and helps to situate him in the France of his time.

He was born on 27 May 1894 at Courbevoie, then as now a seedy and unattractive suburb of Paris. His father, Ferdinand Destouches, was not without education but never managed to achieve more than a subordinate position as an insurance clerk. His mother, whose maiden name was Louise-Céline Guillou, ran a shop for a considerable period in the Passage Choiseul, specializing in old lace. The Passage Choiseul nowadays is a smart arcade of shops not far from the Place de l'Opéra—in an expensive and fashionable part of Paris. Céline in *Mort à crédit* describes it in sinister terms, but it cannot have been badly placed for a business concerned with a luxury product. Céline's mother seems to have

been skilled as a repairer of old lace and also to have passed on to
her son her interest and her knowledge. Late in life at any rate (in
an interview broadcast in 1957 by Radio Lausanne) he made a
point of saying that one of the few valuables he still possessed
was a rare collection of old lace about which he knew a good deal.[1]

We do not know for certain what the circumstances of the
family were really like—Céline's depiction of his childhood in
Mort à crédit certainly makes them far grimmer than is at all
plausible—but it is reasonable to suppose that the level of
existence was that of an urban *petit bourgeois* family of the period.
They were not poor, but there were permanent money problems.
They were not ignorant, but the struggle to keep up a certain
respectability was presumably as soul-destroying then as now.
The parents seem to have had definite if limited ambition for their
son: a solid career in commerce of some kind. Elementary
education, successively at the Ecole Communale (Square Louvois),
then at the Catholic Ecole Saint-Joseph (rue du 29 juillet), and
finally at the Ecole Communale (rue d'Argentueil), seemed
enough for this, but none the less his parents found the money
for—and, more interesting still, had the idea of—sending Louis-
Ferdinand off for quite protracted stays in Germany and England
to learn the languages, in the years 1907-9. An oft-repeated
legend—which Céline did nothing to contradict—alleged that one
of his stays in Germany was cut short by his having been to bed
(at the age of fourteen) with his landlady. Her testimony is, alas,
missing, but the best evidence in favour of *something* of the kind
having occurred is the touching sequence (transferred to England)
to be found in *Mort à crédit* (see below, pp. 73ff.).

Whether Louis-Ferdinand learnt much German or much
English at this point in his life is uncertain, but what is absolutely
clear is that very few French boys aged thirteen to fifteen from his
social background would have travelled abroad at all in the years
1907-9. It would be nice to know whose idea it was. Father, who
apparently had wanted to be a merchant navy officer in sail?
Mother, who had both a business and an artistic sense? Or an
enlightened relative like *l'oncle Edouard* in *Mort à crédit*? It does
seem, however, that father communicated to Louis-Ferdinand his
own love of that sea, and that this, together with these early
journeys which revealed a world beyond the confines of the
Passage Choiseul, no doubt fostered in the child the restlessness

[1] See Pléïade, vol. II, p. 945.

which is such a feature of his life until the last ten years of it. The overall picture is that of a family in which hard work was the parents' lot and in which the only child received care and exhortation directed towards making him aware of the importance of a safe job. This was very understandable too at a time when the real economic pressure on the *petite bourgeoisie* was beginning to be felt. It would be wrong to give the usual modern pejorative force to the label *petit bourgeois* in this kind of context, and we should not be misled either by some of Céline's remarks in the late thirties when he asserts that he was *not* a bourgeois by origin. By 1937 the meaning had changed. . . . But none the less, the ideals (if they can be so described) of his parents must have been stultifying to a boy of Céline's imaginative sensitivity, even if the prejudices they seem to have espoused—including a touch of anti-semitism in father—left a mark. It must again be emphasized that much of what is being suggested here is speculative: the facts are not fully in our possession, and it is only too easy to be over-influenced by Céline's novelistic account of these years in *Mort à crédit*.[2]

If his parents' ardent desire was for him to settle down in a good, quiet, lucrative post, then it was to be disappointed. He had a series of jobs in 'business' between 1909 and 1912—in fact as, roughly, an errand-boy. However, he had ideas of his own about his future. It is not known when he was first inspired by the desire to become a doctor—he maintained that it was quite early—but at least between the ages of fifteen and eighteen he was studying by himself in his spare time. Then in September 1912, at the age of just over eighteen, Céline volunteered as a regular soldier in a cavalry regiment. It could have been to get away from his family and also to cease being an errand-boy, but there was probably another important factor—an immensely strong patriotic streak which remained with him all his life, even if, as will be seen, it showed itself at times in a most peculiar manner. Virtually nothing is known about his army experiences from 1912 until the outbreak of war in 1914. (We possess fragments of a novel covering this period—*Casse-pipe*—the manuscript Céline asserts was stolen in 1944. (See pp. 196ff.)) When war broke out he was a senior NCO and in October 1914 an incident occurred which was to affect the

[2] These years are greatly illuminated by the publication of the first volume of a biography of Céline by François Gibault—*Céline 1894–1932 le temps des espérances* (Mercure de France, Paris, 1977). M. Gibault, lawyer and legal adviser to Céline's widow, has had access to important unpublished letters of the period, many of which are of great documentary interest.

whole of his life. He volunteered for a dangerous front-line mission in Flanders, carried it out successfully, but was gravely wounded on the way back to base. He was awarded the Médaille Militaire (earlier than Pétain, as he enjoyed pointing out in later years) was mentioned in despatches and was invalided out of the army with the rating of 75 per cent invalidity. One arm was seriously affected and severe damage to his ear-drums left him with permanent tinnitus. His war experiences left a deep impression on him: on the one hand he was appalled at the futility and absurdity of war and never ceased to regard it as the greatest of evils, and on the other hand he was proud of his own achievement and of the courage of French soldiers in the First World War. The first of these attitudes emerges in many of his works, notably perhaps at the beginning of *Voyage au bout de la nuit*, in *Nord* and in *Rigodon*. The second is most forcefully expressed after the events of 1940 when, according to him, the French army did *not* stand but ran all the way from Dunkerque to the Spanish frontier.

Over a year was to pass before he was considered fit for sedentary employment. He was posted in May 1915 to the French Consulate General in London where he worked for six months while awaiting definitive release from the army. He stayed on in England until May 1916. This period of his life is sparsely documented, but there is evidence to suggest that it was a time of considerable happiness (see below, p. 186).[3] At all events, on 19 January 1916 he married Suzanne Germaine Nebout at the St Martin's Registry Office in London. She was an *entraîneuse* in a bar according to M. Gibault,[4] who also says that the marriage was not registered also at the French Consulate, so that under French law it could be disregarded . . . Be that as it may, Louis-Ferdinand left his wife in May 1916 and set off for West Africa. The atmosphere of these months in London is vividly evoked in *Guignol's Band I* and *II* (See Chapter 5).

The stay in West Africa (Cameroons) lasted a year. He was employed by the Compagnie Forestière Shanga-Oubangui as a trader, and had experience of isolated existence in the bush which comes through strongly in the African sequences of *Voyage au bout de la nuit*. He contracted severe dysentery which caused him to be invalided home, and of which he was never entirely cured.

[3] See also *Cahiers de l'Herne*, p. 201.
[4] op. cit., pp. 169–70.

Back in Paris in May 1917, he soon made the acquaintance of a remarkable journalist/pseudo-scientist, Raoul Marquis (see below, pp. 67ff.), and a little later on, together with Marquis and others, was employed for a while by the Rockefeller Foundation to give a series of lectures in towns and villages in Brittany on hygiene and the prevention of tuberculosis. He was studying at this time for the *Baccalauréat*, which he obtained at Bordeaux (Part I in April 1919 and Part 2 three months later in July). Thereupon he began medical studies at the University of Rennes. The indiscretion of his marriage in London was forgotten: in August 1919 he married Edith Follet, daughter of the Director of the Faculty of Medicine at Rennes. Their daughter Colette was born the following year.

Qualified as a doctor in 1924 at the age of thirty, with his doctoral thesis *La Vie et l'oeuvre de Philippe-Ignace Semmelweis (1818–1865)* accepted by the Faculty of Medicine in Paris and published in Rennes, with an influential father-in-law to whose practice he could surely have succeeded in due course, Céline seemed set for a comfortable and lucrative medical career. However, only a few months later, in 1925, he left his wife and child in Rennes and took a job with the League of Nations in Geneva. His duties involved a great deal of travelling, and in the following years (up to 1928) he visited England and Africa again, and also Canada, the United States and Cuba. His wife divorced him in 1926. The restlessness which he felt during the years since he left the army was shown in particularly dramatic fashion in London in 1916 and in Rennes in 1925. His third marriage was, however, to turn out very differently. . . .

In 1928 the wanderings were to cease for a while. Leaving the League of Nations, he settled down for ten years as a doctor in Clichy, a working-class suburb of Paris, first in private practice on his own, and then (from 1931 to 1938) at the local municipal clinic. There were some journeys during these years—notably to Germany and to the Soviet Union—but the main features of his life at this time were his medical duties and the beginning of his literary career.

He maintained to the end of his days that what always mattered to him most was his medical vocation and that being a writer was for him quite secondary. One of the clearest statements he ever made about this vocation was in conversation with Marc Hanrez, in 1959, two years before his death:

J'étais très médecin de tempérament; ma vocation n'était pas littéraire. A votre âge, et plus jeune même, j'avais la vocation médicale (dans ma misère, puisque j'étais tres pauvre) qui consiste essentiellement à rendre la vie plus facile et moins douloureuse aux autres. Ma pratique, si vous voulez c'est une mystique,—la seule que j'aie,—et qui ne m'a pas réussi! . . . C'est une espèce d'idéal 'bonne soeur', que j'avais puissamment: se donner entièrement a l'adoucissement des maladies.[5]

(I really did have the temperament of a doctor, and not at all a literary vocation. When I was your age, and even younger, I had a medical vocation (even in my miserable poverty—I really was poor) which means wanting to make life easier and less painful for others. My professional activity, if you like, is a kind of mysticism—the only kind I have—and it's not done me much good! . . . It's a sort of do-gooding idealism which I had very strongly: a total commitment to the relief of illness.)

He also stated that what caused him to start writing (about 1928) was the desire to make enough money to buy a decent flat. Well, maybe, and he must have had the encouragement of knowing—from his doctoral thesis—that he could indeed write (see below, p. 92).

His first two non-medical publications were *Voyage au bout de la nuit* in 1932 (see below, Chapter 1), and the play *L'Eglise* in 1933 (see below, p. 235). *Voyage* was an instant and immense success, and he became famous overnight. Despite the decision to use the pen-name Céline, he was not long able to conceal his true identity, but from that moment on he did his very best to protect himself from the consequences of literary renown. He was most unwilling to be interviewed by journalists and was determined not to become a fashionable *homme de lettres*. This is an important characteristic and one that tells a good deal about his temperament. He was not over-anxious to make money (though he certainly wanted security for his old age), for he could have made a great deal from journalism between 1932 and 1944. He had instead a genuine dislike and even contempt for what we now call the media. He continued to work as a doctor in Clichy up to 1938, he had a number of love-affairs (notably with the American dancer Elizabeth Craig), he had a number of close and devoted friends (such as the writers Lucien Descaves, Marcel Aymé and Lucien Rebatet, the painters Henri Mahé and Gen Paul, and the actress Arletty),

[5] Marc Hanrez, *Céline* (Gallimard, Paris, 1961), pp. 227–8.

and was also (1933–6) writing his second novel, *Mort à crédit*. As far as can be seen, this must have been one of the most satisfying and active periods of his life.

It was impossible for any intelligent person in Western Europe not to be aware from 1933 onwards of the growing threat of war, and Céline certainly became obsessed with this realization. His excursions into 'politics'—*Mea Culpa* (1936), *Bagatelles pour un massacre* (1937) and *L'Ecole des cadavres* (1938)—are examined at length in Chapter 4 below. All that perhaps need be said here is that the last two, with their anti-semitic content, did his reputation enormous damage, involved him in the immediate post-war years in exile and imprisonment and delayed balanced assessment of his overall literary achievement until well after his death in 1961.

If in part these 'political' works were inspired by his genuine hatred of war, none the less Céline's equally genuine patriotism caused him to volunteer for active service at once in August 1939. Rejected on medical grounds for the army, he had a lively period of service as ship's doctor on the *Shella* (running between Marseille and Casablanca) during which the ship was first in collision off Gibraltar and then torpedoed by a German submarine on the way back to Marseille. Thereupon he returned in 1940 to practice in the Parisian suburbs at the municipal dispensary at Sartrouville first, and then (1942) at Bezons. The only important event in the war years that does not require the kind of comment made hereafter in Chapter 4, is his marriage in 1943 to Lucette Almanzor, whom he had met in 1937 when she was a dancer at the Opéra-Comique.

Céline continued to write during the war. *Les Beaux Draps* (1941) was the last of his 'political' texts but he was also working on *Guignol's Band* (the first volume of which appeared in April 1944), and probably also on *Casse-pipe* (the incomplete work about the army, 1912–14).

Céline's pre-war pamphlets, *Bagatelles* and *L'Ecole des cadavres* with their anti-semitic and pro-German context, made it impossible for him to remain in France after the Allied landings in June 1944 if he wished to survive. He and his wife left Paris in July 1944 for Denmark. But they were not allowed to proceed there at once and the story of their enforced wanderings in Germany during the last months of the war is recounted—with relative accuracy—in the trilogy of novels *D'un Château l'autre*, *Nord* and *Rigodon* (see chapter 8). They were first in Baden-Baden, then for some months in Prussia, north-west of Berlin, and finally in Sigmaringen on the upper Danube where the Vichy government in exile was established. In November 1945 came the permission to leave for Denmark, where they arrived after a three-week journey through the wreckage of Germany just before the armistice.

These are the bare facts about the years 1939–45: more is said about them in appropriate context later. It is perhaps worthwhile attempting some assessment of the *kind* of existence Céline led during this period. Again, it should be emphasized that speculation inevitably plays a part in what follows. It is clear that once the war began, Céline's attitude to the Germans changed. If he had in 1937–8 urged an understanding and an alliance with Nazi Germany—and he was far from alone in this as the whole policy of appeasement showed—once war broke out, Germany was for him the enemy and France was bound to be the main victim. He had no love for Soviet Russia, and held traditional French views about the untrustworthiness of Britain. He had nothing but contempt for Pétain and the Vichy government. On the whole, he went on with his work in Paris—as doctor and as novelist—taking no active part in events. He felt, it seems, early on that Germany was doomed and his fears for the future were of two kinds. At a national level he certainly feared Russian domination of Western Europe and would have been willing to fight the Russians. On a personal level he knew full well that rightly or wrongly his life would be in danger when France was freed from German occupation. He considered genuinely that he had in no way betrayed the cause of France and that he had every right to try and survive, so that he took what steps he could—with ultimate success—to save himself and his wife from summary assassination/execution by the French Resistance movement in 1944. Cowardice? Yes, perhaps. But his life is not that of a coward, and it is perhaps more just to say that he was determined to survive and to justify himself.

The experiences in Germany in 1944–5 are described very much in terms of the will to survive—at the price of all sorts of hardships and humiliations. French literature is the richer as a result of this survival by half a dozen important novels. . . . It is clear, too, that the fate of his wife was much at the forefront of his mind during this period. She barely emerges as a character in her own right in the post-war trilogy, but the undertones are clear enough—survival is undeniably her right too.

Denmark—from 1945–51—treated the Célines both well and badly. Well in that a French request in late 1945 for Céline's extradition was not granted. Badly in that he was imprisoned in rigorous conditions for over a year (and his wife for nearly three months).[6] From April 1947 until June 1951 they lived in Denmark in a cottage north of Korsör by the sea. They were on sufferance, no more. Céline's health had been much affected by his stay in prison and those who saw him at this time bear witness to this. The pages about Denmark—mostly in *Féerie pour une autre fois I* (1952)—are the bitterest he ever wrote (which is no mean statement), and are inspired by a defiant insistence on establishing the iniquity of his persecutors.

In 1950 he was tried in absence by a court in Paris on charges of collaboration and given what can only be described as a token sentence, which indeed aroused the wrath of the left-wing press at the time. In April 1951, a military court in Paris accorded him full amnesty and he was free to return to France. In June, he and Lucette left Denmark and, after a stay in Menton and with friends in Paris, they settled down in Meudon, just outside Paris, and began a new life. Céline the traveller had journeyed enough, and virtually never left Meudon for the rest of his life. Madame Veuve Destouches lives there still.

The last ten years, 1951–61, were very productive, as can be seen from the bibliography. Céline again set up in practice as a doctor, and his wife began to give dancing lessons once more.[7] It was a life of seclusion, surrounded by the domestic animals—dogs, cats, birds—which both of them had always loved. But the outside world did impinge from time to time, and in these final years Céline revealed more of himself and his ideas about his art than ever before. He made two recordings in 1957, the weekly *L'Express* published an important interview with him (the interlocutor was Jean-Louis Bory) on 26 May 1960. And, most significant of all, he was persuaded by Gallimard (his publishers ever since 1952), to write in 1955 his *Entretiens avec le Professeur Y*, a work which gives us more information than any other about his attitude to the novel and about his methods of work (see pp. 83ff).

If he kept himself very much outside the main stream of events

---

[6] Interesting information about the stay in Denmark is provided in H. Pedersen, *Le Danemark a-t-il sauvé Céline?* (Plon, Paris, 1975).

[7] I have it on direct authority that in 1975 she could still raise her toes above her head. . . .

during these final years, he was not lonely nor without friends. If the German and Danish experiences had left their mark, if there was great bitterness about the critical silence that greeted his post-war publication, there was none the less still a powerful sense of humour running through his writing, and the originality and artistic integrity which had been visible as early as *Semmelweis* in 1924 were not dimmed.

Now while all Céline's novels have an autobiographical basis, any attempt to link them closely with the life of the author or to use them as source material for his actual life is highly dangerous and misleading. Céline was a myth-maker. He used his own experience of existence, of course, but always with deliberate distortion. A good example is to be found in *Voyage au bout de la nuit*. There is a substantial passage therein describing the narrator's experience on the production line at the Ford factory in Detroit. Céline had indeed been to the Ford factory there, and indeed knew what he was talking about. But he had *not* been on the production line: he went there as a doctor to study industrial medicine, and the results of this visit are also to be found in an article called 'L'organisation sanitaire des usines Ford'.[8] It has been amply shown that *Mort à crédit* does not give a genuine picture of his father and mother. *Guignol's Band I* and *II* are not to be taken as a literal version of his life in London during the First World War. The picture of the Vichy government in exile at Sigmaringen in *D'un Château l'autre*, while very correct in general terms of atmosphere, is not accurate in detail. Once one has accepted the fact that the novels of Céline are no more an accurate transcription of his life than *A la recherche du temps perdu* is an autobiography of Proust, it is reasonable to draw up a kind of concordance of life and work. The coverage of his life—with the reservations just emphasized—would be as follows:

1   *Mort à crédit*. Childhood and adolescence of 'Ferdinand', ending with his decision to join the army.

2   *Casse-pipe*. A fragment only, describing his first night in the army.

3   *Voyage au bout de la nuit*. A different version (not what really happened) of the entry into the army of 'Bardamu'. About a third of the way through *Voyage*, one should insert

[8] First published 1928; reproduced in *Cahiers de l'Herne* op. cit., pp. 27–32.

4   *Guignol's Band I* and *II* ('Ferdinand' in London). Then one would revert to the rest of *Voyage*, which includes his African and American experiences and leaves him qualified as a doctor with already some knowledge of the life of a *'médecin des pauvres'* in the Parisian suburbs.

5   *Féerie pour une autre fois I*. In part—those sections dealing with Paris during the Second World War.

6   *Féerie pour une autre fois II, Normance*. The wartime bombardments of Paris.

7   *Nord*. Germany in 1944—Baden-Baden, Berlin and Prussia.

8   *Rigodon*. First part—journey from Prussia to Sigmaringen, seat of the Vichy government in exile.

9   *D'un Château l'autre*. Sigmaringen, 1944-5.

10   *Rigodon*. Second part—March 1945, Sigmaringen to Copenhagen during the closing days of the war in Europe.

11   *Féerie pour une autre fois I*. Those sections—quite extensive—which deal with his imprisonment in Denmark.

12   Isolated passages in all the works published after *Féerie I* (except *Guignol's Band II*) dealing with his life in Meudon on return from Denmark in 1951.

From *Féerie pour une autre fois I* onwards he speaks in his own persona as Céline, but this does not mean that the works from then on are more accurate as autobiographical sources: there is *always* an element of fantasy and of hallucination.

Indeed, when one looks—in 1979—at the present state of information about the life of Céline, when one knows that not only many of his manuscripts but also a great mass of his correspondence are dispersed, one realizes that it is going to be a long time before an authoritative biography can be undertaken. He clearly took a puckish delight in slightly misleading the various interviewers and acquaintances who talked to him in the last fifteen years of his life. There was one moment in his life when he was indeed vulnerable—the years in Denmark after release from prison. It is sad that the most voluble contact he had at that time was a man of crocodile-like insensitivity and massive self-importance called Milton Hindus: a more sensible interlocutor at this juncture would have been immensely valuable. There is no doubt that Céline was an extremely awkward and difficult person

to know and understand—though his friends were very devoted
to him—and I confess to being relieved that I have not got to
climb up to Meudon and put perceptive questions to the subject
of this book. . . .

We shall not know the truth about large areas of Céline's life
for a good long time yet. But all that can wait: the books are
there for us to read and that is more than enough for the time
being. An explanation of the placing in this study of the chapter
on language has already been given. One other point about the
ordering of the chapters needs to be made. Consideration of the
individual works of Céline could be arranged in a number of
ways: in fact a nearly chronological approach is the most satisfactory with this author. There is a substantial chapter on the
political writings, and some reference later on to certain minor
texts, but the novels themselves—with one exception—can be
handled in the order of publication without confusion. The one
exception is *Guignol's Band II*, *Le Pont de Londres*. This, which
forms a perfectly natural continuation of *Guignol's Band I* (1944),
and was written immediately after it, was not published until 1964,
because the manuscript was 'lost' at the Liberation. I propose to
refer to the work as *Guignol's Band II*, and to treat it with *Guignol's
Band I*, i.e. *out* of chronological order of publication.

CHAPTER ONE

Voyage au bout de la nuit

This, surely, is one of the titles one would like to have hit upon—like *A la recherche du temps perdu, Splendeurs et misères des courtisanes, Wuthering Heights* and *Vanity Fair*, or, indeed, that of Céline's second novel *Mort à crédit*.

The book hit the reading public and the critics with tremendous force when it appeared in 1932. A long, violent and original novel from an unknown author, it nearly won the Prix Goncourt (and indeed should have done!) and *was* awarded the Prix Renaudot, all of which meant publicity. It was an immediate, enormous success, and Céline found himself famous overnight and pretty prosperous very soon. He had hoped by using the pen-name Céline to keep his real identity secret, but that was a vain hope and the public soon learnt at least a certain amount about Dr Destouches.

The critical reception was mixed. There was enthusiasm from both right and left, but there were also denunciations of the alleged obscenity of the book, and reservations about the so-called 'message' it contained. All this, of course, helped mightily in selling the novel to the general public: Céline in 1932 was God's gift to journalists in search of copy.

If you've never read any Céline, then *Voyage au bout de la nuit* (henceforward abbreviated to *Voyage*) is still likely to startle you even now, more than forty years since its first publication. Its view of the human predicament in modern industrial society, its audacity of language, its occasional recurring moments of compassion, its humour and its range of imagination all contribute to this effect. My account of it—and indeed the accounts of all the other works discussed hereafter—is aimed at giving a way into an understanding of its complexities; exegesis being given more prominence than actual comment.

Voyage is told in the first person by a narrator, named Bardamu, and traces his experience from the age of about twenty until his middle thirties. We see him first as a young medical student at the moment when, in a fit of enthusiasm, he volunteers for the army in 1914 at the outbreak of war, and we leave him at a date which is not ever given by himself but which must be around 1932.[1] This takes up 482 pages in the Pléiade edition, and to give some idea of the structure of the work I give the number of pages in that edition which cover the various sections of the narrative. Bardamu's active service during the war takes up thirty-seven pages, then comes a sixty-four-page section in Paris where he is recovering from wounds. Invalided out of the army he sets off to make his fortune in Central Africa (seventy-one pages), then moves to the United States (fifty-one pages), before returning to France to complete his medical studies. The longest single section of the book (106 pages) is devoted to his time in Rancy, a working-class suburb of Paris, as a general practitioner. Next a link passage of thirty pages in Paris, leading to a stay in Toulouse (twenty-eight pages), and followed by a final ninety-page section covering his working at a private mental hospital just outside Paris.

The variety of milieux here is, of course, considerable, and we are introduced to a whole series of episodic characters in the course of the narrative. Only one character besides Bardamu recurs constantly, however. This is Robinson, first met on the battlefield in Flanders and present in every section of the book (except the short link passage before Bardamu's departure for Toulouse), and whose violent death occurs at the end of the novel. The relationship between Bardamu and Robinson is the key structural device employed, and it is through contemplating the actions and attitudes of Robinson that Bardamu attains a kind of acceptance of his destiny. The subject of the book in the most general sense could be said to be Bardamu's voyage of discovery through life, impelled for years by what he once calls 'la manie qui me tracassait de foutre le camp de partout' (p. 229) ('my mania for buggering off from everywhere'), until through the practice of medicine he comes to understand the futility of so much of human existence and recognize the significance of death. But there are many more themes and a very wide range of differing moods,

[1] We are told of one of the characters who is introduced towards the end of the book, Madelon, that she was born during the war and that she looks about twenty—which would take us up to 1934 at least—(pp. 380–81).

some of which will now be described in the course of going through the novel.

The opening pages on the war are justly famous. What emerges from them is not only the horror of war but even more its enormous stupidity. Bravery is the prerogative of those without imagination—

> Quand on a pas d'imagination c'est peu de chose, quand on en a, mourir c'est trop. (p. 23)
>
> (Dying when you've got no imagination isn't so dreadful: but when you *have*, it's too much.)

—and war turns the ordinary individual into an animal intent only on survival. Here at the very start of his first novel is stated this theme of *survival* during the journey to death. It is a theme which recurs constantly in Céline, and which becomes dominant in *Féerie pour une fois I* and *II* and in the trilogy. The tone is often frankly comic, especially at the expense of officers, and even more often sardonic and wry, underplayed and even casual, as is seen in this short passage where Bardamu has been sent on a long reconnaissance patrol on horseback with full jangling equipment:

> Dès que j'eus pris la route, à cause de la fatigue, je parvins mal à m'imaginer, quoi que je fisse, mon propre meurtre avec assez de précision et de détails. J'avançais d'arbre en arbre, dans mon bruit de ferraille. Mon beau sabre à lui seul, pour le potin, valait un piano. Peut-être étais-je à plaindre, mais en tout cas sûrement, j'étais grotesque. A quoi pensait donc le général des Entrayes en m'expédiant ainsi dans ce silence, tout vêtu de cymbales? Pas à moi bien assurément. (p. 39)
>
> (As soon as I'd got underway, try as I might, I was too tired to be able to imagine with any sort of precision or details, what my own murder would be like. I jangled along, from tree to tree. My fine sabre alone, from the point of view of noise was as good as a piano. Perhaps I was to be pitied but in any case I was clearly grotesque. What *was* General des Entrayes thinking of, sending me out here in this silence dressed up in cymbals? He certainly wasn't thinking of *me*, that was clear.)

During this wartime sequence we have the first appearance of Robinson. He and Bardamu meet at night—during this same patrol—and the moment is underlined:

> Après des années et des années, je me souviens bien encore de ce

moment-là, sa silhouette sortait des herbes, comme faisaient des cibles au tir autrefois dans les fêtes, les soldats. (p. 44)[2]

(Even after years and years, I still remember that moment well: his silhouette came up out of the grass, just like used to happen at fairs in days gone by when soldiers popped up as targets at shooting-stands.)

Robinson has had enough of fighting: he wants to try and get taken prisoner. The idea appeals to Bardamu too, and indeed in their early encounters in the book Bardamu has a certain admiration for Robinson as the practical man who believes that action can change one's destiny. But there are no Germans around to capture them that night and they separate at dawn—'le Jour: Un de plus! Un de moins!' (p. 49) ('Day: one more! one less!')—one more day of life, or one less before death; you can look at it either way.

It must not be thought that Céline himself was physically a coward: his Médaille Militaire surely shows he was not. More-over, he is *not* Bardamu, though he clearly agrees with the picture of war that Bardamu gives. The experience of war marked him for life, both physically and psychologically, and in only one of his novels (*Mort à crédit*) is it absent as a theme.

The next section of the work sees him convalescent in Paris at various military hospitals and also engaging in two love-affairs, with Lola, a sexually attractive but deeply stupid American, who none the less inspires him with the first idea of 'journeying', since he feels he must discover for himself the country that produces such admirable animals, and then with Musyne, an actress/violinist who is initially fond of him but who is firmly on the make and deserts him for richer protectors. Later in America he is to recognize the harm they both did him:

Une haine vivace naquit en moi pour ces deux femmes, elle dure encore, elle s'est incorporée à ma raison d'être. (p. 212)

(There grew up in me an undying hatred for these two women—it still lasts, it has become part of my *raison d'être*.)

and these experiences help to make impossible the one human relationship that might have changed his life, as will be seen.

This Parisian interlude is important also in that it contains the first 'hallucinatory' passage in Céline. In the course of a long walk

---

[2] See below, p. 47.

Lola and Bardamu come across an abandoned fair-ground near the Porte de St Cloud, where among other things is a stall called the *Stand des Nations* where one can fire at clay-pipes and balloons and also at a wedding-party, a Mairie and a troop of soldiers in the street below. This triggers off in Bardamu a nervous crisis, as a result of which he is whipped off to a mental hospital, a victim of terror:

> Alors je suis tombé malade, fiévreux rendu fou, qu'ils ont expliqué à l'hôpital, par la peur. C'était possible. La meilleure des choses à faire, n'est-ce pas, quand on est dans ce monde, c'est d'en sortir? Fou ou pas, peur ou pas. (p. 61)
>
> (So I fell ill—feverish—sent mad (so they explained to me in hospital) by fear. It was possible. The best thing to do when you're in this world, is to get out of it—no? Mad or not, afraid or not.)

Now this seemingly desperate statement is not to be taken as a counsel to humanity. He is not *'un homme à messages'* (see below, p. 80): it is totally reasonable for Bardamu to feel this at this juncture, and Céline is doing no more than make this point.

What he is saying throughout this part of the book—and indeed in many different ways throughout all his writings—is that for the vast majority of human beings life is not notably interesting, exciting or particularly worth living. And he has the utmost contempt for sentimental liberals who deny this, and a positive hatred for Marxists who think that by establishing Stalinist Communism they will bring about the millennium.

It is worth remembering that Zola, when he gave in *L'Assommoir* his desolating picture of the Parisian slums of the nineteenth century, was attacked by the left for having 'libelled' the working-classes. The degree of controlled indignation and of genuine compassion in the book gives the lie to such an absurd charge. Céline's picture is not vastly different. Nor is—more recently— Alan Sillitoe's in *Saturday Night and Sunday Morning*. There is no reason to doubt the truth of what all three of them say. Céline's own life brought him for many years into daily contact with the poor, and he is constantly emphasizing how stultifying existence in an industrial society in the twentieth century can be for the great majority of human beings. He is unconvinced by the marvels of our consumer society and contemptuous about our so-called leaders. It is unlikely that events since his death in 1961 would have caused him to change these views.

Bardamu has another important reflection, only a few pages later, which he holds on to for the whole of the book, and indeed which Céline's other narrators later all adopt too. If you are weak, then you will derive strength from stripping those you fear of all the prestige they pretend to possess. You need to learn to consider them as they are, worse than they are, that is to say from all points of view.

> Ça dégage, ça vous affranchit et vous défend au delà de tout ce qu'on peut imaginer. Ça vous donne un autre vous-même. On est deux. (p. 64)
>
> (That frees you, liberates you and protects you beyond all that you can imagine. Gives you another self. There's two of you.)

The sense of being an underprivileged victim in a society which you despise and which, given human nature as you know it to be, you see no way of changing, is what provokes so many remarks of seemingly black pessimism in Céline, but the attitude of defiance just outlined is an element of hope and personal salvation. Adopt it and you may well find yourself in isolation but you will also acquire an independence of mind—almost what Rabelais called 'un mépris des choses fortuites' ('a contempt for things fortuitous').

If Bardamu comes to these conclusions during his period of convalescence in Paris, it is because he is confronted here with the real discovery of the gap between rich and poor. Lola leaves him because he tells her he believes neither in heroism and patriotism nor in the future, but Musyne leaves him for richer lovers. Both are anxious for him to return to the front line as soon as possible: so are the doctors and nurses at the various hospitals where he is treated. War, he concludes, is a device to enable the rich to get rid of the poor in large numbers: we have to agree that there is some evidence in support of this view.

Towards the end of this section there are some fine and moving pages about a walk he takes with his mother in the miserable suburban streets near the hospital. She is full of what Bardamu calls a tragic, resigned optimism, whereas for him 'A vingt ans je n'avais déjà plus que du passé' ('At twenty I already had only a past'). But eventually he is freed from military obligations and is able to begin his 'voyage au bout de la nuit', but not before he has a second brief meeting with Robinson, whose dishonest resourcefulness is briefly revealed.

The African sequence which follows is initially a relatively lighthearted assault on French colonists. The passengers—male and female—on board the elderly ship which takes Bardamu to the West African colony of Bambola Bragamance, are all travelling free or at reduced rates: only Bardamu himself, about to become a minor employee of the Compagnie Pordurière (one might translate this as Pshit & Co.), has paid the ordinary fare. This puts him firmly in the class of the underprivileged once more, and the result is suspicion, ostracism and threat of physical violence. The portraits of the other passengers, and of the French officials and employees in the colony itself, are amusing and sharp, and remind one of similar accounts in English of the parallel milieu on P. & O. liners and in pre-war India. But the descriptions are marked by the medical observations of the writer. All these ignorant and odious people are rotting with disease aided by alcohol:

Les moustiques s'étaient chargés de les sucer et de leur distiller à pleines veines ces poisons qui ne s'en vont plus . . . Le tréponème à l'heure qu'il était leur limaillait déjà les artères . . . L'alcool leur bouffait les foies . . . Le soleil leur fendillait les rognons . . . Les morpions leur collaient aux poils et l'eczéma à la peau du ventre . . . (p. 115)

(The mosquitoes had taken it on themselves to suck them and to distil full into their veins those poisons which stick . . . At that very moment the treponema was already filing away at their arteries . . . alcohol was inflating their livers . . . the sun was cracking open their kidneys . . . crabs were sticking to their pubic hair and eczema to the skin of their stomachs . . .)

As for the indigenous population, Bardamu regards them with a kind of detached pity, but not with the edgy disgust at their white masters:

La négrerie pue sa misère, ses vanités interminables, ses résignations immondes; en somme tout comme les pauvres de chez nous mais avec plus d'enfants encore et moins de linge sale et moins de vin rouge autour. (p. 141)

(The blacks stink of their poverty, their interminable vanity, monstrous resignation; all in all just like our own poor but with still more children and less dirty linen, less red wine around them.)

It is to be remembered that only shortly before the publication of *Voyage*, had appeared Gide's *Voyage au Congo* and *Retour du Tchad*, which had alerted a very wide public in France to the evils of colonialism and to the exploiting activities of the Grandes Compagnies Concessionaires of which Céline's Compagnie Pordurière is an example. The subject was alive: the glories of colonial expansion à la Lyautey were being questioned. But Céline is not really making political points as was Gide. (Nor was he affected by any particular sexual interest in the black population, male or female.)

Bardamu is soon sent off to manage—by himself—a remote out-station in the middle of nowhere. On his way there he meets a French sergeant, Alcide, who has volunteered for a second spell of three years' service in miserable lonely conditions—why? Because he is paying for the education in France of a little niece whom he barely knows and whose parents are dead (see below, p. 116 for the words used about this). If Alcide had been more intelligent, perhaps he would have been able to find a better and less painful way of helping his niece. That is not the point: he makes the sacrifice which he is capable of imagining. And Bardamu watches Alcide sleeping, and reflects sadly that asleep he looks just like anyone else, and that it is a great pity that there is no way of distinguishing between the good and the wicked. This passage is justly famous: one of the emotional summits of the novel and not to be forgotten in view of the grim nature of much of the rest.

Bardamu's stay in the forest out-station Bikomimbo is a disaster. It is described in pages of almost lyrical intensity, strongly atmospheric, as though written through the fever that quickly overtakes him there. His predecessor in the post hands over briefly to him, and disappears in the course of the night: only the next morning does Bardamu realize that it is Robinson who, true to form, has again looked after his own interests. It is not long before Bardamu too leaves Bikomimbo, crosses into the Spanish colony of Rio del Rio, whence (and the whole of this section is a kind of fantasy provoked by fever) he finds himself shipped on a galley bound for America.

From the primitive nastiness of the African jungle he is thus transported to the sophisticated nastiness of the American urban jungle. The 'hallucinatory' section ends when he eventually lands in New York in the cold rain of the morning rush-hour:

. . . il en cheminait déjà tellement d'autres de gens, des petits et des gros qu'ils m'emmenèrent avec eux comme une ombre. Ils remontaient comme moi dans la ville, au boulot sans doute, le nez en bas. C'était les pauvres de partout. (p. 141)

(. . . there were already so many other people going along—big and small alike—that they carried me along with them like a ghost. Like me they were going up into town, to work doubtless, nose downward. The same poor you find everywhere.)

The American experience gives but further reinforcement to what Bardamu is generally coming to accept: everywhere in the world the lot of the poor is the same. In the hall of the New York hotel (where, with his last dollars, he has taken a room for a night or two) he would like to enter into conversation with some of the sleek well-dressed girls seated there, but he fears he might be arrested—'Presque tous les désirs du pauvre sont punis de prison' (p. 200) ('Almost all the poor man's desires are punishable with prison'). He also comes to realize that the excitement of travel, of knowing new countries is an absurdity (this will lead him soon to determine on return to France to undertake his study of medicine):

. . . et l'infini s'ouvre rien que pour vous, un ridicule petit infini et vous tombez dedans . . .

Le voyage c'est la recherche de ce rien du tout, de ce petit vertige pour couillons . . . (p. 214)

(. . . and infinity opens just for you—a laughable little infinity— and you fall into it . . .

A journey is the search for this nothing, this little vertigo for fools . . .)

After this statement on the first word in the novel's title, a few pages later—in the course of a last embittered meeting with the odious Lola—comes a short paragraph which gives the essential clue to the rest of the title's significance. Lola is trying to get rid of him—and does so a little later. He reflects bitterly to himself:

. . . à force d'être foutu à la porte de partout, tu finiras sûrement par le trouver le truc qui leur fait si peur à eux tous, à tous ces salauds-là autant qu'ils sont et qui doit être au bout de la nuit. C'est pour ça qu'ils n'y vont pas eux au bout de la nuit! (p. 219)

(. . . by dint of being chucked out of everywhere, you're bound to finish by finding the thing which scares them all so much—all of those swine, how ever many there are, and which must be at the far end of the night. That's why they don't go to the far end of the night!)

And in the next few pages it would seem that he discovers this 'truc qui leur fait si peur' and uses it with extreme, brutal calm. It is the fear of death. It is not surprising that Céline's greatest admiration in French literature was for Villon ... The triumphant tone of the *Ballade des seigneurs du temps jadis* on the theme of Death the leveller[3] has never been more powerfully re-echoed than in *Voyage au bout de la nuit*.

From New York, Bardamu goes to Detroit where, after a horrifying experience of working on the production line in the Ford factory,[4] and a further meeting with Robinson, again on the run, and destitute in America, he meets Molly, a prostitute who falls in love with him and causes the second great emotional climax of the book. Indeed, the pages about Molly (227–36) contain the essential clues to the understanding of the whole work, and, it could equally be maintained, to the general outlook of Céline on humanity, an outlook which never fundamentally changed throughout his life thereafter. The beauty, gentleness and affection of Molly come very close to deflecting Ferdinand Bardamu from his now determined course (which is the fulfilment of his medical vocation), and these qualities inspire in him at all events intense and touching self-examination and self-reproach. It is too late. . . . He cannot now accept the existence Molly offers him. . . . If he had known her before *cette garce de Musyne* and *cette fiente de Lola* who had absorbed all his youthful enthusiasm ...

Mais il était trop tard pour me refaire une jeunesse. J'y croyais plus ... Je l'aimais bien, sûrement, mais j'aimais encore mieux mon vice, cette envie de m'enfuir de partout, à la recherche de je ne sais quoi, par un sot orgueil sans doute, par conviction d'une espèce de supériorité. (p. 229)

---

[3] De plus parler je me desiste:
Le monde n'est qu'abusion.
Il n'est qui contre mort resiste,
Ne qui trouve provision.

(I'll say no more about this:
The world is merely deceit.
There is no one who can resist Death,
Nor find protection against it.)

[4] Céline had visited the Ford factory in 1926, and published a short treatise ('La médicine chez Ford', reproduced in *Cahiers de l'Herne*, op. cit., pp. 27–32) on the subject of the use of physically inferior personnel in the production-line work force.

(But it was too late to refashion myself a youth. I didn't believe in it any more! . . . I was fond of her, of course, but I liked my vice even better, this desire to run away from everywhere in search of God knows what, driven by a silly pride doubtless, my belief in some kind of superiority.)

In saying this, Bardamu does not spare himself; and, much as I distrust 'autobiographical' criticism *à la manière de* Sainte-Beuve, I think it is fair to extend this to Céline himself. There is here a tough, non-self-pitying statement about the position of the intelligent victim of modern society—victim in part indeed because of his temperament, and with a fair dose of masochism—but felt and genuine. It is because of this toughness and overall lack of sentimentality that the closing lines of the first half of the novel have such an intense emotional effect:

Pour la quitter il m'a fallu certes bien de la folie et d'une sale et froide espèce. Tout de même, j'ai défendu mon âme jusqu'à présent et si la mort, demain, venait me prendre, je ne serais, j'en suis certain, jamais tout à fait aussi froid, vilain, aussi lourd que les autres,[5] tant de gentillesse et de rêve Molly m'a fait cadeau dans le cours de ces quelques mois d'Amérique. (p. 230)

(I doubtless needed a great deal of foolishness to leave, a foolishness of a dirty and calculating sort. All the same I've defended my soul up to now and if tomorrow death came to fetch me, I'm sure I would never be quite as cold, nasty, heavy as the others—Molly made me a gift of so much sweetness and dreams during those few months in America.)

From this moment on, the novel changes abruptly in subject matter and Bardamu stirs no more from France—and indeed only briefly from Paris and its suburbs. Half a page carries us over the five or six years of his medical studies, and then we launch into the long account of his life as a doctor in Garenne-Rancy, a miserable, sordid working-class suburb of Paris. The rest of the novel is coloured deeply by the medical experience, and the understanding of this grows steadily as the work proceeds. Also from now on, Robinson, from being a mysterious episodic figure, turns into a major character, barely absent from the narrative.

It would be a pity to recount the plot of the rest of *Voyage* in any detail. It will be perhaps enough to say that the main

[5] See below, p. 240.

plot-line hereafter concerns Robinson. In Rancy, in order to make
a substantial sum of money, he agrees to help in the killing of an
eccentric old woman, Madame Henrouille, whose son and
daughter-in-law want her out of the way. The booby-trap that
was meant to kill Madame Henrouille explodes in Robinson's
face and he is temporarily blinded. The whole affair is covered
up and Robinson is sent away to Toulouse with Madame Henrouille (they now have a kind of understanding), where Robinson
falls briefly in love with a girl called Madelon and where eventually
he does kill Madame Henrouille. He tires of Madelon and returns
to Paris. She follows him, and shoots him in exasperation.
Throughout all this, Ferdinand Bardamu, who recounts it, is
moving towards his final position of despairing resignation. I
want to make two kinds of comment on this second half of the
novel. First to indicate the importance and meaning of Robinson,
and secondly to point out some passages which take up themes of
general Célinian significance.

From the moment of that memorable first meeting in the front
line in 1914, Bardamu has had a curious admiration—even
respect—for Robinson, as the kind of man who really believes
that his fate in life depends on his own actions and resourcefulness. Robinson wants to be taken prisoner by the Germans in
order to survive the war. Interesting idea, Bardamu seems to say.
Robinson has devised an effective way of raising money during
the war by playing on the feelings of the relatives of war casualties.
Bardamu again seems to approve. Robinson has defrauded the
Compagnie Pordurière in Africa of substantial sums of money
and leaves Bardamu to carry the can. Reasonable again, feels the
latter. In America, where Bardamu fully expected him to succeed,
Robinson fails completely and returns to France. Bardamu is for
the first time somewhat surprised. From his re-appearance (in
Rancy) Robinson is judged differently by Bardamu, who now
begins to see through the inefficacy of Robinson's independent
outlook. As Bardamu grows in perception about the realities of
the human condition, about its miseries if you are poor, about its
futilities if you are rich, about the terrible way in which the
innocence of children turns into the cruelty, selfishness and
ignorance of adults, about the ignorant, crass stupidity and uselessness of 'leaders', about the rarity of love and the triviality of
sexual desire, about the grotesque escape routes men seek through
gluttony and alcoholism, about the only eternal verities of pain,

old age and death, so Robinson's continual efforts to fight his
destiny seem more and more petty and less and less estimable.
However, there comes even for him a moment of truth which
moves Bardamu, gives rise to some of the most impressive and
compassionate pages of the novel and leaves us with Céline's
final statement about the 'voyage au bout de la nuit' as the novel
ends. Whereas at an earlier stage—when he was temporarily
blinded—Robinson was unwilling to accept the notion of his own
death, there comes a time when he almost seems to welcome it, to
provoke its onset. It has been suggested that Robinson is a kind
of *double* of Bardamu: that he represents *action* as opposed to
passive *acceptance*. There is some truth in this, but it is of limited
utility. Robinson is rather to be thought of as an average, deluded
human being who never really has a chance and who only realizes
this dimly very late on. Bardamu can see this clearly from the
Rancy section onwards and knows that he is powerless to affect
the course of events—even if he thought it right to do so. The
death of Robinson none the less is treated with the same emotional
involvement that has been noted at key points in the novel already,
and is made all the more effective by being described in almost
clinical terms by the watching Bardamu. A very great deal of
nonsense has been written about the desolating, grinding
nihilism of Céline. (The same sort of rubbish was, of course,
written in the nineteenth century, first about Balzac, then Flaubert
and, most obviously of all, about Zola. Perhaps it is one of the
tests of literary distinction to provoke contemporary critical
idiocy? No one had said anything quite as silly about Eugène Sue,
Champfleury, Bourget, Mauriac or Malraux: understandably!)
What there is in Céline can much more truly be described as an
understanding of the immense, worldwide misery to which the
great majority of human beings are condemned, an understanding
which is never sentimentalized, but which is profoundly derived
from the clinical standpoint of the doctor. In this respect Céline
is a descendant of Zola: *L'Assommoir*, as I've said, was attacked
by the left on the grounds that it was a libel on the working
classes, and *Voyage* shocked communist critics because it contained no note of revolt and—seemingly—no note of hope (see
below, p. 124). Zola and Céline could reply with the same voice,
even if their intentions were profoundly different, to the effect
that their aim was the faithful representation of a certain state of
affairs. Just as in Zola there is at times a sense both of indignation

and of compassion, so there is in Céline. And if Zola was to go on to write *Les Trois Villes* and *Les Quatre Evangiles*, Céline was once to venture upon a similar terrain in *Les Beaux Draps* (see below, pp. 165ff.).

My remarks about the remaining 350 pages of *Voyage*, pointing out the main themes and moods of the work, are directed to showing the humanity of the authorial standpoint concealed as it often is by the apparent neutrality of the narrator Bardamu. This neutrality, this detachment wears thin on countless occasions: 'les circonstances où le bonhomme se trouve' is a subject which cannot be treated dispassionately, especially by an author who seeks above all to transmit *emotion* and not ideas (see below, pp. 80 ff.).

Céline's ability to evoke atmosphere has been seen in the foregoing pages, but nowhere is his skill more visible than in the pages devoted to Rancy (237ff.). The whole of this section is impressive: it is studded with isolated sentences whose evocative power is due to a mixture of simplicity of diction and sophistication of imagery.

> Les maisons vous possèdent, toutes pisseuses qu'elles sont, plates façades, leur coeur est au propriétaire. Il envoie son gérant, la vache . . . La lumière du ciel à Rancy, c'est la même qu'à Détroit, du jus de fumée qui trempe la plaine depuis Levallois . . . Faut avoir le courage des crabes aussi, à Rancy, surtout quand on prend de l'âge et qu'on est bien certain d'en sortir jamais plus. (p. 238)

> (The houses take hold of you, piss-coloured as they are, flat façades, their heart belongs to the owner. He's never to be seen. Wouldn't dare show himself. He sends his agent, the swine . . . The light's the same in the sky over Rancy as over Detroit, smoke juice which soaks the plain right from Levallois . . . You need the tenacity of crabs too, in Rancy, above all when you start getting old and you know quite well you'll never get out again.)

To see the sun one needs to leave Rancy, covered as it always is by industrial smoke, and climb up for instance to Sacré-Coeur. From there one can see Rancy:

> C'était nous, et les maisons où on demeurait. Mais quand on les cherche en détail, on les retrouve pas, même la sienne, tellement que c'est laid et pareillement laid tout ce qu'on voit.
> Plus au fond encore, c'est toujours la Seine à circuler comme un grand glaire en zigzag d'un point à l'autre.
> Quand on habite à Rancy, on se rend même plus compte qu'on est

devenu triste. On a plus envie de faire grand'chose, voilà tout. (p. 241)

(There we were, and the houses we lived in. But when you try to look closely, you can't find them—even your own—because it's all so ugly, everything you see is identically ugly.

Further on again, the Seine is still flowing round, zigzagging from one bridge to another, like a great gob of spit.

When you live in Rancy, you don't even realize any longer you've become sad. You no longer want to do much, that's all.)

The visual picture of Rancy is paralleled by impressions of its inhabitants, especially of course of Bardamu's patients, and the most vividly presented of these is Bébert, the little nephew of his concierge. The language used about him is of infinite tenderness. It's safer to love children if you need to express love, because there's always a chance that a child will grow up into less of a shit than most human beings, and as for the gentle, delicate slum victim Bébert:

Sur sa face livide dansotait cet infini petit sourire d'affection pure que je n'ai jamais pu oublier. Une gaîté pour l'univers. (p. 242)

(Over his livid face there flitted that infinite little smile of pure affection I've never been able to forget. Kind of cosmic cheerfulness.)

Alcide, Molly, Bébert . . . three human beings who stand out in *Voyage* and who represent a kind of hope for humanity . . . Simple, uneducated, natural, good . . . they affect and modify the attitudes of Bardamu . . . even if he maintains his detachment from the ordinary miseries and nastiness of human conduct. Bébert falls victim to a rare kind of typhoid and despite all the efforts of Bardamu—including specialist consultation, which enables Céline to express angry contempt for the impersonality of certain kinds of medical research—he dies. Bardamu vainly questions himself about his responsibility in all this:

Je cherchais quand même si j'y étais pour rien dans tout ça . . . J'ai fini par m'endormir sur la question, dans ma nuit à moi, ce cercueil, tellement j'étais fatigué de marcher et de ne trouver rien. (p. 288)

(All the same I was trying to see if all of that was anything to do with me . . . I finished falling asleep over the question, in the coffin of my personal night, exhausted from walking and finding nothing.)

The members of the Henrouille family have been introduced

before the death of Bébert. Much of the material concerning them is comic—notably, for instance, the first confrontation between Bardamu and old Madame Henrouille (pp. 354–7)—and indeed continues to be so throughout, though with elements of very black humour at times. Céline used them essentially to make two points: first to give a picture of the horrible rapacity, small-mindedness and selfishness of the *petite bourgeoisie* represented by M. and Mme Henrouille: secondly to show how the hopelessness of old age can sometimes be transformed into surprising energy, and a contempt for death once a new purpose in life has been acquired, as in the case of old Mme Henrouille when she survives the attempt on her life arranged by Robinson:

> Etre vieux, c'est tomber dans cette insipide relâche où n'attend plus que la mort. Le goût de vivre lui revenait à la vieille, tout soudain, avec un rôle ardent de revanche. Elle n'en voulait plus mourir du coup, plus du tout. De cette envie de survivre elle rayonnait, de cette affirmation. (p. 319)

> (Being old is a question of falling into that insipid giving-up where you've nothing else to wait for except death. The old woman's taste for life came back to her all of a sudden, together with an ardent role of revenge to play. She didn't want to die straight off anymore, not at all. She was radiant with this desire to survive, with this affirmation.)

For Robinson, however, the accident which blinds him temporarily induces a despair and an expressed intention of suicide which he is none the less too much of a coward to carry out. In a key passage, Bardamu reflects on the nature of cowardice:

> Lâche qu'il était, je le savais, et lui aussi, de nature, espérant toujours qu'on allait le sauver de la vérité . . . On dirait qu'on peut toujours trouver pour n'importe quel homme une sorte de chose pour laquelle il est prêt à mourir et tout de suite et bien content encore . . .
> Robinson n'était pas prêt à mourir dans l'occasion qu'on lui présentait. Peut-être que présentée autrement, ça lui aurait beaucoup plu . . . En somme la mort c'est un peu comme un mariage. (pp. 324–5)

> (Coward as he was by nature—I knew and he too—always hoping he was going to be saved from the truth . . . You'd think you could always find—for any man—some sort of thing for which he's ready to die, straightaway and what is more quite happily . . .

Robinson wasn't ready to die in the situation presented to him.
Perhaps, presented differently it would have pleased him a lot . . .
In fact, death is not unlike a marriage.)

These two attitudes to death are revealing. Death is indeed at the
end of the 'voyage au bout de la nuit'; acceptance of that is what
men fear (as was seen above in the case of Lola), but if you have a
role to play, you will not fear its onset. Alternatively, if life seems
to hold no role for you, it may be that death will be at length
accepted with relief—we shall see Robinson come to this.

After Rancy, there is a short period for Bardamu in Paris itself,
notable mainly for another 'hallucinatory' section. Bardamu and
Tania, a dancer, spend a long day together and end up drinking
far into the night at a bar near the Place du Tertre.

Nous venions d'arriver au bout du monde, c'était de plus en plus
net. On ne pouvait aller plus loin, parce qu'après ça il n'y avait plus
que les morts. (p. 359)

(We'd just arrived at the end of the earth—it was more and more
obvious. You couldn't go farther, because after that there was
nothing but the dead.)

And suddenly before him the dead begin to appear in the skies
in their thousands—beginning with Bébert and including many of
his patients and others he has known. But, fortunately, Molly is
not among them . . . yet.

Bardamu shortly afterwards sets off for Toulouse where he
finds Robinson nicely installed, his eyes on the way to recovery,
making a quiet income along with old Mme Henrouille and with
a girl called Madelon, by showing tourists around the crypt of a
church which contains a kind of charnel-house with well-
preserved, long-buried corpses. Perhaps the most revealing
passage of this part of the book is about a day spent in the country
with Madelon and Robinson. They have a rather miserable
morning in a rowing boat under the hot sun, but in the afternoon
they find themselves invited on board a luxury houseboat to join
a party of somewhat inebriated 'rich' people. Nowhere in the
book does the sense of the barrier between rich and poor emerge
more clearly than in these pages (pp. 392–8), especially perhaps in
the following phrases:

Ils ont une certaine manière de parler les gens distingués qui vous
intimide et moi qui m'effraye, tout simplement, surtout leurs

femmes, c'est cependant rien que des phrases mal foutues et pré-
tentieuses, mais astiquées alors comme des vieux meubles. Elles
font peur leurs phrases bien qu'anodines. On a peur de glisser
dessus, rien qu'en leur répondant . . . C'est excitant, mais ça vous
incite en même temps à trousser leurs femmes rien que pour la voir
fondre, leur dignité, comme ils disent . . . (pp. 393–4)

(Smart people have a certain way of speaking which intimidates you,
and me, it scares me, nothing more complicated than that—above
all their women, and yet it's nothing more than badly stuck-together
pretentious sentences—but polished up like old furniture. Their
sentences frighten people, even though they're anodine. You're
afraid of slipping on them, just by replying to them . . . It's exciting,
but it incites you at the same time to have it off with their women,
just to see what they call their dignity, melt . . .)

When Robinson finally pushes Madame Henrouille down the
steep stairs of the crypt, Bardamu prudently leaves Toulouse at
once, and is lucky to find a job at a private mental home just
outside Paris, at Vigny-sur-Seine. Not very long afterwards
Robinson appears, having had more than enough of Madelon
(and of her mother too). But Madelon is tenacious and follows him
to Vigny-sur-Seine. In a remarkable final thirty pages of the
novel, Madelon and Robinson together with Bardamu and a
complaisant Slovak nurse at the hospital called Sophie, spend a
long evening together at an open-air fair in the Paris suburbs.
Roundabouts, Big Dipper, stalls of all kinds (including notably
the *Stand des Nations*, unchanged since Bardamu had seen it years
before at St Cloud, with Lola, and once again at Rancy); plenty of
entertainment, indeed, but Madelon is determined to provoke a
show-down with her reluctant Robinson. On their way back to
Vigny in a taxi, she shoots him, jumps out of the taxi and disappears. Robinson lives only for an hour or two. I know of no
description of death in a work of fiction that is more vivid or
affecting than these underplayed and simple few lines:

Il nous tenait par la main. Chacun une. Je l'embrassai. Il n'y a plus
que ça qu'on puisse faire sans se tromper dans ces cas-là. On a
attendu. Il a plus rien dit. Un peu plus tard, une heure peut-être,
pas davantage, c'est l'hémorragie qui s'est décidée, mais alors
abondante, interne, massive. Elle l'a emmené. (p. 487)[6]

(He held our hands. One each. I kissed him. There's nothing else

[6] See also below, p. 108, for further quotation from this section.

one can do in those cases without making a mistake. We waited. He said nothing else. A bit later—an hour perhaps, not longer—the haemorrhage set in—copious, internal, huge. It carried him off.)

Bardamu has some five pages of reflection after this. He walks in the small hours along the banks of the Seine, and certain truths come to him. . . . The death of Robinson is almost for him, we may feel, like the revelations that come to Marcel at the end of Proust's *Le Temps retrouvé*. (Céline had equivocal views about Proust, but on balance had a definite admiration for his achievement.) Robinson, he feels, decided upon his own death: he could have avoided it. This was the moment when he was able to accept a notion stronger than death itself, whereas earlier at the time of his blinding he had been unable to conceive anything of the kind. It all amounts to a question of ultimate acceptance of the lot of humanity. As Bardamu thinks of himself he understands that for him the time has not yet come to have such heroic notions. Life for him will go on, as it will for the majority of suffering human beings. Dawn is on the way. The lock gates on the river begin to move. The day's work is about to commence in the grim and dirty first light:

> Voici que reviennent de plus loin encore les hommes. Ils s'infiltrent dans le jour sale par petits paquets transis . . . Il faudra bien qu'ils crèvent tous un jour aussi. Comment qu'ils feront?
>
> Ils montent vers le pont. Après ils disparaissent peu à peu dans la plaine et il en vient toujours des autres, des hommes, des plus pâles encore, à mesure que le jour monte de partout. A quoi qu'ils pensent? (p. 492)

> (These are the men coming back from even farther away. They infiltrate themselves into the dirty day in shivering little groups . . . They'll all have to die one day too. How will they manage?
>
> They go up towards the bridge. After, they disappear little by little into the plain and still others arrive, men, even paler ones, as fast as the day breaks all round. What are they thinking of?)

In the riverside café which has already opened, the clientele want to hear all the details of Robinson's death. The policeman, Mandamour, who was a friend of Robinson, and has taken charge of the body, has drunk too much. He has to be restrained from demonstrating the genuine fire-dance. . . . He falls asleep. . . . Outside, from the river comes the whistle of a tug. And with an image that already prefigures one that Céline was to use more than

twenty years later (see below, p. 88) to describe how he seeks to
affect the sensibility of his readers, the book ends thus:

> Il appelait vers lui toutes les péniches du fleuve toutes, et la ville
> entière, et le ciel et la campagne, et nous, tout qu'il emmenait, la
> Seine aussi, tout, qu'on n'en parle plus. (p. 493)

> (It called towards itself all the barges of the river—all of them—and
> the whole town, and the sky and the countryside, and us, took
> everything along with it, the Seine as well, everything, and there's
> no more to be said.)

This final sentence is not one of desolation as one might easily
think. 'Qu'on n'en parle plus' could perhaps be thought to mean
no more than weary disgust with all that has happened. But the
real sense is that a chapter is closed. Life does have to go on:
Bardamu has completed his 'voyage au bout de la nuit', and he
knows now what there is at the end of the journey. Death indeed,
but not yet for him. A page is turned.

CHAPTER TWO

Mort à crédit

If you bring off a massive success with your first novel, the newspaper critics are all ready to pounce on your second, and to explain that they were of course taken in the first time round by a certain facility, a certain freshness and novelty.

It's not too surprising that Céline's second novel, *Mort à crédit* (1936), had a mixed reception. To the unperceptive it looked, perhaps, like a repeat of *Voyage*, with the addition of some erotic material—the only work of Céline where this occurs, incidentally. Few at the time of its appearance saw how the style of Céline had evolved in the four years between the two novels. But there were enough favourable articles for the book to have an enormous sale. And there are many people now who would consider it his greatest novel.

This time the narrator is simply called Ferdinand. Apart from the thirty-page opening section which shows Ferdinand as a doctor (follow on from *Voyage*, we assume) the novel is written in flash-back, and deals with Ferdinand's childhood and adolescence. It is in some ways a more violent and more outspoken book than *Voyage*, but it is also very much more comic. There are plenty of places in *Voyage* where a tough but puckish humour is present: *Mort à crédit* is for long periods very funny indeed. *Voyage*, as we have seen, is often written from a 'medical' standpoint: *Mort à crédit* even more so, with a concentration (some would say) on the natural functions, and a famous erotic passage (cut in certain popular editions, but found in full in the Pléiade text, on the grounds presumably that if you can afford to buy the Pléiade you are not corruptible).

There is a curious structural similarity between the two works. In each there is a first half which covers a substantial period of time and which moves from one milieu to another, and in each there is a second part where a major character other than the narrator takes over—Robinson in *Voyage* and Courtial des Pereires in *Mort à crédit*. Both works reflect the same overall point of view about the human condition and both end in the same mood of despair tinged with acceptance of the future. It is again important to stress that although there is clearly auto-biographical material in *Mort à crédit*, it is heavily transposed as always with Céline: the picture Ferdinand gives of his parents and of his childhood has points of contact with the experience of Céline—topographical for instance—but is by no means to be taken as a realistic re-creation of that experience.[1]

I shall leave aside, when discussing *Mort à crédit*, the attitudes which are carried on from *Voyage* and concentrate instead on its new characteristics. But first, a brief indication of the relative length of the various sections of the novel, using for this purpose page references to the Pléiade text. There is an initial section (pp. 501–33) forming a kind of prologue set in the present, which needs to be examined. Then (pp. 533–688) comes the first of two massive blocks of linear narrative, namely, childhood of Ferdinand, mostly in Paris, but including a stay in Dieppe and an epic excursion to Newhaven. Ferdinand is then sent (pp. 688–758) to England to learn the language. He does not do so, but he learns a lot about the English. Returning home under a cloud, he has a violent row with his father and is looked after for a while by his uncle Edouard (pp. 758–815), who eventually finds him a job as secretary/factotum to an inventor/scientific journalist called Courtial des Pereires. Their activities in and around Paris are covered in the second massive narrative block (pp. 815–975). A series of disasters causes Courtial to leave Paris and engage in experimental agriculture in a bleak and remote part of the country-side not far from Paris—Blême-le-Petit. This section (pp. 975–1062) ends with the suicide of Courtial and the return of Ferdinand to Paris where once again Edouard looks after him. The final section with Edouard (pp. 1063–182) shows Ferdinand in a mood of distraught hopelessness, only able to express a desire to get away from his present existence and from himself: he will join the army.[2]

[1] Proof of this is to be found in the pages of François Gibault, *Céline 1894–1932: le temps des espérances*, op. cit., which includes letters written from young Louis-Ferdinand Destouches to his parents during childhood and adolescence.

[2] The ending of *Mort à crédit* does not of course tie in with the opening of *Voyage*. It leads directly, however, to the unfinished fragment *Casse-pipe*. (See below, Chapter 6.)

The narrator, Ferdinand, is only seventeen at the end of the book, but by then he's had immense experience of a good many aspects of life. He knows about poverty and what it does to people, he knows about the loneliness of adolescence, he knows too that some people can be kind even if most are selfish, ignorant and self-seeking. He has discovered, first sex, and then, momentarily in England, something that is nearer to love. And while he sees through the charlatan side of Courtial from the very start of their time together, he develops an undoubted admiration for certain of his qualities, is as fond of him as he can be of anyone, and is broken by his death.

Ferdinand is not a nice little boy who only needed a bit of luck to make him into a good solid citizen. He is a tough, silently rebellious but extremely sensitive little boy, living from an early age in a fantasy world of his own creation and defending himself by all the means in his power against the efforts by adults to encroach upon his personality. The most striking single feature in him is undoubtedly his creative imagination (seen, for example, in the hallucinatory passages) and his ability to exploit dramatic situations. It may at first seem odd to suggest this, but there is an extraordinary similarity between Céline's narrator Ferdinand and Proust's narrator Marcel. Their social circumstances could hardly be more different, and their attitudes to the process of living are poles apart, *but* both have the same early understanding of the world around them, both have the same instinctive ability to control to some extent the reactions of the adults most closely concerned with them. In Marcel's case it may be, for instance, the exploitation of his nervousness to constrain his mother's affection. In Ferdinand's case it may be the exploitation of his near predilection for vomiting to infuriate his exasperating father:

> Moi du coup l'idée me montait de tout dégueuler sur place . . . **Papa** était là . . . Il a juste eu le temps de me raccrocher après l'arbre . . . j'ai tout, tout dégueulé dans la grille . . . Mon père il a fait qu'un bond . . . Il a pas tout esquivé . . . 'Ah! saligaud! . . .' qu'il a crié . . . Il avait en plein écopé sur son pantalon . . . (p. 598)

> (All of a sudden I had the idea of vomiting it all up on the spot . . . Papa was there . . . He had just time to grab me past the tree . . . I brought it all, all up in the gateway . . . My father jumped . . . He didn't get out of the way of it all . . . 'Ah! little wretch!' he cried . . . It had got him full on his trousers . . .)

Both Marcel and Ferdinand have grandmothers who are of great importance to them, both of whom die, without their grandsons ever expressing genuine feeling for them until too late. Both Marcel and Ferdinand find their youthful imaginations stimulated by the Middle Ages: Geneviève de Brabant and Gilbert le Mauvais set up infinite reverberations in the mind of the young Marcel, and in the case of Ferdinand it is the 'Légende du Roi Krogold' (allegedly found in a children's picture book series called *Les Belles Aventures Illustrées*) which provides him with an escape from the depressing reality of his existence, and which he recounts in part in the course of the novel. I throw out this line for reflection: I do not wish to suggest more than that Céline had before him the most notable depiction of childhood in the whole of French literature—that by Proust; that there is evidence that Céline knew the work of Proust well; that despite certain early dismissive remarks he conceded the originality of Proust (especially in the domain of language); and that Proust is one of the very few twentieth-century authors whom he sometimes talked about without contempt. I think it quite likely that in the first half of *Mort à crédit* he may have found it amusing—it would have been typical of him—to give a first-person narrative account of a childhood very different in social assumptions from the cosseted existence of the young Marcel. I make no suggestion of plagiarism, and have no desire to push the parallel too far. I am just planting the idea that the two greatest French novelists in the twentieth century have here some common ground. The difference is that while Marcel remembers things like hawthorn hedges, Ferdinand remembers that:

> D'ailleurs j'ai eu de la merde au cul jusqu'au régiment, tellement j'ai été pressé tout le long de ma jeunesse. (p. 534)
>
> (And furthermore I was shit-arsed until I joined the regiment, because I'd been in such a hurry all my youth.)

The smell is different, of course.

Before looking rapidly at the main lines of the narrative, I must say something of two other characters—Courtial des Pereires and Edouard. The first of these steps into the novel unannounced slightly over half way through:—'Des hommes comme Roger-Martin Courtial des Pereires on en rencontre pas des bottes . . .' (p. 815) ('Men like Roger-Martin Courtial des Pereires don't grow on trees'). That sentence introduces him, and for 200 pages,

Ferdinand's life is totally dominated by him. And it is an active happy, educative existence too. Courtial has, Céline tells us elsewhere, a real life model, a man called Raoul Marquis (see above, p. 35)[3], whom he knew well at the end of the First World War, and who, under the pen-name of Henri de Graffigny, published an immense number of 'scientific' treatises for the masses. The list of his publications—beginning in the 1880s—takes up twenty-four pages of the printed catalogue of the Bibliothèque Nationale, and it should be said at once that as examples of vulgarized 'popular science' they are not absurd. Marquis (like Courtial) was a keen aeronaut and made a large number of balloon ascents in the late nineteenth century. Many of his manuals are of a strictly practical kind, while others deal with more esoteric topics. Three titles will serve to indicate some of his interests (all three relevant to *Mort à crédit*): '*A travers l'espace: aventures d'un aéronaute*', ('Through space: adventures of an aeronaut'), '*L'automobile actuelle en 20 leçons*' ('The modern motor car in 20 lessons'), '*Les Rayons qui tuent et les radiations utiles*' ('Rays that kill and useful radiations'). Now Courtial is equally prolific and full of ideas, and genuinely believes in his mission of bringing scientific knowledge to the people. But at the same time he is feckless and a gambler, and in part a charlatan, having a great contempt for the subscribers to his magazine *Le Génitron* 'le périodique favori (vingt-cinq pages) des petits inventeurs-artisans de la Région Parisienne' (p. 815) ('the favourite magazine (twenty-five pages) for the artisan inventors of the Paris region') and something of a well-intentioned crook too. Ferdinand is no dupe: he quickly sees through Courtial, but he admires him too, learns a great deal from him and leads a free and contented existence as his secretary. Courtial is no Robinson: he is genuinely an idealist, though a distinctly crazy one, and Céline presents him in a highly sympathetic if comic light. Underlying the absurdities and the human weaknesses of Courtial there are enthusiasms and buoyant optimism which affect this whole long section of the book and which implant in Ferdinand an interest in the world about him together with a healthy scepticism. We are led to conclude that the infectious curiosity of Courtial is an admirable and even touching quality, and one that totally redeems him in the eyes of the author.

Edouard is the other character for whom Ferdinand has

[3] See also François Gibault, op. cit., pp. 191–204.

respect and indeed affection. From him Ferdinand receives nothing but understanding and kindness, and even if a sort of adolescent pride prevents him from responding explicitly, he is grateful, and indeed feels something near to embarrassment at the selfless help which Edouard affords him. We have seen in *Voyage* how Céline generates an overpowering emotional atmosphere by careful underplaying: this device is used to the full in all the pages dealing with Edouard and Ferdinand, and in particular in the final twenty pages of the novel which are amongst the most humane and affecting ever written by Céline. Edouard in fact touches Ferdinand just as Molly got through to Bardamu, and is the character who most clearly manifests the qualities of warmth and tenderness which Céline admires in man.

In *Mort à crédit* as in *Voyage* there is no clearly defined plot-line. Both books recount the manifold experience of living, through the eyes of a narrator, and there is plenty of incident in both, but they do not seek the kind of strong dramatic plot à la Balzac. They are not about 'love' nor 'success', nor even 'failure': they are perhaps about development of personality and growth of understanding and they certainly deal realistically with events and characters on the way. They are not naturalistic slices of life, but carefully modulated impressions of reality, varying extensively in tone and mood. If in *Voyage* the emphasis is eventually on resignation to the lot of mankind, in *Mort à crédit* the youth of the narrator and the comic warmth that surrounds the character of Courtial cause the ultimate impression to be one of hope. Ferdinand is undoubtedly in the deepest despair at the end of the novel after the death of Courtial, yet he has worked out a temporary solution for his problems—he wants to get away, to join the army. But he envisages a return later. . . . Edouard tries hard to persuade him to stay and receives the reply:

> Je voudrais bien mon oncle . . . Je voudrais bien! . . . Mais c'est pas possible, je te jure! . . . Plus tard mon oncle! . . . Plus tard? Tu veux pas? . . . Je ferais rien de bon mon oncle, tout de suite . . . (p. 1082)
>
> (I'd like to, uncle . . . I'd really like to! . . . But I swear it's not possible! . . . Later, uncle! . . . Later? . . . Don't you see? . . . I wouldn't do anything good, uncle, straightaway . . .)

It may be useful to highlight certain of the important passages of the book. Not surprisingly, the opening pages have been very carefully worked. They are an intense and bitter meditation on death. Alone in his room during a night of storm, Ferdinand, now a doctor, reflects on the death of his old concierge, Madame Bérange:

> C'était une douce et gentille et fidèle amie. Demain on l'enterre rue des Saules. Elle était vraiment vieille, tout au bout de la vieillesse. (p. 501)
>
> (She was a gentle, kind, faithful friend. Tomorrow she will be buried in the rue des Saules. She was well and truly old, at the far end of old age.)

He thinks of all who have visited him in his room who knew her too. He would like to write and tell some of them about her death:

> A qui vais-je écrire? Je n'ai plus personne. Plus un être pour recueillir doucement l'esprit gentil des morts . . . pour parler après ça plus doucement aux choses . . . Courage pour soi tout seul! (p. 501)
>
> (Who am I going to write to? I've got nobody any longer. No longer another being to greet gently the kind spirit of the dead . . . to talk more gently to things after that . . . Courage for oneself alone!)

Those whom he might write to are far away, have forgotten . . . he can therefore express all his hatred:

> Je le ferai plus tard s'ils ne reviennent pas. J'aime mieux raconter des histoires. J'en raconterai de telles qu'ils reviendront, exprès, pour me tuer, des quatre coins du monde. Alors ce sera fini et je serai bien content. (p. 502)
>
> (I'll do it later, if they don't come back. I prefer telling stories. I'll tell such stories that they'll come back from the four corners of the world, just to kill me. Then it'll be over and I'll be nice and happy.)

This opening page, with its mixture of tenderness and revolt, sets the tone for the whole novel. It cannot too often be emphasized: Céline, despite all his bitterness, theatrical violence and defiance, is essentially compassionate. Remembrance of this in reading *Mort à crédit* is the key to understanding it. The opening page is there to point the way to the discerning reader. So indeed are the very curious thirty pages or so that follow. Ferdinand is shown at his work as a doctor and also as a writer (there is even a reference to someone who has read *Voyage*), and there is the first mention of a manuscript that he prizes greatly, part of which has been lost by his secretary: it is the medieval 'Légende du Roi Krogold' and several pages of it are quoted. Full of poetry and imagination is what I am, he seems to be saying—even if the text is really pretty feeble.[4] There are also references to his war wounds, notably to the head injury which affected his hearing for life, caused chronic insomnia, and an almost permanent tinnitus:

> Je bourdonne toujours et tellement des deux oreilles que ça peut plus m'apprendre grand'chose. Depuis la guerre ça m'a sonné. Elle a couru derrière moi, la folie . . . tant et plus pendant vingt-deux ans . . . (. . .) Quand je trouverai le Bon Dieu chez lui, je lui crèverai, moi, le fond de l'oreille, l'interne, j'ai appris. Je voudrais voir comment ça l'amuse? Je suis chef de la gare diabolique. (pp. 525–6)

> (I can hear rumblings all the time, and to such an extent in both ears that that can no longer teach me much. The ringing has gone on since the War. Madness has been running behind me . . . so much, and increasingly, for twenty-two years . . . (. . .) When I meet the Good Lord, at his place, I'll burst the inside of his ears for him, the inner ear, I will—I know about that. I'd like to see if He finds that funny? I'm the Devil's station-master.)

This disability, added to malaria contracted in Africa—truly suffered by Céline, it should be said—occasionally causes the onset of fever and hallucination and indeed this part of the book contains a notable passage (pp. 524–5) resultant upon such an attack. It is the presence of his mother who comes to help look after him that triggers off the rest of the book, the reconstruction of his childhood and adolescence. It is not the taste of a madeleine dipped in tea, but an onset of malarial fever which brings back over the next 500 pages all Ferdinand's past. No good-night kiss from his mother but a slanging match between them in which Ferdinand declares all his contempt for his dead father:

> Je lui répète qu'il était sournois, hypocrite, brutal et dégonflé de partout! Elle retourne à la bataille. Elle se ferait tuer pour son Auguste. Je vais la dérouiller. Merde! . . . Je suis pas malarien pour de rire. Elle m'injurie, elle s'emporte, elle respecte pas mon état. Je me baisse alors, je lui retrousse sa jupe, dans la furie. J'y vois son mollet décharné comme un bâton, pas de viande autour, le bas qui godaille, c'est infect! . . . (p. 532)

---

[4] Céline elsewhere alludes to the loss of the manuscript of 'Krogold'. My guess is that there never was such a work, and that the feebleness of the 'extracts' in *Mort à crédit* is partly deliberate mystification and partly because some later passages are narrated by Ferdinand when very young.

(I repeat to her that he was sly, hypocritical, brutal and an out-and-out coward. She comes back to the attack. She'd gladly die for her Auguste. I'm going to beat her up. Shit! . . . I've not got malaria for nothing. She yells at me, gets carried away, doesn't respect my state of mind. So I lower my head, pull up her skirt, in my fury. I can see her calf withered like a stick, no meat around it, the stockings all wrinkled. It's disgusting! . . .)

Then begins the long section devoted to childhood. Father is shown as a bad-tempered failure. He'd wanted to be a merchant navy officer, but has ended up with a dead-end job as an insurance clerk. Mother runs a shop selling old lace, loving her husband (even if he often beats her), surrounding Ferdinand with all kinds of infuriating, well-intentioned, but misconceived solicitudes. They are always short of money. They live (for most of the time) in the Passage des Bérésinas—a smoky gas-lit arcade near the Opéra (now the sleek Passage de Choiseul)—deprived of sunlight and fresh air.

Father and mother constantly nag at Ferdinand and he is constantly being punished by them both. They also have frequent and violent rows. In the course of one of them, Ferdinand (who is seven or eight years old at most of this point) reflects thus:

De mon côté, je préfère personne. Pour les gueulements et la connerie, je les trouve pareils . . . Elle cogne moins fort, mais plus souvent. Lequel que j'aimerais mieux qu'on tue? Je crois que c'est encore mon papa. (p. 553)

(For my part, I prefer no one. For yelling and stupidity, they're both the same . . . She hits less hard, but more often. Which would I prefer to see killed? I think it would still be papa.)

The grotesque uncles and aunts are paraded before us, and also two persons who make an attempt to understand and care for Ferdinand—his grandmother Caroline and his uncle Edouard. Caroline buys him a little dog. Ferdinand at first treats it as his father treats him—with blows. The dog lies down whimpering as though asking for pardon. Just like me, thinks Ferdinand. But he prefers caressing the dog, in fact, and is intrigued when it gets an erection. Caroline takes him to the cinema:

'T'as aimé ça?' qu'elle me demandait Caroline. Je répondais rien, j'aime pas les questions intimes. 'Cet enfant est renfermé' que prétendait les voisins . . . (p. 554)

('Did you like that?' Caroline asked me. I didn't answer, I don't like personal questions. 'That child is very secretive,' the neighbours used to make out . . .)

And Caroline it is who secretly buys him copies of *Les Belles Aventures Illustrées* (disapproved of by his father) in which he will find eventually the story of 'Le Roi Krogold . . .'

The first significant appearance of uncle Edouard is a scene of high farce. 'Il était moderne l'oncle Edouard, il réussissait très bien dans la mécanique' (p. 536) ('Uncle Edward was up to date, had a knack with mechanical things'), and one day he invites Ferdinand and his parents and grandmother for a run in the country in a primitive early motor car. This gives rise to a remarkable four pages in which the punctuation is that of Céline's definitive manner.

> On a rempli les réservoirs. Le gicleur a bavé partout. Le volant avait des renvois . . . Y a eu des explosions horribles. On a remis ça à la volée, à la courroie . . . On s'attelait dessus à trois ou six . . . Enfin une grande détonation! . . . Le moteur se met à tourner. Il a pris feu encore deux fois . . . (p. 557)

> (The tanks were filled. The carburettor jet slobbered all over the place. The steering-wheel belched a bit . . . There were some frightful explosions. We had another go, full force, at the belt . . . Harnessed together, three, six of us . . . Finally a huge detonation . . . The motor began to turn over. It caught fire twice more . . .)

The whole section, well sustained, is an early example of what it is convenient to call Céline's 'epic manner': the recipe is not unlike that of Rabelais—fantasy built on to a realistic foundation and expressed in a highly coloured cascade of flippant imagery.

Ferdinand goes to school, falls ill—(another long 'hallucinatory' passage of remarkable inventiveness (pp. 574–81)—begins to learn about the differences between rich and poor, acquires some sexual information, grieves at the death of his grandmother Caroline, and is taken one summer to Dieppe where his mother tries with moderate success to sell her lace to the holiday-makers. The section concerning Dieppe (pp. 603–16) introduces what is to become a favourite theme in Céline—the sea and ships. It includes also a remarkably funny 'epic' account of a trip to Newhaven and back on a rough day: one would not expect a description of sea-sickness to be particularly amusing, but there is little doubt that Céline brings it off through verve and fantasy.

Ferdinand obtains his '*Certificat d'études*' and starts a career 'dans le commerce'. The sixty-odd pages which cover this part of his existence—two jobs from which he is sacked—are again largely comic in tone but they also show the mounting despair and anguish of Ferdinand as he finds himself always pushed around and bullied. And they also contain the one detailed, explicit erotic description in the whole of Céline. There are, of course, plenty of incidental sexual references throughout his works, but as he said on more than one occasion, he did not think that 'love'—and even less the sexual act—was an interesting subject for literature. But it was presumably necessary for the young Ferdinand to have a sexual initiation and when it comes to the point Céline gives a great deal of explicit physiological detail. Ferdinand and a fellow apprentice, Robert, first witness a series of sexual encounters between their *patronne*, Madame Gorloge, and Antoine, an employee. They are hidden—like Marcel when he observes the encounter between Charlus and Jupien—and find the spectacle most informative: it might be noted that the same extravagant use of butter as received such publicity in the film *Last Tango in Paris* is to be found here. Then, a day or two later, Madame Gorloge seduces Ferdinand himself, with no holds barred one might say . . . (pp. 663–70). And after the seduction he finds that a valuable jewel he was about to deliver to a customer has disappeared from his pocket. He is sacked and his parents have to pay for the jewel: Ferdinand cannot persuade his parents that he is not a thief. At this point of crisis, Edouard comes to the rescue with the suggestion that Ferdinand's business career would be greatly helped if he knew a foreign language, and he is despatched to learn English at Meanwell College, Rochester.

The English section is one of the best parts of the book. The atmosphere created is compelling, the narrative at Ferdinand's level more detached than when he is expressing his misery and hatred at home: the impressions of a broken-down English private school gained by a French adolescent are convincing and very funny in places, and, above all this, is the remote and gentle figure of Nora, young wife of the headmaster of Meanwell College for whom Ferdinand feels first desire and then, at length, something stronger which he barely understands. Ferdinand refuses to utter a word of English but he quite likes his life at Meanwell College—it is for him a period of irresponsible isolation:

Pendant trois mois j'ai pas mouffeté: j'ai pas dit hip! ni yep! ni, youf! . . . J'ai pas dit yes . . . J'ai pas dit no . . . J'ai pas dit rien! . . . C'était héroïque . . . Je causais à personne. Je m'en trouvais joliment bien . . . (p. 721)

(For three months I didn't open my trap: I didn't say hip! nor yep! nor youf! . . . Didn't say yes . . . didn't say no . . . I didn't say nothing! It was heroic . . . I talked to no one. I was pretty happy like that.)

The school is on its last legs, all the pupils gradually leave to join a newly founded school nearby. The headmaster takes to drink, and Nora comes at night to make love with Ferdinand before committing suicide.

Ferdinand first arrives at Rochester late on an autumn Sunday night, alone. At once the atmosphere is seized in a descriptive passage that extends over several pages, subtle, sensitive and full of extraordinary images. It opens in this fashion:

La ville commençait là tout de suite. Elle dégringolait avec ses petites rues, d'un lumignon vers un autre . . . C'était poisseux, ça collait comme atmosphère, ça dansait autour des becs . . . c'était hagard comme sensation. De loin, de plus bas, il venait des bouffées de musique . . . le vent devait porter . . . des ritournelles . . . On aurait dit d'un manège cassé dans la nuit . . . (p. 691)

(The town began there at once. It ran downwards in little streets, from one feeble lamp to another . . . It was sticky, a clinging kind of atmosphere . . . it danced about around the street lamps . . . it gave a feeling of unease . . . From afar, from further down, came gusts of music . . . the wind must have brought them . . . refrains . . . Sounded like a broken down roundabout in the night . . .)

The picture of Nora is built up gradually throughout these pages. At first Ferdinand is simply inspired by lust: at night in the dormitory when he is not having a little quiet sex with one of the other boys, he masturbates while thinking of her. But gradually—without the word 'love' ever being pronounced—his feelings seem to change, the description of Nora takes on a kind of tender idealization:

Elle émanait toute l'harmonie, tous ses mouvements étaient exquis . . . C'était un charme, un mirage . . . Quand elle passait d'une pièce à l'autre, ça faisait comme un vide dans l'âme, on descendait en tristesse d'un étage plus bas. (p. 729)

(Total harmony emanated from her, all her movements were

exquisite . . . It was a spell, a mirage . . . When she left one room for
another, there was a kind of emptiness in your soul, you went down
one more storey in sadness.)

Nora is indeed someone who, like Molly in *Voyage*, leaves a mark
on the narrator's sensibility, and for the reader stands out, clear
and warm, in the grimness of Ferdinand's life so far. Ferdinand
returns to Paris wise beyond his years: his childhood is over.

His life at home is about to end too. After a while, hostility
between him and his father becomes more intense. Ferdinand
returns home late one evening rather drunk, and, threatened by
his father, knocks him out, collapses himself and is taken away
by Edouard—Edouard being the only one who understands him
at all. Ferdinand soon feels guilty at being dependent on Edouard
and wants to look for a job, but Edouard has this in hand and will
soon find him something. A conversation between them on this
prefigures the end of the novel, and concludes in this way:

> 'Dans quelques jours je te dirai . . . Je vais avoir quelque chose de
> très bien! . . . Je le sens! . . . J'en suis sûr! . . . Mais il faut rien
> brutaliser! . . . Et j'espère que tu me feras honneur! . . .'—'Oui mon
> oncle! . . .' (p. 815)

> ('I'll tell you in a few days . . . I'm on to something very good! . . .
> I feel it! . . . I'm sure of it! . . . But no good rushing things! . . .
> And I hope you'll be a credit to me! . . .'—'Yes, uncle!')

Indeed, Edouard is as good as his word. Ferdinand is taken on
by Courtial des Pereires, and the novel takes a totally new turn.
What we observe in the long section devoted to their adventures
together is the growing amusement and contentment of Ferdin-
and and the amount he learns from Courtial, who is tireless in his
desire to inform and educate:

> Toujours je l'ai connu prêt à me sacrifier une heure, deux heures,
> et davantage, parfois des journées entières pour m'expliquer
> n'importe quoi . . . Tout ce qui peut se comprendre et se résoudre,
> et s'assimiler, quant à l'orientation des vents, les cheminements de la
> lune, la force des calorifères, la maturation des concombres et les
> reflets de l'arc-en-ciel . . . Oui! Il était vraiment possédé par la
> passion didactique. (pp. 837–8)

> (I've always known him ready to give up an hour, two hours, more
> for me, sometimes whole days to explain to me no matter what . . .
> Everything that can be understood and solved and assimilated,
> regarding the direction of winds, the movements of the moon, the

power of stoves, the ripening of cucumbers and the reflections of
the rainbow . . . Yes, he was genuinely possessed by the mania for
teaching.)

If it were not for the unfortunate need to make money, Courtial
would remain a pure idealist, but in his troubled existence—
harried somewhat by his more hard-headed wife—he has to
resort to well-meaning but dubious subterfuges to survive. He
is not so much in pursuit of personal happiness—a quest that we
know, from the character of Robinson in *Voyage*, to be futile in
Céline's view—but rather of universal enlightenment, and there
is in him a streak of the selflessness that is to be found in all the
characters whom Céline presents in a favourable light. The view
we get of Courtial handling the ideas and demands of his clientele
of minor inventors, of his 'educative' balloon ascents in little
provincial towns, of his weakness for betting on horses, and of
his fear of his wife, is undeniably both comic and human; and his
ceaseless eloquence is a major factor in the development of
Céline's style in the novel. The Paris section ends with the sacking
of Courtial's office in Paris by a horde of infuriated '*petits inven-
teurs*'—related in the now familiar epic hallucinatory manner:

> Tout vole en éclats! . . . La boiserie cède! crève! s'éparpille! Tout a
> sauté! . . . Une avalanche de vitrerie . . .! la ferraille . . . les glaces . . .
> les plafonds suivent dans la cascade! . . . (p. 942)

> (Everything shatters to bits . . . The woodwork yields, collapses,
> disintegrates! Everything went up! . . . An avalanche of glass . . .!
> bits of metal . . . the mirrors . . . the ceiling next came cascading
> down! . . .)

After this disaster Courtial has to flee from Paris. He buys a
farm at Blême-le-Petit where he proposes to do two things.
First to cultivate vegetables in a scientifically advanced manner
(*radio-tellurique*, he calls it, with electric shocks passed through the
soil by wires), and then to establish the 'Familistère Rénové de
la Race Nouvelle', a kind of *pension de famille* for city children,
who, while being educated by Courtial, would do all the work
on the farm. . . .

Of course, both projects come to grief. The local peasantry
becomes hostile, all the vegetables rot, the children all turn out
to be uncontrollable delinquents—very good at stealing food from
other farms when the money runs out. Eventually Courtial can
bear it all no longer; he shoots himself. The imaginative idealistic

dreams of Courtial are shattered—like Robinson's dreams of happiness—and Ferdinand is left once more to pick up the pieces of his own life.

He returns to Paris with nothing but the clothes he is wearing, and is once more received by Edouard, who understands, who wants to help him, who lodges him, clothes him, feeds him. But Ferdinand—like Bardamu in this—cannot bring himself to remain with Edouard as a liability: he is too discouraged, too disillusioned, too miserable. He must go away—somewhere, anywhere, for at least a time. The last fifteen pages of the novel are amongst the most effective and most moving ever written by Céline. Edouard tries eloquently and at length to persuade Ferdinand to stay for a while and recover, but Ferdinand can for the most part only reply briefly with phrases like 'Je sais pas mon oncle!... Je voudrais bien mon oncle' ('I don't know, uncle... I'd like that, uncle'), 'Oui, mon oncle' ('Yes, uncle'), 'Non, mon oncle' ('No, uncle'). He insists that he will join the army at once:

'Je t'aime bien mon oncle, tu sais!... Mais je peux plus rester!... Je peux plus!... T'es bien bon toi, avec moi!... Je mérite pas mon oncle!... Je mérite pas!...'
'Pourquoi ça que tu mérites pas?... dis petit con?...'
'Je sais pas mon oncle!... Je te fais du chagrin aussi!... Je veux partir mon oncle!... Je veux aller m'engager demain...'
(p. 1078)

('Uncle, I'm very fond of you, you know that!... But I can't stay any more!... I can't any more!... You're so good to me, you are! I don't deserve it, uncle!... I don't deserve it!...'
'Why do you go on about not deserving it?... tell me why, you silly idiot?...'
'Uncle, I really don't know!... I'm hurting you too!... I want to get away uncle!... I want to go and join up tomorrow...')

And despite all the affectionate efforts by Edouard, he holds to this (the final lines of the novel are quoted below, p. 119).

Thus the work ends with Ferdinand grown up, and at a further turning point in his career. From birth onwards we are all engaged in paying for death by instalments: the process of living makes us pay all the time in terms of experience and suffering, and no one can avoid entering into this hire-purchase agreement. But, of course, once you have understood this, it gives you a certain strength and a certain ability to cope with existence: this is what Ferdinand has acquired at the end of *Mort à crédit*. It's a more difficult work to read than *Voyage*: the language is becoming more consistently violent and idiosyncratic and the author's intentions are not so immediately clear on first reading. But it has tremendous vitality and humour, and, like *Voyage*, an emotional charge of high intensity.

CHAPTER THREE

Language

The quotations from *Voyage* and *Mort à crédit* given in the last two chapters give some idea of the flavour of the style of Céline. The main characteristics of his mature manner are to be found—from time to time—in *Voyage*, but the first novel is relatively conventional and unadventurous, especially when looked at in retrospect. *Mort à crédit* certainly shows a stylistic development and gives us many indications of things to come, but the real change comes just after it, when from 1936 to 1938 Céline indulged in political polemic. Indeed, this change of subject matter seems to have accelerated the process of evolving a really personal and idiosyncratic style.

It is because the reputation of Céline rests very considerably upon his achievements in the use of the French language and also because his definitive manner is both original and at first even disconcerting, that it is desirable to look carefully at this side of his work *before* examining the subsequent writings.

The problems involved in a full-scale stylistic analysis of the entire run of his works—many thousand pages of text—are such that we shall have to wait many years before any satisfactory over-all statement can be made.[1] There is a secondary problem—already mentioned—in a work of the present kind, written in a foreign language and directed at a foreign public, since questions of style cannot be usefully handled in translation. What I propose to do in this chapter, therefore, is bound to be something in the nature of a compromise. I shall give an account of the critical theories underlying Céline's manner of writing and try to indicate some of the main characteristics of this manner. The critical

---

[1] The only works by Céline for which anything approaching a critical text is available are those in Pléiade, vol. II, 1974 (edited by Henri Godard): *D'un Château l'autre*, *Nord* and *Rigodon*. Jean-Pierre Dauphin has prepared a complete critical text of *Entretiens avec le Professeur Y*, based on the collation of *five* MS versions, which I have been able to consult, and which, it is to be hoped, will soon reach print.

theories are mainly to be culled from his *Entretiens avec le Professeur Y.* (henceforward abbreviated to *Entretiens*). I hope that even readers who know no French at all will be able to get the main points.

Those scholars who have begun to work on the textual problems of Céline's manuscripts are quite clear about one thing: his effervescent and apparently spontaneous style is the result of an enormous amount of detailed and meticulous rewriting. Not only are there in some cases several manuscript versions of substantial sections of text, but there are also countless corrections of individual words and phrases, which testify not only to a great insistence on exactness of meaning, but also to equal insistence on rhythm and tonal aptness. Since the days of Flaubert such labour is of course not unusual in a novelist, and indeed of the *major* novelists since Flaubert only perhaps Zola has been able to avoid it. In his recorded monologue, 'Louis Ferdinand Céline vous parle' (see above, p. 26, note 7), Céline is most emphatic about the difficulties of writing. To those who tell him they admire his *facilité* he retorts that he is not *facile du tout* and that writing is for him an intensely painful and complicated process. One of his main criticisms of contemporary writing is precisely its looseness and lack of concentration—products of idleness in the writer. The Impressionists, he says, for example, were extremely hard working but no one wants to work as hard as they did nowadays.

Another theme we find recurring from an early stage is his contempt for what he calls the academic style in French. By this he means the kind of style acquired through a *lycée* education, based on seemingly immutable principles of clarity and exactitude dating at least from the eighteenth century. He refers to it variously as 'le style de Voltaire', 'le style d'Anatole France', 'le style du bachot', 'le style du journal habituel'. It was marvellous in the hands of Voltaire, but it's dead now, he protests, and nothing live can ever be written in this manner again. That is why he has sought a new and different mode of expression.[2]

What Céline achieved was a manner of writing which was *emotionally* rather than intellectually based. 'Je ne suis pas un homme à *idéâs*: je suis un homme à *style*' ('I'm not a man of ideas: I am a stylist') he says in the recorded monologue of 1957.[3] In

[2] This set of views is implicit as early as *Voyage* (Pléiade, vol. I, pp. 393-4). It is first stated explicitly in *Bagatelles pour un massacre*, op. cit., see below, p. 145.

[3] See Pléiade, vol. II, p. 934.

the *Entretiens* he outlines in some detail his thought on all this, but it is interesting to note that one of the key sustained images he uses in that text is already to be found in a letter he wrote eleven years earlier (in 1944) to a critic, Claude Jamet, who had written a perceptive and intelligent article about him. Jamet publishes the letter at the end of his article, four years later.[4] The significant passages are these:

> Il me semblait qu'il y avait deux façons de raconter les histoires. La classique, l'habituelle, l'académique qui consiste à se faufiler d'un incident à l'autre, virer, tourner en surface, si j'ose dire, avec cent cahots, trébuchages, rattrapages tant bien que mal (. . .) le chemin des voitures dans la rue . . . et puis, l'autre, descendre dans l'intimité des choses, dans la fibre, le nerf, l'émotion des choses, la viande, et aller droit au but, à son but, dans l'intimité, en tension poétique, constante, en vie interne, comme le 'métro' en *ville interne* droit au but, une fois le choix fait, il faut rester dans la même conviction, dans la tension intime, une fois pour toutes, dans l'intimité de la vie, tenir ainsi l'histoire.

> (It seemed to me that there were two ways of telling stories. The classic, normal, academic way, which consists of creeping along from one incident to the next, twisting, turning on the surface, if I may say so, into all sorts of jerks, hesitations, restarts for better or for worse (. . .) the way cars go along in the street . . . and then, the other way, which means descending into the intimacy of things, into the fibre, the nerve, the feeling of things, the flesh, and going straight on to the end, to its end, in intimacy, in maintained poetic tension, in inner life, like the *métro* through an *inner city* straight to the end, once the choice is made, it's essential to stay in the same conviction, in the same intimate tension, once and for all, in the intimacy of life, to seize the story in this fashion.)

This is the first use by Céline that has so far come to light, of an image—contrast between *surface* and *métro*—which he develops much more fully in 1955 in the *Entretiens*. Before I get down to the consideration of that text, however, there is another short passage worth noting which contains the same essential notion, published this time after the *Entretiens*. It is a short statement (published in an edition of Rabelais transcribed into modern French) entitled *Rabelais il a raté son coup*[5] ('Rabelais didn't bring

---

[4] Claude Jamet, *Images mêlées de la littérature et du théâtre* (E.L.A.N., Paris, 1948). (Reference due to the courtesy of M. J.-P. Dauphin.)

[5] La Bibliothèque de l'Etoile, Productions de Paris, 1957; Reproduced in *Cahiers de l'Herne*, pp. 44-5.

it off'). The writer whom Céline we know admired most was Villon, and he sees Rabelais as in the same tradition and hostile to the Renaissance which he regards as destructive. There is certainly a link between Villon and Rabelais, but this view is somewhat perverse in that it disregards Rabelais's enthusiasm for the culture of Greece and Rome, cultures despised by Céline. In this little text he points out that the use Rabelais made of the French language did not in fact find favour and survive. What triumphed linguistically—with, in his view, dire results for the future—was the academic style of Amyot, the translator of Plutarch who was so greatly admired by Montaigne and others of his generation:

> Rabelais avait voulu faire passer la langue parlée dans la langue écrite: un échec. Tandis qu'Amyot, les gens maintenant veulent toujours et encore de l'Amyot, du style académique. Ça c'est écrire de la m . . . : du langage figé. Les colonnes d'un grand quotidien du matin, qui se flatte d'avoir des rédacteurs qui écrivent bien, en est plein. (. . .) Rabelais, oui, il a échoué, et Amyot a gagné. La postérité d'Amyot, c'est tous ces petits romans émasculés qui paraissent de nos jours dans les meilleures maisons d'édition. Des milliers par an. Mais, des romans comme ça, moi j'en fais un à l'heure. (. . .) Ce qu'il y a en effet de bien chez Rabelais, c'est qu'il mettait sa peau sur la table, il risquait. La mort la guettait, et ça inspire la mort! c'est même la seule chose qui inspire, je le sais, quand elle est là, juste derrière. Quand la mort est en colère. Il n'était pas bon vivant, Rabelais, on dit ça, c'est faux. Il travaillait. Et, comme tous ceux qui travaillent, c'était un galérien.

> (Rabelais had wanted to insert the spoken language into the written language: a failure. Whereas Amyot, people now still want more and ever more of Amyot, of academic style. That means writing sh-, congealed language. The columns of a famous daily paper which prides itself in having journalists who write well are full of it. (. . .) Rabelais failed indeed, and Amyot won. Amyot's posterity it's all those emasculated little novels that come out nowadays from the best publishers. Thousands of them a year. Well, novels like that, I make one of them an hour. (. . .) The great thing about Rabelais is that he stuck his neck out, took risks. Death was waiting for him, and death inspires alright! indeed it's the only thing that does inspire, don't I know it, when it's there, just behind you. When death is angry. He wasn't a pleasure seeker, Rabelais, people say so, but it's wrong. He worked. And like all those who work, he was a galley-slave.)

These remarks contain the kernel of Céline's reflection on the use of language. Emotion counts more than reason, and naturalness of expression more than order and clarity. Man is condemned to death and if he is to achieve greatness as an artist he must work like a galley-slave. There is no other way.

Although even a cursory glance at Céline's early works shows at once that these notions were present from the start, it is not until after the war that we begin to find him formulating them in positive fashion, and despite occasional texts like the letter to Jamet, the main effort at a considered statement did not come until the *Entretiens avec le Professeur Y* in 1955. If we are to believe his account of the starting-point of this work—and, even though one must always regard his remarks in this kind of context as a compound of fact and fiction, there is no reason to disbelieve him here—his publishers (by now Gallimard) were anxious for him to engage in some publicity about himself. And so he agreed to give an interview. 'Le Professeur Y' insists that it should occur in a public place, so a rendezvous is arranged in the Square des Arts et Métiers. It soon appears that 'Professeur Y' is a pseudonym, and that his real name is Colonel Réséda—a name which has in turn resonances of a Resistance code-name. Their conversation, or more accurately perhaps, Céline's long monologue punctuated by occasional interventions from his interlocutor, forms the book.[6] It contains a certain amount of self-justification, it moves into fantasy once or twice and is often very amusing, but it also develops a number of serious statements about his art, and it is these that we must now examine.

The first suggestion from the interviewer is that they should have a philosophical conversation. Céline is unwilling:

> ... je suis hostile! ... j'ai pas d'idées moi! aucune! et je trouve rien de plus vulgaire, de plus commun, de plus dégoutant que les idées! les bibliothèques en sont pleines, et les terrasses des cafés! . . . (p. 19)
>
> (... I'm against that! ... I don't have any ideas myself! none! and I don't know anything more vulgar, more common, more disgusting than ideas! libraries are full of them and so are café terraces! . . .)

And he proceeds to launch an attack on philosophers as corrupters of youth—this of course at a time when the post-war existentialist vogue was at its height.[7] 'Je laisse les *idéâs* aux camelots! toutes les *idéâs*! aux maquereaux, aux confusionnistes! . . .' (p. 22) ('I leave *ideas* to hawkers in the streets! all ideas! to the pimps, to the muddlers!') What claim therefore does he make for himself? He is an inventor. Quite a modest one, but he *has* invented something. What?

> L'émotion dans le langage écrit! . . . le langage était à sec, c'est moi qu'ai redonné l'émotion au langage écrit! . . . (. . .) retrouver l'émotion du 'parlé' à travers l'écrit! c'est pas rien! c'est infime mais c'est quelque chose! . . . (pp. 22–3)

> (Emotion in the written language! . . . the language was dried up, I'm the one who has brought back emotion into the written language! . . . (. . .) to rediscover through writing the emotion of the *spoken word*! it's more than nothing! it's minute, but it's something at least! . . .)

This indeed is the central notion of the book. But it is some time before it is fully discussed: Céline has a number of points to make first, two of which must be mentioned here.

There is a considerable section devoted to what he calls 'le chromo' (i.e. chromolithograph, cheap colour print). This is used as a term of abuse to describe all forms of feeble, sentimental commercial literature. 'Le chromo' is what the public wants and never tires of, and it is furnished by the mass of standard novelists who are out of date, like academic painters of the nineteenth century before Impressionism. Moreover, such writers seem unaware that the cinema can do this kind of thing much better than they. But the cinema is none the less 'tout en toc, mécanique, tout froid . . . il est infirme d'émotion . . .' (p. 28) ('all sham, mechanical, cold . . . emotionally feeble . . .'). True emotion, true lyricism is only attainable in art by immensely subtle and patient effort:

> . . . l'émotion est chichiteuse, fuyeuse (. . .) évanescente (. . .) la rattrape pas qui veut la garce . . . que non . . . des années de tapin acharné, bien austère, bien monacal, pour rattraper et de la veine! un petit bout d'émotion vibrée! grand comme ça! . . . (p. 35)

> (. . . emotion is hard to catch, fleeting (. . .) evanescent! (. . .) not to be seized, the bitch, by just anyone . . . not at all . . . years of desperate work, austere, monastic labour in order to seize it, and

[7] He had good reason to dislike the author he variously calls *Jean-Baptiste* or *Tartre* (see below, pp. 183 and 238–9).

you need luck too! just a little scrap of quivering emotion, no bigger than this! . . .)

Linked with this is the use—by Céline at all events—of the first person singular, inevitable, essential indeed in lyricism. In this part of the argument Céline lets fall—in passing and without development—an extremely important statement about his own use of *je*:

> . . . moi, la modestie en personne! mon 'je' est pas osé du tout! je ne le présente qu'avec un soin! . . . mille prudences! . . . je le recouvre toujours entièrement, très précautionneusement de merde! (p. 66)

> (. . . me, I'm modesty personified! My use of 'I' isn't at all daring: I only employ I with great care! . . . with infinite prudence! . . . I always coat it completely, taking every precaution, with shit.)

We have already seen a clear example of this technique in the picture of Ferdinand's childhood in *Mort à crédit*. All Céline's works from *Voyage* through to *Rigodon* have a first-person narrator—Bardamu, Ferdinand and eventually Céline—but it is a great mistake to identify any of these too closely with the author himself.

The second point we must examine is a brief but useful development on the use of slang. Slang is an effective literary device for the *'auteur lyrique'*, but it must be used with great discretion, otherwise its shock effect is lost and it quickly palls:

> L'argot est un langage de haine qui vous assoit très bien le lecteur . . . l'annihile! . . . à votre merci! . . . il reste tout con! . . . (. . .) l'émoi de l'argot s'épuise tres vite (. . .) un livre tout entier d'argot est plus ennuyeux qu'un 'Rapport de la Cour de Comptes' . . . (. . .) piment admirable que l'argot! . . . mais un repas entier de piment vous fàit qu'un méchant déjeuner! (pp. 71-2)

> (Slang is a language of hatred which enables you to stun your reader . . . to destroy him! . . . he's at your mercy! . . . completely shaken! . . . (. . .) the emotion of slang is quickly exhausted (. . .) a whole book in slang is more boring than an (=) Official Treasury Report . . . (. . .) slang's a marvellous spice! . . . but a whole meal of spice only makes a miserable lunch.)

It must be said that Céline adheres very closely, and no doubt very wisely, to this principle: there is a good deal of slang in his novels, but it is very carefully manipulated and rarely, as a result, loses its impact. Moreover he believed that genuine slang is disappearing. In a short article published in 1957 in the periodical *Arts*[8] he explains this point of view:

> Non, l'argot ne se fait pas avec un glossaire, mais avec des images de la haine, c'est la haine qui fait l'argot. L'argot est fait pour exprimer les sentiments vrais de la misère. (. . .) L'argot est fait pour permettre à l'ouvrier de dire à son patron qu'il déteste: tu vis bien et je vis mal, tu m'exploites et roules dans une grosse voiture, *je vais te crever* . . .

> (No, slang is not made up from a glossary, but from images of hatred, it's hatred that creates slang. Slang is made to express real feelings of poverty. (. . .) Slang is made to allow the workman to tell his boss, whom he loathes: your life's easy, my life's tough, you exploit me and you go around in a big car, *I'm going to get you* . . .)

But he goes on to add that the only slang that is being created is that of an artificial kind used by amateur pimps at bar counters, or that of a snob public pronouncing it with an English accent.[9] His own slang, as will be seen, is of a very traditional kind.

The key pages of the *Entretiens* are essential reading for anyone who wishes to understand the art of Céline. They come about halfway through the book (pp. 95–123) and I must now talk about them in some detail. His interlocutor sums up the situation thus on p. 95:

> 'Vous, le plus grand écrivain du siècle, l'inventeur du style que vous dites, le Bouleverseur des Lettres Françaises . . . le Malherbe actuel en somme! *enfin Céline vint*,[10] c'est bien ça?'

> ('You, the greatest writer of the century, the inventor of the style you talk about, the Disruptor of French literature . . . the modern Malherbe in fact: *at length came Céline*, that's right isn't it?')

But the key revelation, says Céline, 'le moment de mon trait de génie' ('the moment of my flash of genius'), is yet to come. And it is then given in a series of brilliant, witty and incisive pages of what one may reasonably call 'vintage Céline'. He starts by saying that he had a sudden revelation about language which he compared with Pascal's revelation on the Pont de Neuilly of 'le sentiment du gouffre' ('the sensation of the abyss'). However, his revelation did not come to him in a *carosse* like Pascal—'le Pascal,

---

[8] Reproduced in *Cahiers de l'Herne*, p. 39.

[9] This predilection for a mild English accent is still to be found in certain Parisian milieux of an idle rich kind—traditionally the 16th *arrondissement*.

[10] Reference to Boileau, *Art Poétique*, Chant I, 'Enfin Malherbe vint . . .'.

dans une "deux chevaux", je voudrais le voir un peu du Printemps
à la rue Taitbout! . . . c'est pas un gouffre qu'il aurait peur' ('old
Pascal, in a Citroen 2 CV, I'd like to see him coping between the
Printemps and the Rue Taitbout! . . . it's not an abyss he'd be
afraid of')—but on the steps of the Métro station Pigalle. At one
period in his career while living in Montmartre he had to make an
almost daily journey across Paris to Issy. How was he to go?
Bicycle, on foot, by bus—or by Métro (the line is direct, the old
Nord-Sud, Porte de la Chapelle—Mairie d'Issy)? The answer is of
course the Métro—'le noir Métro? ce gouffre qui pue, sale et
pratique? . . . le grand avaloir des fatigués? . . . ou je restais dehors?
je bagottais? *be or not to be*? . . .' (pp. 100–101) ('the dark Métro?
stinking dirty but useful abyss? . . . the great swallower of the
exhausted? . . . or should I stay outside? and run? *be or not to
be*? . . .'). There follows an extended figure of speech—an expansion of what we saw earlier in the letter to Claude Jamet—
contrasting *surface* reality with *underlying* truth created by the
artist. On foot or by bus you perceive only the irritating 'cine-
matic', 'visual' reality of our times:

. . . l'autobus? . . . cet angoissé monstre grelottant hoquetant
bégayeur à chaque carrefour? . . . qui perd des heures à être poli . . .
à pas écraser la rombière . . . (. . . .) ou je fonçais à pied? . . . par
les rues? une! deux! . . . (. . .) la surface est pleine d'intérêt! . . .
tous les trucs . . . tout le Cinéma . . . tous les plaisirs du Cinéma! . . .
pensez! . . . pensez! . . . les minois des dames, les postères des dames,
et toute l'animation autour! les messieurs qui piaffent! . . . (p. 101)

(. . . bus? . . . that tortured monster shivering, hiccoughing, stutterer
at every crossroads? . . . which loses hours through being polite . . .
not knocking women down . . . (. . .) or rush off on foot? . . .
through the streets? left! right! . . . (. . .) the surface is full of
interest! all the tricks . . . total Cinema . . . all the pleasures of the
Cinema! . . . just think! . . . think! . . . women's faces, women's
bottoms and all the activity around! the gentlemen showing off! . . .)

And there follows a catalogue of the interesting things one sees
on the 'surface'.
There is, however, a disadvantage in all this:

. . . mais attention! ensorcellures! vous voilà film . . . transformé
film! film vous-même! et un film c'est que des anicroches! de bout
en bout! . . . qu'anicroches pertes de temps! carambolages! . . .
(. . .) la Surface est plus fréquentable! (pp. 101–2)

(. . . but watch it! bewitchment! you're now a film . . . changed into a film! yourself! and a film is nothing but snags! from start to finish! . . . snags which waste time! collisions! . . . (. . .) the Surface isn't viable any more!)

So without further hesitation, Céline chooses the Métro. He will embark all his readers therein and hurl them in a dream, non-stop, to their destination. There are no traffic-jams or other hold-ups in his *métro émotif*:

... dans un rêve! . . . jamais le moindre arrêt nulle part! non! au but! au but! direct! dans l'émotion! . . . par l'émotion! rien que le but: en pleine émotion . . . bout en bout! (p. 102)

(. . . in a dream! . . . not the least halt anywhere! no! on to the end! to the end! straight! emotively! . . . through emotion! simply to the end: with full emotion . . . start to finish.)

But this state of emotional excitement can only be attained if a special operation has been conducted on the rails of the *métro émotif*: the rails, normally straight, have to be specially stream-lined ('profilés') and bevelled ('biseautés'):

... ses rails rigides! . . . je leur en fous un coup! . . . il en faut plus! . . . ses phrases bien filées . . . il en faut plus! . . . son style, nous dirons! . . . je les lui fausse d'une certaine façon, que les voyageurs sont dans le rêve . . . qu'ils s'aperçoivent pas . . . le charme . . . la magie, Colonel! la violence aussi . . . (p. 103)

(. . . its firmly fixed rails! . . . I hit them bloody hard! . . . no more of them! . . . its nicely elongated sentences . . . no more of them! . . . its style, as it were! . . . I deform them in a particular way, so the passengers are in a dream . . . so they don't notice . . . spellbound . . . magic, Colonel, violence too . . .)

Moreover, the readers/travellers are not alone in the Métro: the whole surface world is packed in with them:

Les maisons, les bonshommes, les briques, les rombières, les petits pâtissiers, les vélos, les automobiles, les midinettes, les flics avec! entassés, 'pilés émotifs'! dans mon métro émotif! je laisse rien à la Surface! . . . tout dans mon transport magique! . . . (pp. 103–4)

(The houses, the passers-by, the bricks, the women, the pastry-boys, the bikes, the cars, the shop-girls, the fuzz too! piled up, emotively crushed! . . . inside my emotive métro! I leave nothing on the Surface! everything inside my magic vehicle! . . .)

If the rails are not cunningly modified in the manner indicated—

'si vos rails sont droits, Colonel, du style classique, aux phrases
bien filées . . .' (p. 112) ('if your rails are dead straight, Colonel,
in classical style, with elongated sentences')—then there will be
the most terrible accident and you will kill all your passengers.

There is one more stage to his sustained image of the *métro
émotif*. To hold these specially constructed rails in place there
must of course be sleepers. These in Céline's writings are the
three dots . . . which have been apparent in all the quotations just
given, and which appear in all his works, sparingly in *Voyage*,
more extensively in *Mort à crédit*, until by *Féerie pour une autre
fois I* they have virtually replaced all other forms of punctuation
except the exclamation mark and the occasional ordinary full
stop. They are almost comparable to the pointing of a psalm:
they divide his text into rhythmical rather than syntactical units,
permit extreme variations of pace and make possible to a great
extent the powerful hallucinatory lyricism of his style:

> Mes trois points sont indispensables! . . . (. . .) Pour poser mes rails
> émotifs! . . . simple comme bonjour! . . . sur le ballast? . . . vous
> comprenez? . . . ils tiennent pas tout seuls mes rails! . . . il me faut
> des traverses! . . . (pp. 115–16)

> (My three dots are essential! . . . (. . .) To lay down my emotive
> rails! . . . clear as daylight! . . . on the ballast? . . . get it? . . . my
> rails won't hold firm by themselves! . . . I have to have sleepers! . . .)

One may feel that the image is as forced as the famous 'steppes
of Russia' passage in *Madame Bovary*. The section needs to be read
in its entirety, however, and from the full text, with its flippant
asides and its joyous parody of the literary interview, there
emerges a compelling view of what Céline aims at achieving by
his idiosyncratic handling of language. He sums up the effect he
seeks to obtain in a passage describing the reactions of the reader
of 'un livre émotif . . . une de mes oeuvres' ('an emotive book . . .
one of my works'). The reader first finds himself disconcerted,
because he begins to have the curious sensation that there is
someone inside his head who is reading to him willy-nilly. That,
says Céline, is the secret of Impressionism:

> Pas simplement à son oreille! . . . non! . . . dans l'intimité de ses
> nerfs en plein dans son système nerveux! dans sa propre tête! (. . .)
> que quelqu'un lui joue comme il veut sur la harpe de ses propres
> nerfs! (pp. 122–3)

> (Not just in his ear! . . . no! . . . in the intimacy of his nerves! right

inside his nervous system! inside his own head! (...) as though
someone is playing at will on the harp of his very nerves!)

This is a most imaginative and telling way of conveying what
goes on in the reader's consciousness if he finds himself able to
take Céline, and the author's ability to produce this extraordinary
sensation is one of his principal and most original merits. There
is undoubtedly an almost hypnotic effect induced by the emotional
charge of the language used as it is by Céline, an effect equalled in
our century in French only by a very different writer—Proust.

The bewildered colonel—who, by this time, despite one visit
to the nearby *pissotière*, has lost control of his bladder and is
seated with his feet in a pool of piss—is given one further piece
of help about Impressionism. An Impressionist, in order to
represent truth, insists upon his right to deform reality in the
process. If you plunge a stick into water, says Céline—and he
sees this instance again in his recorded monologue—it will
appear bent. If you want it to appear straight in this circumstance,
what must you do?:

> Cassez-le vous-même, pardi! avant de le plonger dans l'eau! cette
> bonne blague! tout le secret de l'Impressionisme! (...) Ainsi de
> mon style émotif! et de mes rails si *ouvragés*! *profilés 'spécial'* ! (pp. 123–4)
>
> (Break it yourself, for God's sake, before plunging it in the water!
> what a good joke! the whole secret of Impressionism! (...) Just the
> same with my emotive style! and with my carefully constructed rails
> 'specially' bevelled!)

If Céline affects you, then this is how he does it—to take up
his own version of the process. It is by an assault on the reader's
nerves which transports him, like it or not, far beyond the
terminus of Mairie d'Issy into the special world of the author's
vision . . . a world that the reader recognizes as very real . . . but
which he knows to be an impressionistic version of reality. The
stick seems straight enough . . . but Céline has bent it . . . the rails
of the Métro run straight, straight, straight into infinite distance
. . . bevelled, however, by Céline . . . so that the train will not
crash . . . and the sleepers flash by . . . unperceived . . . beneath
us. As is so often the case, Gide hit upon a splendid formula when
he said of Céline 'Ce n'est pas la réalité que peint Céline, c'est
l'hallucination que la réalité provoque'[11] ('It is not reality that
Céline depicts, but the hallucination that reality provokes').

[11] See *La Nouvelle Revue Française* (April, 1938), p. 295.

It is time to illustrate some of the ways in which Céline achieves his aim of rendering emotion by means of a carefully 'stream-lined', 'bevelled' version of the spoken language. All that can be done here is to offer some main-line suggestions which may help readers to see what the problem is like—and the size of it!—and which may perhaps increase awareness with regard to the effects being attempted by the author. It must be emphasized that what follows is far from being a proper professional exercise in stylistics.

There are of course many differences between the 'spoken' and the 'literary' language. They are less obvious in a language which is minimally inflected. Indeed in English the differences are more obvious between what might be called 'illiterate' and 'literate' utterance—with due allowance made for dialectal variants and eccentricities of pronunciation. They are at their most obvious in a highly inflected language like German: an example would be the apparently well-attested decline in speech of the genitive case, replaced more and more by constructions with the preposition, *von*. In French we have perhaps a midway position in which phonetic observations play a considerable part. Few people, for instance, ever articulate all the sounds in a phrase like 'Je ne sais pas', and it gets reduced often enough to 'sais pas'. Also in French certain verb forms have to all intents and purposes disappeared from the spoken language—the past definite and the imperfect subjunctive tenses are examples. It is important to emphasize that there are in French quite clearly two standards of 'correctness' (or better 'acceptability') of usage, one spoken and one written. Anyone who has had experience in teaching the writing of French will often have had to explain that a particular turn of phrase or a particular handling of tenses belongs to the spoken language—where it is universally employed—but that it is better not to use it in formal writing. Now as we have seen, for Céline 'formal writing' represents a dead activity, of no interest and with no future for the artist. For him the language which is still alive—and which therefore has artistic potential—is the spoken language. Its utilization by the artist is, however, a matter of very considerable difficulty and delicacy: it can easily become monotonous; it must be handled in such a way as to convey various kinds and various levels of emotion; it must be cunningly adapted and even deformed by the artist in order to give a sense of variety and richness which ordinary colloquial speech often

does not possess, or only possesses sporadically. In fact, it must
be enriched by devices of a specifically 'literary' kind, such as
images and the exploitation of rhythm and tonality. Céline's
language measures up to all these requirements, and is as a result
a highly successful and very sophisticated literary medium,
personal to him.

It must not be thought that he was incapable of 'formal'
writing. The first text of any substance by him which we possess
is his doctoral thesis for the Faculty of Medicine (Paris, 1924),
La vie et l'oeuvre de Philippe-Ignace Semmelweis. It is written in a
perfectly conventional literary manner—as is hardly surprising—
but every now and again there are extraordinary flashes of
imagination which prefigure the highly original writer he was to
become. The first introductory chapter (five pages long), in which
he sketches the state of Europe during the generation preceding
the birth of Semmelweis in 1818, gives striking examples of the
force of his imagination even at this juncture and in this rather
unlikely context. He explains the advent of Napoleon after the
Revolution in these terms:

> Au cours de ces années monstrueuses où le sang flue, où la vie gicle
> et se dissout dans mille poitrines à la fois, où les reins sont
> moissonnés et broyés sous la guerre, comme les raisins au pressoir,
> il faut un mâle.
>
> Aux premiers éclairs de cet immense orage, Napoléon prit l'Europe
> et, bon gré mal gré, la garda quinze ans. (pp. 14–15)
>
> (During these monstrous years when blood flows, when life spurts
> up and dissolves in a thousand breasts at once, when loins are
> harvested and crushed by war like grapes in a wine-press, the need is
> for a male.
>
> At the first flashes of lightning of this immense storm, Napoleon
> possessed Europe, and for better or for worse, kept her for fifteen
> years.)

There are no syntactical eccentricities here, no idiosyncratic
punctuation, no traces of colloquialism. Instead there is a very
conscious formal patterning of clauses, a highly literary vocabulary and several carefully devised and powerful images. The
manner is well fitted to the subject matter, and one can see in this
short chapter a degree of confidence with words and their handling which he was never to lose.

La vie et l'oeuvre de Philippe-Ignace Semmelweis is an account of the
life and sufferings of a little-known Viennese doctor of the

nineteenth century, whose discoveries in the domain of asepsis in surgery were long despised and laughed at, the whole presented as a piece of medical history in an academic context. When Céline came to write his first literary works—from about 1928 onwards (*viz.* the play, *L'Eglise*, and *Voyage*)—the subject matter became that of all his subsequent narrative works except the ballet scenarii: 'les circonstances où le bonhomme se trouve', as he put it himself in later life (see above, p. 26). All the novels are first-person narratives, and all of them have connections with the life of the author, usually much transposed indeed, but none the less linked with personal experience in a wide range of milieux. The situations described often have powerful emotional undertones, the characters introduced are mostly 'victims' of society, very often poor and uneducated even if not stupid. (The number of prosperous characters is small, and very few of them emerge sympathetically.) To handle this kind of material Céline forges a language which in its fundamental features does not alter from *Voyage* through to the last work, *Rigodon*, but which develops in certain other respects very strikingly.

The range of words on which Céline draws, and his idiosyncratic devices of syntax, are already largely established in *Voyage*. Already in the opening pages of that first novel are to be found the kinds of image which the reader soon comes to associate with his particular sensibility. What does change are such things as narrative method, rhythmical devices, use of punctuation (notably) and authorial standpoint. In *Voyage* there are substantial sections of relatively conventional writing—carefully constructed 'grammatical' sentences with ordinary punctuation and ordinary sequence of tenses. This is still the case in *Mort à crédit*, though the quantity of such writing has diminished.

The first big change comes in fact in 1937 with the polemical *Bagatelles pour un massacre* (henceforward abbreviated to *Bagatelles*), where the staccato utilization of three dots occurs throughout the work and modifies the whole tone of the writing. *L'Ecole des cadavres* of the following year shows a temporary reversion to more standard syntax (it was hurriedly written), but, broadly speaking, all his subsequent writings follow the stylistic pattern set in *Bagatelles*, with of course variations dictated by the changes in subject matter.

The vocabulary of Céline is approximately that of an author like Balzac with the addition of a considerable twentieth-century proletarian element of familiar speech. I say Balzac deliberately, for Céline needs a wide-ranging vocabulary drawing upon technical terms for his coverage of a broad area of human experience. What he has done is to extend very substantially the kind of vocabulary which Balzac used only in a few special contexts—notably in his depiction of the underworld in *Splendeurs et misères des courtisanes*. He also invents words too, rather in the manner of Rabelais. They do not tend to be words that one would expect to pass into the language, but rather words that are effective in a specific (and often unique) context, and whose meanings are deducible from that context. What can be claimed for him is an immensely high literary awareness of the resources of French and an acute ear for the striking and the picturesque in colloquial utterance. His lexicographical knowledge—like that of Balzac, Hugo and Gautier, for instance—is very extensive. This enables him to avoid monotony when handling the spoken language, which is only too often restricted in scope and not easily sustained at length without its limitations being obvious. Low-life novels are in fact often low-level.

The sources of Céline's vocabulary are then two-fold. First, he has available his knowledge of the literary language of French from Villon onwards, with a particular emphasis on centuries other than the seventeenth and eighteenth. Secondly, he has a close knowledge of proletarian speech patterns of the period 1900–39, drawn from his childhood in Paris, his three years in the army (1911–14) and from his life as a doctor in the working-class suburbs of Paris from 1928 onwards. He has also two specialized vocabularies which prove to be rich sources of imagery—that of medicine and that of sea-faring.[12]

I am now going to give examples of some of the characteristics of Céline's vocabulary that lie outside standard literary French. He uses his colloquialisms with discretion, and while the reader certainly gets the impression of a vivid and picturesque language far removed, shall we say, from that of Voltaire or Anatole France, at the same time he is rarely baffled by incomprehensible words even if he is not a specialist in slang. This is because Céline's use of slang is carefully governed by context. With a little practice, it is possible to guess correctly the meaning of

---

[12] He spent a good number of years—on and off—as a ship's doctor. In his novels and in some of his letters there is ample evidence of his love of the sea. The most striking examples occur in *Mort à Crédit* and *Guignol's Band II* (*Le Pont de Londres*).

many of his slang terms because of their context. He does not employ ephemeral 'in-words' which are fashionable for a while and then disappear, such words are most often the invention of restricted social groups (e.g. the Ecole Polytechnique in France, the wartime RAF officers' mess). Instead he tends to use words that have existed for some considerable time,[13] and which have their historical origins in two areas in particular—the underworld and the army. The underworld may well be a 'restricted social group' but in a country that has had compulsory military service for a very long time, the army certainly is not. Moreover, at least since the time of Balzac and Eugène Sue,[14] the underworld has exercised fascination on an ever-growing public: we pass via Carco to Genet and San-Antonio and there's lots of money in it for discerning publishers. So the language of the underworld has found its way into the dictionaries of slang too, and also into the minds of those people who have the money and the inclination to buy books.

The examples that follow are selected from the whole run of Céline's works (except the play *L'Eglise* and the ballet scenarii) from *Voyage* to *Rigodon*. There is no attempt here at a serious classification, nor at a statistical approach. What is being briefly illustrated is the *kind* of word that Céline mixes in with standard French to give the particular flavour of what he calls 'style parlé'.

First I list some of the words that originate from the army and the underworld: that these should be grouped together is not a piece of anti-militarism but rather the recognition of the fact that there is much overlap between the two, the result no doubt of the presence of a good number of ex-prisoners in the ranks, and even more perhaps of the need felt by prisoners and soldiers alike for a private language of defence against authority. Some of these words have a long history—even back to the time of Villon—but most of them seem first attested in print in the nineteenth century. They occur everywhere in Céline, but those with a specific military sense are found above all in the wartime sequence at the beginning of *Voyage* and in the unfinished novel *Casse-pipe* (set in

[13] This means that most of them are to be found in, for example, G. Esnault's widely available *Dictionnaire historique des argots français* (Larousse, Paris, 1965).

[14] To be strictly accurate one should go back a great deal further—to Villon in the fifteenth century, for whom Céline had the greatest admiration. But the use of 'thieves' jargon' as 'underworld slang' virtually disappears from written French after Villon until the nineteenth century.

a cavalry regiment pre-1914). The following are all to be found in these two texts, but most of them occur elsewhere as well: *amoché* (= wounded, damaged), *bleu* (= recruit), *boucaner* (= bribe, corrupt), *cabot* (= corporal), *canard* (= rifle), *droper* (= run), *feuille* (= ear), *gluant* (= baby), *gougnafe* (= rogue), *jus* (= coffee), *juteux* (= warrant-officer), *mouscaille* (= mud, shit; misery), *pelure* (= wretch), *piston* (= captain), *pouloper* (= run hard), *rondin* (= turd), *zouave* (= cunning bastard, sly character). Here are a few more examples of this sort of word taken at random from other novels (as indicated): (*Mort à crédit*) *cambuse* (= room), *crounir* (= die), *pétard* (= arse), *pige* (= year); (*Bagatelles pour un massacre*) *auber* (= cash), *bourguignotte* (= tin-hat), *être fleur* (= be broke); (*Ecole des cadavres*) *coton* (= tough job), *douiller* (= pay); (*Les Beaux Draps*) *carbi* (= coal), *piffer* (= like); (*Guignol's Band I*) *bouzine* (= vehicle), *chocotte* (= tooth); (*Guignol's Band II*) *barda* (= sack, kit), *se maquer* (= procure a prostitute), *micheton* (= whore's client);[15] (*Féerie pour une autre fois I*) *blèche* (= soft, cowardly), *clebs* (= dog); (*Féerie pour une autre fois II, Normance*) *goutte de nib* (= nothing at all), *zébi* (= prick, penis); (*D'un Château l'autre*) *perlo* (= tobacco), *pingre* (= thief); (*Nord*) *bamboula* (= orgy), *dab* (= old man), *se gourer* (= make a mistake); (*Rigodon*) *astibloche* (= bait, worm), *plombe* (= hour).

This list—which could be very greatly expanded of course—does not mean to suggest that the words only occur in the novels mentioned. They are to be found generally in Céline, from start to finish: this kind of traditional slang has a substantial place in his works. More interesting perhaps are his exploitation of what is a relatively rare technical field in literature, that of medicine, and his creations of words. The medical terminology does not need illustration (though I shall illustrate his use of it in imagery, see below, pp. 109ff.)—the words are clear in their context—but it is necessary to say something about their effect on Céline's writing. One of the first impressions a new reader often has when coming to him is that he is much concerned with the human body and its functioning. Precise descriptions of wounds in battle and of symptoms of physical illness, bleeding, vomiting, of defecation, urination—all these are frequently found. (*Very* few descriptions of copulation occur, which makes him unusual as a twentieth-century writer: he didn't think it an interesting topic.) This physiological insistence is of course the result of his medical

[15] *Guignol's Band I* and *II* contain a great deal of underworld slang.

experience: he regards it as an essential part of human existence, not pleasing, but not revolting either, and one that is under-stressed in most of the representations of life that we call literature. One can readily understand his feeling for Villon and Rabelais. (And I'm tempted to add the reminder that Balzac was considered vulgar and almost obscene by many nineteenth-century critics because he had dared to suggest that money was a major force in human affairs. . . .) But no more than these authors is he porno-graphic.[16] There is only one sexual encounter really described in detail in the whole of Céline—the episode of Madame Gorloge in *Mort à crédit* (see pp. 667ff.)—and that is present much more as a stage in the general disillusionment of the young Ferdinand than for titillating erotic reasons. It is what is to be expected of an author whose main leitmotiv is the human journey towards death, and who expresses himself on the subject of love on the second page of his first novel—'L'amour c'est l'infini mis à la portée des caniches' (p. 12) ('A poodle's glimpse of the infinite—that's what love is').

It is only to be expected that a writer with so extensive a knowledge of the French language[17] should be intrigued by the possibilities of inventing words. There are many examples: some already in *Voyage*, rather more in *Mort à crédit*, and an enormous increase in *Bagatelles* and thereafter. Indeed, this sudden flood of lexical invention is one of the reasons why *Bagatelles* marks a turning-point in his literary development and why it is an im-portant text.

A number of these words are highly idiosyncratic and we can fairly attribute their invention to Céline. But there are some which may well have been picked up by him from elsewhere, even if they are not attested in recent dictionaries. There is a nice example of this (in Céline's favour as it happens) with regard to the verb *discutailler* (= to go on making finicky points). The admirable *Petit Robert* dictionary gives this as first attested in 1940: it occurs, however, in 1932 in *Voyage* (p. 441) and until someone finds it in print earlier than this, we can call it a creation by Céline. . . . In *Mort à crédit* we find a certain number of terms of scientific fantasy in connection with the inventor Courtial des Pereires

---

[16] I have no desire to be drawn into controversy on the nature of pornography—an issue which seems to have been ducked by ministers, Parliament and the judiciary. I owe to a colleague and to *Le Canard enchaîné* a simple and telling definition of a pornographic book: it is one that you are meant to read with one hand.

[17] He knew at least English and German quite well too.

(such as *cosmologonique, radio-tellurique, ondigène, Néo-Pluri-Rayon-nante, radiogrométrique*), but the principal linguistic inventions to the first two novels are in the domain of imagery. However with *Bagatelles* there comes a great change. It is partly caused no doubt by the move to a polemical subject, but it represents a new dimension in his writing which opens up all sorts of possibilities— grotesque, violent, obscene, contemptuous and often very funny.

As though he wished to proclaim this new departure with a flourish, he uses in the first half-page of *Bagatelles* (seventeen lines of print) *eight* neologisms. Examination of them will show several of his standard procedures. He is saying in his opening paragraphs —and this sharpens the point of his invented words—that he is genuinely a *raffiné* even if he does not write like officially con-secrated, refined stylists such as Gide, Duhamel, Colette and others. What you have to do in order to be so considered is '*troufignoliser* . . . l'adjectif . . . *goncourtiser* . . . merde! *enculagailler* la *moumouche, frénétiser* l'insignifiance, babiller ténu dans la pompe (to babble with subtle pomposity), *plastroniser, cocoriquer* dans les micros.' Now to anyone with a fair knowledge of French, none of these italicized words presents any great difficulty of approxi-mate comprehension: the passage gets through alright. But if you look at what has gone on in these instances, a particular tone emerges which adds a great deal to the text. *Troufignoliser*: the starting-point here is the verb *fignoler* which means 'to execute with care and attention to detail'. *Fignoler l'adjectif* would have been a possible example of the refined style he is mocking. The first device is to make *fignoler* into *fignoliser*. The termination *-iser* most frequently (like the ending -ize in English verbs) has the sense of 'make'—*diviniser* (= make divine), *neutraliser* (= make neutral), etc.—so the effect here is *rendre fignolé*. But if we also know that *troufion, troufignard* and *troufignon* are words of varying degrees of popular usage all best translated into parallel English as 'arse-hole', we see that Céline's new word is contemptuous and not in *style raffiné* at all. *Goncourtiser* uses the *-iser* termination again, and picks up Céline's frequently expressed scorn for the kind of commercial novel so often crowned by the Académie Goncourt. (It is not really malicious to point out that in 1932 *Voyage* was beaten into second place for the Prix Goncourt by a quite un-memorable work, *Les Loups*, by Guy de Mazeline.) *Enculagailler* starts of course from *enculer* (= to bugger), but it has been transformed into a more picturesque verb by use of the termination -*ailler* which is pejorative and also indicates repeated action— as in verbs like *disputailler*, *ecrivailler*, *tirailler*. He could have written *enculailler*; but perhaps for reasons of euphony and extra force, he supplies the further syllable -*ag*.[18] It becomes a more vigorous (!) word as a result: traces of *gaillard* perhaps? *Moumouche* is an example of the common feature of reduplication in child language—like *caca*, *dada*, *pipi*—and serves to trivialize the image still further. Moreover, *mouche* has more than one meaning: the most likely here is that of 'fly', but it could also be a 'bull's-eye' (of a target) . . . I will take this up again in a few moments. *Frénétiser* is made telling by its attachment to *l'insignifiance*, as a kind of contradiction in terms. *Plastroniser* is based on *plastronner* (= to posture, throw out one's chest). *Cocoriquer* seems to me to be an entirely felicitous creation on the noun *cocorico* (= cock-a-doodle-doo) and describes succinctly and agreeably the behaviour of certain celebrities in front of a microphone.

The eighth new word on this half-page occurs a few lines later. Céline develops his line of thought by saying that with a bit of practice he could easily write in the manner described—all things are possible with a little effort. And he adds:

> On arrive à tout . . . comme dit le proverbe espagnol: 'Beaucoup de vaseline, encore plus de patience, Elephant *encugule* fourmi.'
>
> (Everything is possible—as the Spanish proverb has it 'Plenty of vaseline and even more patience, Elephant bulugger ant.')

Just to show that he can do other things with the word *enculer* (and he uses this word a lot in *Bagatelles*), he gives an agreeable variant on *enculagailler*. More gentle, perhaps? slightly Spanish? More flippant too, and owing something again to the trivializing effect of reduplication. And its use with *fourmi* strengthens the view that *moumouche* = fly.

This kind of thing becomes standard practice in Céline from *Bagatelles* onwards. Its full savouring does certainly require a fair degree of linguistic sophistication, but part of the pleasure of reading the later Céline lies in sensitizing oneself to the ingenious overtones this technique affords. Here are a few more which are not too hermetic: (*Bagatelles*) *culacagneux, pantachiotes*; (*Ecole des cadavres*) *chèvres et chouteries, dosatages, éclatouiller, explosiller,*

[18] Also because addition inside a word of a syllable -*av* or -*ag* is frequent as a joke device (known in French as *javanais*).

larbinisé, vachardise; (*Les Beaux Draps*) *beubeurres, crocro, susuques*; (*Féerie I*) *blablatter, ménopauserie, ovationner*; (*Féerie II*) *existenglaireux*; (*Rigodon*) *cacographes, déconophones*.

There are also other more obvious inventions which border on the pun, such as *Céphalo-Bills* (*Bagatelles*) as a pejorative term for intellectuals, and many others which are really images—such as the description (again *Bagatelles*) of Maurice Thorez as *le bébé-Führer*.[19] Material of this kind, unlike the straight use of popular terminology, pulls out from the reader quite specific intellectual responses. None the less, insofar as it represents a kind of rejection of what he conveniently called 'le style raffiné', it has the same kind of emotional effect on the reader. He is confronted with an unusual, irreverent, and—as the author himself might have said—piss-taking employment of language.

Even more effective in uprooting traditional notions about how to write French is Céline's adoption of certain 'ungrammatical' features of the spoken language. Here again we can only point to some of the procedures most commonly found.[20] The most frequent of all is syntactically unnecessary repetition (pleonasm), elevated into a deliberate stylistic device:

Elle a duré des semaines *la maladie de Bébert*. (*Voyage*, p. 272)

(*It* lasted for weeks, *Bebert's illness*.)

Mais *j*'avais plus rien à imaginer *moi* sur *elle la mer* à présent. (*Voyage*, p. 489)

(But *I*, I didn't have any more to imagine about *it myself, the sea*, for the time being.)

Mon *père il* tenait un beau cocard. (*Mort à crédit*, p. 616)

(*My father, he*'d got a hell of a black eye.)

Si je tuais l'*Helsey*, au pistolet, c'est encore moi qu'irais en caisse ... Et puis *il* existe peut-être pas le *Helsey*! (*Bagatelles*, p. 35)

(If I shot that character *Helsey* with a pistol, I'd be the one to go to jail ... Anyway, perhaps *he* doesn't even exist, *Helsey*.)

[19] Thorez, the leader of the French Communist Party for many years, is thus dismissed as one who would *like* to be a Hitler but had not the stature. The rotundity of Thorez's face, giving him an air of benevolence despite his hard-line Stalinism, explains the use of *bébé*.

[20] N.B. the translations in this section are only literal guides to the meaning—that is to say it is sometimes impossible to give an equivalent syntactical idiosyncracy in English. Indeed, the next few pages won't mean much to someone who knows no French grammar *at all*.

Bien sûr que je ne suis pas le seul aux *'certains ennuis'*! Mais les autres qu'*en* ont-ils fait de leurs *'certains ennuis'*? (*Nord*, p. 394)

(Agreed, I'm not the only one to have *'certain difficulties'*, but the others what have they done about *them*, about their *'certain difficulties'*?)

This device has many uses. It certainly gives a familiar, colloquial tone on most occasions, but it can also be used for emphasis, for vituperation, for ironical effect. Found continuously in Céline from *Voyage* to *Rigodon*, it is not, however, used to excess, and eventually the reader comes to accept it as a normal kind of diction which helps to give him the sensation Céline is seeking— 'Le lecteur qui me lit! il lui semble, il en jurerait, que quelqu'un lui lit dans la tête! . . .[21] ('The reader who reads me! it seems to him, he'd swear to it, that someone is reading to him inside his head! . . .')

The reader will have noticed in two of the above examples the suppression of the negative *ne*—'j'avais plus rien' and 'il existe peut-être pas'. One would soon tire of counting the many examples of this standard feature of the spoken language. But sometimes the pronoun subject disappears too—'Y avait personne avec lui' (*Voyage*, p. 45) ('Was no one with him'), and sometimes the omission of a *ne* almost seems to emphasize the negative—'Je faisais semblant de pas le regarder (*Mort à crédit*, p. 613) ('I pretended not to look at him'). Another frequent colloquial device is the substitution of adjective for adverb—'Je fuis affreux dès qu'on me cause' (*Mort à crédit*, p. 696) ('I run terrible as soon as anyone speaks to me') or 'Ils me regardaient horrible' (*Mort à crédit*, p. 1006) ('They looked horrible at me').

Perhaps the most fruitful of all the liberties Céline takes with standard written French is the willingness to disturb normal word order for reasons of tonality of emphasis. The quotation a few lines above from *Mort à crédit* (p. 613) gives a good idea of this if continued through to the end of the sentence—'Je faisais semblant de pas le regarder mais au beurre noir qu'il avait l'oeil' ('I pretended not to look at him, but a black eye is what he had'). A few pages earlier in *Mort à crédit* (p. 607), we have the following phrase which comes from a description of a vessel entering the port of Dieppe in rough weather—'L'amarre en poupe a encore un grand coup gémi' ("The after mooring-rope once again loudly

[21] *Entretiens*, p. 122; see also above, p. 89.

groaned'). Unlike the preceding instance, this is a particularly *literary* effect, if only because *gémir* is never transitive in ordinary speech. Invert *a* and *encore* and you have a rather limp alexandrine: he was wise to avoid that. . . . Another literary example is almost *précieux* in tone—'Joyeusement alors gambadante ma famille sur les gazons de l'été revenu, je la vois d'ici par les beaux dimanches' (*Voyage*, p. 69) ('Joyfully gambolling my family on the lawns of newly arrived summer, I can see them from here on fine Sundays'). In both these cases there is an attempt at a kind of lyricism: in the first the content is perfectly serious, as often in Céline when ships and the sea are the subject, but in the second, this manner is placed in violent contrast with the sentence which follows immediately (and which has some interesting balancing of phrases):

> Cependant qu'à trois pieds dessous, moi papa, ruisselant d'asticots et bien plus infect qu'un kilo d'étrons du 14 juillet pourrira fantastiquement de toute sa viande déçue . . .
>
> (Meanwhile three feet below, I, daddy, streaming with maggots and much more disgusting than a kilo of bank holiday turds, will be rotting fantastically with all his disappointed flesh . . .)

('Moi papa' is taken as third person singular in view of the verb form *pourrira*: the effect is one of depersonalizing the speaker.) Sometimes the shift of one word by one place in the sentence has a highly dramatic effect. In *Bagatelles* (p. 106) there is a torrential long sentence describing the fate of the innocent schoolchild under the yoke of official *lycée* education (quoted more fully below, p. 144), which ends thus with a veritable cascade of vituperative epithets at the expense of the teaching profession:

> . . . la pire clique parasiteuse, phrasuleuse (. . .) énucoïde, désastrogène, de l'Univers: le Corps stupide enseignant.
>
> (. . . the worst possible, parasitical, phrase-making (. . .) eunuchoid, disaster-producing, clique in the whole Universe, the teaching stupid profession.)

My view is that the placing of *stupide* is a stroke of polemical genius.

Cascades of epithets are frequently found in Céline, especially in polemical contexts. He did not have warm feelings towards M. Georges de Girard de Charbonnière (that name would have put him off to start with, and why not?), of the French Legation in Copenhagen in 1945, who caused his arrest and none the less failed after much effort to persuade the Danish government that there was a case for Céline's extradition to France as a traitor. M. de Girard de Charbonnière is contemptuously nick-named 'Hortensia' in *Féerie I* from which the following passage is taken:

> . . . Gaëtan Serge d'Hortensia, l'Assesseur nègre de l'Ambassade, représentant l'Union des Cinglés, diplomatiques, politiques, coloniaux, et ectoplasmiques, qui m'inspire au jour levant! c'est pas l'obsession que nul être de haut moral serait tourné chagrin fou grossier grelottant cheveux blancs? (p. 51)

> (Gaëtan Serge Hydrangea, negroid Adviser to the Embassy, repre-senting the Association of diplomatic, political, colonial and ectoplasmic Dim-wits, who comes to inspire me at sunrise! it's surely not obsessive to say that no one of seriousness could avoid becoming melancholy, mad, coarse, trembly, white-haired?)

This process of accumulation is very often found. Should it be discussed in connection with syntax or under the heading of imagery? In so far as the lists are dependent in part on the *order* of words, I have thought it reasonable to use this device as a kind of link between syntax and imagery, all the more so because so many passages from our author raise multiple points of vocabulary, syntax, punctuation and imagery almost simultane-ously. Here are two more passages to illustrate this. First a sentence from *D'un Château l'autre* describing the extraordinary Hohenzollern castle of Sigmaringen:

> Dans ce *sacristi va comme je te pousse biscornuterie quinze* . . . *vingt manoirs superposés* se trouvait une bibliothèque mais une *bath* . . . oh là *youyoue!* cette richesse! inouïe! . . . *nous y reviendrons je vous raconterai* . . . (p. 105)

> (In this blessed all over the place deformation, fifteen . . . twenty manor-houses one on top of each other, was a library, a super one, oh yumyum, riches, unheard of . . . we'll go back there, I'll tell you about it . . .)

There is quite a bit to be said about these few words! *Sacristi* (or *sapristi*) is a slightly antiquated expletive: *sacré* would be more normal in this context, but more obvious too and devoid of the punning religious connotation of *sacristi*. *Va comme je te pousse* is a standard colloquialism meaning 'no matter how, anyhow' and fits the overall remarks about the confusion of styles in the castle. *Biscornuterie* is a Céline neologism on the existing adjective *biscornu* meaning 'deformed, twisted', and adds a further vivid notion to *va comme je te pousse*. The three dots between *quinze* and *vingt* are a good clear instance of how this punctuation device is used from *Bagatelles* onwards. (There will be more about this in a moment.) What we need to ask here is how this particular nuance could have been conveyed in a more conventional style. *Quinze manoirs superposés* (the basic structure) is (un)grammatically connected with *ce*. So one would have to recast the sentence at this point anyway, even without the qualification *quinze . . . vingt*, and one would end up with something like 'où il y avait quinze ou même vingt manoirs superposés'. How much more live and telling is Céline's solution! *Une bath* pulls us back into colloquialism with a jerk. *Bath* or *bat'* is attested in the early nineteenth century in the sense of 'good'. But *youyoue* immediately is a Célinian appreciative noise—not unlike 'yum-yum' in English. (I cannot see how it can have any connection with the nautical term *youyou* = dinghy.) And finally we see the three dots being used once more to allow the reminiscence to continue unimpeded by the break of a full stop which would normally be required.

My second example is slightly longer. It comes from *Nord* (p. 482). Céline has been recounting a memory from October 1914 when in the front line on the banks of the river Lys in Flanders, his regiment was joined during the dark of night by a stream of unseen women—'de demoiselles et de dames, bourgeoises, ouvrières'—who obligingly lifted their skirts for the soldiers under fire from the opposite bank of the river, spoke no words and went away. He continues:

> . . . les *bonnes moeurs* mettent dix mois, dix ans, à faire traîner les fiançailles, *d'un sport d'hiver l'autre, vernissage l'autre,* surprises parties, *ruptures d'autos, petits grands gueuletons, alcools formids, rots, bans,* Mairie, mais s'il le faut, les circonstances font copuler des régiments *méli-mélo de folles amoureuses* sous des voûtes d'obus, mille dames *à la fois! à la minute!* . . . pas d'histoires! . . . *trous dans la nature?* . . . morts partout? *dzigui! dzigui! amours comme des mouches!*

(. . . accepted standards of behaviour require engagements to last ten months, ten years, from one ski-resort to another, one private viewing to another, surprise parties, writing off of cars, nice little big blow-outs, super spirits, belches, banns, (=) Registry Office, but if need be, circumstances can make whole regiments of frenzied

women copulate away, all jumbled up beneath arching shell fire a
thousand at once . . . per minute . . . honestly! . . . slits in thin air?
. . . corpses everywhere? . . . Jigzig! Jigzig! copulating like flies.)

I have quoted this because it is a very representative passage of
mature Céline. No one would want to suggest that any profound
verity is being enunciated here: our author is not *un homme à
idéas*. If all we get from this passage is that bourgeois morality
tends to crack under wartime conditions, then we can thank him
kindly for telling us something we know already. What is
interesting in the content of this passage is the view it gives—
from the outside—of what post-war prosperous society (*Nord* is
of 1960) has happily given to the media as its image, followed by
the wry comment that copulation is no more than a jig-jigging of
the buttocks anyway.

There are quite a few points of detail to examine. *Les bonnes
moeurs* is in contrast with what follows at the end of the passage
and is ironical in context. *D'un sport d'hiver l'autre*—this is a turn
of phrase much affected by Céline (even used in the title *D'un
Château l'autre*): strictly here it should mean 'from one kind of
winter sport to another', but clearly we must understand 'from
one winter sports holiday to another'. *Vernissage l'autre*—same
structure but with the reasonable suppression of *d'un*. *Ruptures
d'auto* is distinctly odd. With the word *rupture* we expect for
instance, *de fiançailles*, but attached to *autos* it is unexpected, and
suggests that, if one is rich, when one tires of a particular car one
throws it away and buys another. *Petits grands gueuletons* gives a
sharp shift in tone and leads naturally to the *alcools formids*, *rots*.
Having got as far as that one may proceed to marriage—*bans*,
Mairie. *Méli-mélo de folles amoureuses*—grammatically one needs
some kind of link with *régiments*, but this is deliberately sup-
pressed, without any loss to clarity, because of the sense of *méli-
mélo* (= confusion). In French it is normally only a noun, but in
Céline's sentence it has an almost adverbial sense. *A la fois! . . . à
la minute!* is another instance of the economy provided by the use
of the three dots. *Trous dans la nature* uses the colloquial sense of
nature (= landscape, scenery). English does not quite have this;
one might translate 'il a disparu dans la nature' as 'he has vanished
into thin air', but behind this meaning is that of welcoming
'vaginas in the open air'. The final section beginning '*Morts
partout?*' evokes elliptically the presence of death, the enemy fire
all around contemporaneous with the movements of copulation,

of human beings procreating like flies. This whole passage reflects Céline's overall view of human sexuality, many times expressed in his works. The union between two human beings is a good and excellent thing: orgasm brings to the human animal a transcendental experience for a few seconds—but this does not merit a mass of literature.[22]

So far I have been illustrating—in a casual and selective fashion—the basic materials of which the style of Céline is constructed. What counts ultimately with any author is the way in which he uses these materials, and so I now move on to the consideration of words in association with each other, of what may loosely be called imagery. I am not going to be concerned with the formal figures of speech—simile, metaphor, metonymy, synecdoche, etc. Indeed, I am going to allow myself much latitude in selecting examples from Céline, some of which are certainly formal literary images, but others of which can best be described perhaps as representative Céline idiosyncracies—*phrases typiques*, one might say. There is an undeniable richness of invention, an imaginative profusion and a high degree of sophisticated allusion and intelligence in our author in this domain. Yet I must say once more that all I can attempt here is the examination of a woefully inadequate number of examples, in the hope you will find it easier as a result of what I say, to reach your own conclusion on what is in fact a vast topic.

There are, broadly speaking, two main kinds of literary effect sought by Céline. On the one hand there are many polemical, ironical, corrosive and even violent statements, and on the other hand there are also passages of sensitivity and even tenderness. The sources of his imagery are, as one would expect of a highly intelligent and very well read author, extremely diverse, and future generations of readers are going to need quite a few footnotes if they are to pick up all the twentieth-century literary and political references: Duhamel is still just about known and so are Daladier and De Brinon, Vailland won the Prix Goncourt and Mauriac is still a Gaullist saint, but in a hundred years' time they will all probably have the same degree of relative obscurity as Guizot or Paul Bourget. There are, however, three specialized

[22] Cf. his contemptuous reference in *Bagatelles* to D. H. Lawrence (p. 113): 'la bravoure inouïe de ses messages sexuels . . . (une pauvre bite de garde-chasse pour 650 pages)' ('the unheard-of courage of his sexual messages . . . (a game-keeper's miserable prick for 650 pages)').

sources of inspiration for Céline which will need illustration. These are his medical vocabulary, his life-long interest in ships and the sea, and his passionate love of ballet.

The medical vocabulary, or, more broadly, the medical *attitude*, produces a whole range of striking and unusual linguistic effects, some of them in appearance blunt, coarse and, to some people, obscene. The last word should be rejected, unless it means no more than physiologically frank. I say again that there is virtually *no* pornographic or erotic material in Céline's works, but there is a great deal of reference to the physical functions—defecation, urination, vomiting, menstruation. Disease and old age are part of the human condition which the doctor observes every day of his life: Céline's view is that since the Middle Ages (when literature did not shy away from reality), these subjects have been carefully excluded from literature, and so he restores them to their place as an essential part of the human predicament. And who is to say that he has not right on his side? Death from cancer, from meningitis, from general senility may not be as pretty as death by the sword, or by the noble poison of Phèdre, but it is a very great deal more frequent. According to M. le Docteur Destouches, life is both a 'voyage au bout de la nuit' and a 'rigodon', and what we are all engaged upon is purchasing a 'mort à crédit'. He is well qualified to make clinical observations on it all.

But Céline, despite his apparently pessimistic, destructive view of the human condition, was at the same time—and this is of extreme importance for the proper understanding of him—an idealist too. Like Villon whom he so much admired, and like Baudelaire (whom he never mentions as far as I know), he sees life in opposing ways. Beside the rotting corpses of the *Ballade des pendus* we find the grace and beauty of the *Ballade des dames du temps jadis*, beside the desolation of *Spleen*, the awareness of the existence of *Idéal*. This aspect of Céline's work is more fully discussed in the chapters dealing with the individual novels, but some of my examples here will show it too.

For simplicity I divide these examples into three categories. First some instances of the medical inspiration, next those of a polemical or ironical kind, and then, more generally, those of a neutral descriptive kind, including references to the sea and to ballet.

The death of Robinson from a bullet-wound at the end of *Voyage* (p. 437) is described in a way that is both moving and vivid: it is the feeling we have of observing it through the eyes of the doctor, Bardamu, that makes it especially effective, as in these two sentences that follow the onset of the massive internal haemorrhage which causes death:

> Son coeur s'est mis à battre de plus en plus vite et puis tout à fait vite. Il courait son coeur après son sang, épuisé, là-bas, minuscule déjà, tout à fait à la fin des artères, à trembler au bout des doigts.
>
> (His heart began to beat faster and faster and then very fast indeed. His heart, it was running after his blood, away there, already minute, right at the end of the arteries, exhausted with trembling at the finger-tips.)

Towards the end of *Mort à crédit* (p. 1020) is a description of the body of a suicide—Courtial des Pereires—who has blown his brains out. The narrator this time is the young Ferdinand, but he already has a dispassionate eye for disagreeable physical spectacles:

> C'est plus qu'un trou sa figure . . . avec des rebords tout gluants . . . et puis comme une boule de sang qui bouchait . . . au milieu . . . coagulée . . . un gros pâté . . . et puis des rigoles qui suintaient jusqu'à l'autre côté de la route . . . Surtout ça coulait du menton qu'était devenu comme une éponge . . .
>
> (His face is no more than a hole . . . with the edges all sticky . . . and then something like a ball of blood blocking it . . . in the middle . . . coagulated . . . a big blot . . . and then there were trickles oozing across to the other side of the road . . . it was flowing particularly from the chin which had become a kind of sponge.)

The point I would wish to make about this—and there are many similar passages in Céline—is that to write with such precision and imagination about such a spectacle, demands the ability to observe it without revulsion. Some qualification here is needed none the less. The presence in Céline's narratives of very explicit descriptions of both the grace and the imperfection of the human body certainly indicates a preoccupation with the purely physical. But this preoccupation is easily misunderstood by the lay reader and is liable to seem an obsession. Céline injects into his descriptions of this sort the kind of detachment regarding what to most people is physically repulsive which every medical student *has* to acquire from the moment when early on in his training he has to enter an anatomy laboratory and begin dissection. Céline does this quite deliberately because he holds that the common tendency to ignore the miseries of human suffering and to shun the reality of death is a prime cause of man's cruelty to man. Villon had the same 'obsession' and the same compassion and it is not surprising that Céline admired him so greatly.

Bagatelles contains a remarkable series of pages about a hospital for venereal diseases in Leningrad (see below, pp. 127–8 for some extracts), and in *Guignol's Band I* there is a description of another hospital, this time in the East End of London during the First World War, from which comes this passage about patients suffering from chronic disease:

Il y en avait de drôles de bouilles (. . .) qui s'en allaient par portions comme ci, comme ça, un jour un oeil, le nez, une couille et puis un bout de rate, un petit doigt, que c'est en somme comme une bataille contre la grande mordure, l'horreur qu'est dedans qui ronge, sans fusil, sans sabre, sans canon, comme ça qu'arrache tout au bonhomme, que ça le décarpille bout par bout, que ça vient de nulle part, d'aucun ciel, qu'un beau jour il existe plus complètement écorché à vif, débité croustillant d'ulcères, comme ça à petits cris, rouges hoquets, grognements et prières, et supplications bominables. (p. 111)

(There were some pretty curious characters there (. . .) who were falling apart bit by bit, one day an eye, the nose, a testicle and then a chunk of spleen, a little finger, it's in fact a kind of battle against the insistent gnawing, the horror within which eats away, without rifle, without sabre, without cannon, just snatches everything away from the chap, takes him apart bit by bit, coming from nowhere, from no heaven, so that one fine day he is no more, totally flayed alive, chopped up crunchily by ulcers, with little groans, red hiccoughs, gruntings and prayers, and terrible pleadings.)

Ferdinand at this stage is not a doctor himself, but as he helps in this hospital the vocation is forming: at least a doctor can bring comfort and, with luck, even alleviate pain. Yet there is no point in glossing over the miseries of terminal illness. . . .

These three examples are of course all related to a 'medical' context. But the influence of a life of general practice, the detached clinical observation which such a career fosters are detectable in all sorts of non-medical contexts in Céline. Here are some obvious instances, listed with minimal comment:

Voyage Dans le kiosque à côté près du métro, la marchande s'en fout de l'avenir, elle se gratte sa vieille conjonctivite et se la purule lentement avec les ongles. (p. 472)

(In the kiosk of the metro the stall-keeper doesn't give a damn about the future, she scratches her long-standing conjunctivitis and turns it purulent gradually with her nails.)

Féerie I [In 1944 in Paris, Céline receives a visit from an old friend and her son. He suspects that they have come to look over his flat, believing that he will be assassinated at the Liberation] Je retourne au jeune homme là au mur, le dadais ingrat . . . (. . .) Il se trifouille la poche . . . c'est pas grave . . . tous les jeunes gens se trifouillent les poches . . . un revolver? une érection? (p. 17)

(I look back at the young man there against the wall, unprepossessing lout . . . (. . .) He's fiddling about in his pocket . . . doesn't matter . . . all young men fiddle about in their pockets . . . a revolver? an erection?)

Nord [An aside on the subject of *les mondains*—i.e. wealthy, 'cultured' persons] . . . eux les mondains, la différence, parlent tout le temps, gardent rien pour eux, sont en scène . . . au lit, encore! . . . ils ne sont vraiment simples qu'aux W.C. . . . et un peu au moment du râle . . . (p. 596)

(. . . the well-to-do, the difference is they talk all the time, keep nothing to themselves, always performing . . . in bed, still! . . . they are only truly natural when they are on the lavatory . . . and a little bit at the moment of the death-rattle . . .)

Rigodon [An aside, very much in the spirit of Villon, on the subject of inescapable and unforeseeable death] . . . ce qu'on ne voit pas qui compte dans la vie, ce qui se voit s'entend n'est que mascarade, coups de gueule, théâtre! . . . ce qui se passe au fond de votre prostate qu'est intéressant, ce millionième de gamète qui décide qu'il en a assez, qu'il obéit plus aux ordres, qu'il va travailler pour son compte, foutre des marquises et du petit ami! qu'il va proliférer et hop! vite, pour lui, lui-même! vous la fosse! hop! vous le verrez jamais ce millionième d'anarchiste gamète crasseux cancéreux! . . . vous saurez même pas qu'il a existé! . . . (p. 832)

(what one doesn't see is what counts in life, what can be seen, heard, is mere masquerade, shouting, theatre! what goes on deep in your prostate is what's interesting, that millionth part of a gamete who decides he's fed up, won't obey orders any more, is going to work for himself, too fucking bad for Mesdames les marquises and for the boy-friend! is going to proliferate, and fast too, for him, himself! You into the grave! out! you'll never see this one millionth part of an anarchical gamete, filthy and cancerous . . . you'll not even know he existed! . . .)

After these somewhat grim examples, it must be stressed that it is his medical experience that also provokes in Céline some of his tenderest passages, as will be seen during the examination of the individual novels. The opening pages of *Mort à crédit* (pp. 501–2) show exactly what I mean by this (see above, p. 69).

My second category—images of a polemical or ironical kind— is so vast that the instances here given are bound to be disparate. Céline is essentially an attacking writer, one who protests with all the vigour and violence at his command against man's inhumanity to man, against false and lying recipes for human happiness, against the grotesque futility of so much of human existence, against the ignorance and stupidity of our so-called 'leaders', against the soul-destroying influence of press, radio, cinema and publicity, and also against the sentimental and commercial exploitation of human sexuality in the arts. His whole work is in fact an indictment of our modern consumer society, and he was one of the first writers to speak out on this theme. The examples that follow are pretty representative of his corrosive and aggressive side, and again need little elucidation. They are presented chronologically rather than in any grouping of topics:

Voyage [About the managing director of the *Compagnie Pordurière* in W. Africa] . . . son passé rempli de plus de crapuleries qu'une prison de port de guerre. (p. 146)

(his past more full of dirty tricks than a prison in a naval port.)

Mort à crédit [Of an extremely obstinate woman] Quand elle s'était vouée à un truc, elle se vrillait dedans comme un boulon, fallait arracher toute la pièce! . . . c'était extrêmement douloureux! . . . (p. 987)

(When she's decided to devote herself to something, she'd gimlet her self into it like a bolt, so the whole block would have to be pulled away . . . It was very painful . . .)

Bagatelles [On how reputations are commercially fabricated in our time] Comment le plus infime crétin, le canard plus rebutant, la plus désespérante donzelle, peuvent-ils muer en dieux? . . . déesse? . . . recueillir plus d'âmes en un jour que Jésus Christ en deux mille ans? . . . Publicité! Que demande la foule moderne? Elle demande à se mettre à genoux devant l'or et devant la merde! . . . (p. 38).

(How can the most minimal cretin, the most repulsive creep, the most hopeless minge, how can they be transmuted into gods? . . .

goddess? . . . gather in more souls in one day than Jesus Christ in two thousand years? . . . Publicity! What does the modern public want? It wants to go down on its knees before money and before shit! . . .)

L'Ecole des cadavres [Epigraph to the book] 'Dieu est en réparation' ('God is being mended').

[On what will happen to millions of ordinary soldiers in the war to come] Ça va, Madame la Marquise, très bien! Des agonies peu banales! vous finirez en vraies dentelles! Plein les barbelés! Vous finirez transparents, frémissants aux moindres rafales, ondoyants aux bouffées d'obus. Quels trépas! Héros de viandes rouges! Limés, repassés, fondus, lustrés, empesés, mousselinés par les tanks, vaporeuses résilles ardentes, oriflammes d'or et de sang. (p. 150)

(Everything, Madame la Marquise, is going well. Most unusual death-agonies! you'll end up really like lace! the barbed-wire will be full! you'll end up transparent, quivering at the least volleys, swaying in the breeze of passing shells! What ways to die! Heroes of red meat! Filed down, ironed, melted, glazed, starched, mashed by the tanks, burning filmy hair-nets, oriflammes of gold and blood.)

[On the President of France in 1938] nous ne sommes plus sous Louis XIV. Les pets de Monsieur Lebrun ne font tressaillir l'Europe. Ils ne font même tressaillir personne, ce sont des pets vraiment pour rien. (p. 254)

(We are no longer under Louis XIV. Monsieur Lebrun's farts do not make Europe tremble. They don't in fact make anyone tremble, they are truly useless farts.)

Les Beaux Draps [On French denunciations to the German occupying forces] La France est bourrique, c'est plein la Commandatur des personnes qui viennent dénoncer . . . (. . .) Au nom de la Patrie toujours! donner le copin, la copine . . . Comme ça ne perdant pas une minute! . . . Le Fiel est Roi! . . . Regardez la gueule du trèpe, c'est du long cauchemar en figures. C'est tout obscène par le visage. Parties honteuses remontées au jour. (pp. 9–10)

(France is a country of informers, the Commandatur it's full of people come to squeal . . . (. . .) For the good of their Country of course! give away friends, girl-friends . . . Just like that, not a minute wasted! Bile is King! Look at the expression of the mob, a long nightmare of faces, that's what it is. Really obscene face. Pudenda exposed to the light of day.)

Féerie II, Normance [Only suffering humanity is of interest: the rest merely copulate without thought and produce new cannon-fodder] . . . question des hommes et des femmes y a que les malades qui m'intéressent . . . les autres, debout, ils sont tout vices et méchancetés . . . (. . .) encore en plus qu'ils parlent d'amour en vers, en prose, et en musique, qu'ils n'arrêtent pas! culot! et qu'ils engendrent! acharnés fournisseurs d'Enfer! et péroreurs! et que ça finit pas de promettre! . . . et que ça s'enorgueillit du tout! et bave et pavane! (pp. 71–2)

(. . . as far as men and women are concerned, I'm only interested in those who are ill . . . the rest of them on their feet, they're all vice and nastiness . . . moreover they go on talking about love in prose and in verse and in music, and never stop! what a nerve! and procreate away! determined suppliers of Hell! and speechifyers! never tired of promising, proud of it all, dribbling and preening themselves!)

D'un Château l'autre [On what it is like being in prison: reflections on his incarceration in Denmark after the war] . . . je voudrais y voir, Mauriac, Morand, Aragon, Vaillant, et tutti, leur galoubet, après six mois! ah Nobels! Goncourts et frutti! cette révélation! . . . et forte chiasse! toute leur jean foutrerie sous eux! (p. 96)

(I'd like to see Mauriac, Morand, Aragon, Vaillant, all hear their tune after six months! ah Nobels! Goncourts and sundry! what a revelation! . . . and strong colic! all their crap under them!)

Nord [Two comments on the difference between VIPs and you and me] . . . les guerres qui font rage sur sept fronts et sur toutes les mers n'empêchent pas le caviar . . . la super-écrabouillerie, bombe Z, lance-pierre, ou tue-mouche, respectera toujours les *delikatessen* des hautes tables . . . Ce n'est pas demain que vous verrez Krouk-rouzov se nourrir de singe! Nixon à la nouille à l'eau, Millamac à la carotte crue . . . les hautes tables sont toujours 'Raison d'Etat' . . . (p. 305)

(. . . wars raging on seven fronts and on all the seas don't stop the caviar getting through . . . the super-pulping, Z bomb, catapult or fly-swatter will always spare the delikatessen for the tables of the great . . . You'll have to wait a long while before you see Krukruschev eating corned beef! Nixon on boiled noodles, Milla-mac [Macmillan] on raw carrots . . . the tables of the great are always of 'national importance'.)

. . . le vrai rideau de fer c'est entre riches et les miteux . . . les questions d'idées sont vétilles entre égales fortunes . . . l'opulent nazi, un habitant du Kremlin, l'administrateur Gnome et Rhône, sont culs chemises, à regarder de près, s'échangent les épouses, biberonnent les mêmes *Scotch*, parcourent les mêmes golfs (...) ... et merde du reste! . . . babioles! galvaudeux suants trimards, mégotiers, revendicateurs, à la niche! ce qu'ils pensent de nous là sûr! ... (p. 417)

(... the true iron curtain is between the rich and the threadbare ... differences of ideas are trifles between people of equal wealth ... the opulent Nazi, an inhabitant of the Kremlin, the managing director of Gnome and Rhone, are indistinguishable if you look closely, they exchange wives, knock back the same Scotch, walk about the same golf-courses (...) ... and don't give a shit for anyone else ... trifles! botching, sweating drudges, pickers-up of fag-ends, malcontents back to your kennels! that's what they think of us for sure! ...)

Rigodon [Céline talking to a friend, indicates what the history books will say of our age in 3,000] 'Les hommes blancs ont inventé la bombe atomique, peu après ils ont disparu.' Tu veux que je te dise comment? (...) plusieurs thèses: ils se sont disparus dans les guerres, et par l'alcoolisme, l'automobile, et le trop manger . . . d'autres auteurs sont plutôt d'avis qu'ils ont succombé aux religions et fanatismes succedanés, politiques, familiaux, sportifs, mondains, toutes leurs religions, catholique, hébraique, réformée, franc-maçonnerie ... (p. 729)

('White men invented the atomic bomb, and shortly afterwards became extinct.' You want me to tell you how? . . . several theories: they disappeared through wars, and alcoholism, cars and too much eating . . . other authors incline rather to the opinion that they succumbed to ersatz religions and fanaticisms,—political, familial, sporting, fashionable,—all their religions, Catholic, Jewish, reformed, free-masonry ...)

[A glimpse of the jet-set in the future] . . . ils se font éjecter, de Passy, leur seizième étage, par super-jet conditionné, direct Golgotha ... sept minutes ... photographiés aux 'oliviers'... Monsieur en Joseph . . . Madame en Marie ... les enfants, anges évidemment . . . retour avant l'apéritif! depuis que chaque homme moteur au cul va où il veut, comme il veut, sans jambes sans tête, il n'est plus qu'une baudruche, un vent . . . il ne disparaîtra même pas, c'est fait ... (pp. 827–8)

(... they'll be shot off from their sixteenth-storey flat in Passy by conditioned super-jet, non-stop to Golgotha ... seven minutes ... photographed by the 'olive trees' ... Monsieur as Joseph, Madame as Mary . . . the children, angels of course . . . Home by drinks time! ever since every man, engine at his arse goes where he wants, as he wants, without legs without head, he's no more than a bladder, a wind . . . he won't even disappear, it's happened already . . .)

My third category of examples gives a necessary contrast. The dominant tone in Céline is indeed that of a kind of twentieth-century *Spleen*, as has been suggested, but this would be much less effective were it not set into relief by the presence of his own kind of awareness of beauty. He is always touched by human physical beauty, by the contemplation of a splendidly formed human body which moves with grace. Nowhere, of course, can this be seen to greater advantage than in the ballet. There are many moments when human kindness (nearly always seen in the humbler of his characters), warmth and altruism are allowed to cut across the more common disenchantment of the medical standpoint, and the innocence of childhood too. And from time to time his love of the sea and of ships gives rise to evocations of atmosphere of an almost lyrical kind. Then, finally, there are moments of overpowering sadness from which all traces of irony are absent, but which express movingly the resignation and compassion he feels about the lot of mankind. Once more the examples require little in the way of comment: they illustrate in various ways the points just made, and this time I have grouped them accordingly.

PHYSICAL BEAUTY

Voyage [Molly] Il me souvient comme si c'était d'hier de ses gentillesses de ses jambes longues et blondes et magnifiquement déliées et musclées, des jambes nobles. La véritable aristocratie humaine, on a beau dire, ce sont les jambes qui la confèrent pas d'erreur. (p. 227)

(I can remember as though from yesterday her tenderness, her long pale legs, wonderfully slender and with well defined muscles, noble legs. Genuine human aristocracy, whatever you say, is conferred by the legs, there's no doubt whatsoever.)

Mort à crédit [the wife of the Headmaster of Meanwell College, Rochester—Nora] Ses mains, c'étaient des merveilles, effilées, roses, claires, tendres, la même douceur que le visage, c'était une petite féerie rien que de les regarder. (p. 712)

(Her hands were marvellous, tapering, rose-coloured, light, tender, the same gentleness as in her face, it was a magic spectacle just to look at them.)

Bagatelles Dans une jambe de danseuse le monde, ses ondes, tous ses rythmes, ses folies, ses voeux sont inscrits! . . . Jamais écrits! . . . Le plus nuancé poème du monde! . . . émouvant! (. . .) c'est Dieu! C'est Dieu lui-même! (p. 11)

(In the leg of a dancer, the whole world, its waves, all its rhythms, its fantasies, its desires all are inscribed! . . . Never written! . . . The most subtle poem in the world! . . . moving! (. . .) it is God! it is God himself!)

Guignol's Band II [Virginia. Here one could quote a very large number of examples. In no other work does Céline describe quite so often the grace and beauty of one of his characters: there is an element of nostalgia and of happiness in all he has to say of Virginia] Elle reste pas en place . . . elle bondit, pirouette, en lutin . . . dans la pièce tout autour de moi . . . Quels jolis cheveux! . . . quel or! . . . quelle gamine! . . . (. . .) Quels bleus reflets clairs et puis mauves . . . ses yeux me prennent tout . . . (p. 28)

(She doesn't stay still . . . she leaps up, pirouettes like an elf . . . in the room all round me . . . What lovely hair! . . . what gold! . . . what a child she was! . . . What reflections, light blue then mauve . . . her eyes really get me.)

D'un Château l'autre [Hilda von Raumnitz, sixteen-year-old daughter of a Prussian nobleman—now SS chief in Sigmaringen—and his slinky Levantine wife] Hilda pour la garcerie (caractère féminin secondaire) était aussi joliment douée! . . . cheveux blonds cendrés . . . pas cendrés 'au pour', véritables! . . . et jusqu'aux talons . . . vraiment la belle animale boche . . . et genoux fins, chevilles fines . . . très rares . . . fortes cuisses, fesses serrées, musclées . . . le visage pas tellement aimable, ni câlin . . . (pp. 160–61)

(Hilda was also very talented at bitchery (secondary female characteristic) . . . ash-blond hair . . . not false, natural! . . . and down to her heels . . . genuinely a fine Boche animal . . . slender knees, slender ankles . . . very rare . . . powerful thighs, tight, well formed buttocks . . . face neither pleasant nor caressing . . .)

HUMAN KINDNESS AND HUMAN SUFFERING

Voyage [Alcide, a French sergeant who has volunteered for an extra tour of duty in West Africa in order to pay for the education of his orphaned niece] Il avait offert sans presque s'en douter à une petite fille vaguement parente des années de torture, l'annihilement de sa pauvre vie, dans cette monotonie torride, sans conditions, sans marchandage, sans intérêt que celui de son bon coeur. Il offrait à cette petite fille lointaine assez de tendresse pour refaire un monde entier et cela ne se voyait pas. (pp. 159–60)

(He had, almost without realizing it, offered up to a little girl vaguely related to him years of torture, the destruction of his poor life, in this torrid monotony, without conditions, without bargaining, with no other interest than that or his kindness of heart. He was offering to that far-away little girl enough tenderness to re-create a whole world and it didn't show.)

Mort à crédit [Ferdinand's mother and father make it up—*à leur façon*—after a violent quarrel] Elle venait l'embrasser. La tempête l'abandonnait . . . Il se relevait jusqu'à la fenêtre. Il faisait semblant de chercher quelque chose dans le fond de la cour. Il pétait un solide coup. C'etait la détente. Elle pétait aussi un petit coup à la sympathie, et puis elle s'enfuyait mutine, au fond de la cuisine. (p. 540)

(She came and kissed him. The storm was leaving him . . . He got up and went over to the window. He pretended to be looking for something at the end of the courtyard. He gave a good solid fart. End of the tension. She gave a small fart too, in sympathy, and then she fled pertly, off into the kitchen.)

Les Beaux Draps [From a passage describing the sufferings of the poor in Paris during the wartime winter of 1940] Et les vieillards qui refroidissent fatalement plus vite que tout le monde . . . vu qu'ils sont déjà presque gelés . . . qu'étaient si contents de leur tisane . . . comment qu'on va leur rechauffer? . . . leurs rhumagos? . . . leur bourdaine? . . . c'est des problèmes qui dépassent l'homme . . . (pp. 207–8)

(And the old men who inevitably got cold more quickly than anyone else . . . since they're nearly frozen to start with . . . who were so happy with their hot drinks . . . how on earth are we to keep them warm? . . . their rheumatism? . . . their laxative? . . . these are problems too great for man to solve . . .)

THE SEA

Mort à crédit [Childhood memory of watching ships fighting their way into the harbour at Dieppe during a storm] Les bourrasques deviennent si denses qu'elles bâillonnent. On étouffe dessous . . . Le vent grossit la mer encore . . . elle gicle en gerbes haut sur le phare . . . elle s'emporte au ciel. Mon père enfonce sa casquette . . .

Nous ne rentrerons que la nuit . . . Trois pêcheurs rallient démâtés
. . . Au fond du chenal leurs voix résonnent . . . (. . .) On ne
s'intéresse plus nous autres que dans les voyages au long cours.
(p. 608)

(The squalls become so thick that they gag you. You stifle . . . The
wind further increases the sea . . . it spurts up high in columns upon
the light-house . . . it reaches out to the sky. My father pulls his
cap down harder . . . We won't go home before night . . . Three
fishing-boats come in dismasted . . . Their voices resound across
the harbour channel . . . (. . .) But we, we're only now interested in
deep sea voyages.)

Guignol's Band I (The Port of London) Je voudrais que toutes les
routes soient des fleuves . . . C'est l'envoûtement . . . l'ensorcellerie
. . . c'est le mouvement de l'eau . . . Là comme ça, sans vouloir,
hanté, juste au clapotis de la Tamise . . . je restais là, berlue . . . le
charme est trop fort pour moi surtout avec les grands navires . . .
tout ce qui glisse autour . . . faufile, mousse . . . les youyous . . .
l'abord Sud des Docks . . . cotres et brigantines au louvoye . . .
amènent . . . drossent . . . frisent à la rive . . . à souple voguent! . . .
C'est la féerie! . . . on peut le dire! . . . Du ballet! . . . ça vous
hallucine! . . . (pp. 139–40)

(I wish that all roads were rivers . . . Fascination it is . . . sorcery . . .
it's the movement of the water . . . There I was, unintentionally,
haunted, just by the rippling sound of the Thames . . . I stayed
there, spell-bound . . . the attraction was too strong for me,
especially with the big ships . . . everything that is gliding around
there . . . slipping by, foaming . . . the dinghies . . . the Southern
approach to the docks . . . cutters and brigantines tacking . . .
coming alongside . . . drifting . . . touching the shore . . . cunningly
sailing! . . . It's enchantment! . . . really! like a ballet . . . it gives
you visions . . .)

Guignol's Band II [Part of an extended simile in which a ship moored
in the port of London is likened to a bird] . . . sans toile, il partirait,
si les hommes s'acharnaient pas, le retenaient par cent mille souquées
à rougir, il sortirait tout nu des docks par les hauteurs, il irait se
promener dans les nuages, il s'élèverait au plus haut du ciel, vive
harpe aux océans d'azur, ça serait comme ça le coup d'essor, ça
serait l'esprit du voyage, tout indécent, y aurait plus qu'à fermer les
yeux, on serait emporté pour longtemps, on serait parti dans les
espaces de la magie, du sans-souci, passager des rêves du monde!
(p. 319)

(. . . the ship would leave under bare poles if men were not striving

to hold it back by numberless shameful taut ropes, it would leave
the docks, naked, high in the air, moving about amongst the
clouds, it would rise to the highest heaven, living harp in the sky-
blue oceans, that would be the moment of takeoff, the spirit of the
journey, altogether indecent, you'd just have to shut your eyes, be
carried away for a long while, journeying in the wide spaces of
magic, with no cares, passenger of the dreams of the world!)

The moments of sadness which I referred to earlier, are of
much importance in the works of Céline. They are less easy to
illustrate in brief quotations since they tend to be carefully
prepared and built up over a number of pages. Very often they
occur at key moments in narrative—the closing pages of *Voyage*,
the opening and closing pages of *Mort à crédit* are obvious
instances. But once we are aware of this manner in Céline,
isolated sentences in quite unlikely contexts acquire a curiously
moving aura. The most impressive example is undoubtedly to be
found in the concluding fourteen pages of *Mort à crédit* (pp.
1068–82): indeed, many would say that these pages are amongst
the most impressive ever written by our author. Ferdinand, now
aged about seventeen, has emerged from childhood, has cut away
from the stifling and nagging atmosphere of his home, has
escaped as secretary to the harmless eccentric Courtial des
Pereires, but now finds his world shattered by Courtial's suicide.
His only resource is his uncle Edouard, who has always believed
in him and helped him. In these final pages, Edouard does nearly
all the talking: Ferdinand can say little more than 'oui, mon
oncle', and 'non, mon oncle'. He is deeply aware of the kindness
of Edouard—and it is a great compliment to Edouard that
Ferdinand comes to seek him out at this juncture—but he is convinced that he must strike out afresh for himself, go away, be
dependent on no one; he will join the army in fact (see *Casse-pipe*).
Edouard hopes to persuade him to delay this for a week or two.
However, the feeling grows during these pages that Ferdinand
will hold to his resolution, despite his real gratitude to and
affection for Edouard. The passage which follows constitutes the
actual end of the novel: it is a classic instance of 'l'émotion par la
langue parlée', under-played, on a down-beat and very accom-
plished:

> —Dis donc je laisse ma porte ouverte! . . . Si t'as besoin de quelque
> chose aie pas peur d'appeler! . . . C'est pas une honte d'être malade
> . . . j'arriverai immédiatement! . . . Si t'as encore la colique tu sais

où sont les cabinets? . . . C'est le petit couloir qu'est à gauche! . . .
Te trompe pas pour l'escalier! . . . Y a la 'Pigeon' sur la console . . .
T'auras pas besoin de la souffler . . . Et puis si t'as envie de vomir . . .
t'aimes pas mieux un vase de nuit? . . .
—Oh! non mon oncle . . . J'irai là-bas . . .
—Bon! Mais alors si tu te lèves passe-toi tout de suite un pardessus!
Tape dans le tas! n'importe lequel . . . Dans le couloir t'attraperais
la crève . . . C'est pas les pardessus qui manquent! . . .
—Non mon oncle. (p. 1082)

('Look, I'll leave my door open! . . . If you need anything, don't be
afraid to call out! . . . No need to be ashamed of being ill, I'll come
at once! . . . If you get a stomach-ache again, you know where the
lavatory is? . . . Down the little corridor on the left! . . . Don't go
down the stairs by mistake! . . . There's the hand-lamp on the
little table . . . Don't bother to blow it out . . . And, if you feel sick
again . . . perhaps you'd like a jerry?'
'Oh, uncle, no . . . I'll go to the lavatory . . .'
'Alright! but, look, if you get up, put an overcoat on at once.
Help yourself! doesn't matter which . . . you'll catch your death
in that corridor . . . There's no shortage of overcoats! . . .'
'No, uncle.')

This is a mood more overtly found in the early Céline. His
circumstances after the war did not lend themselves so readily to
such demonstrations of sentiment. However, such sentiment does
exist in the later works, even if it is often camouflaged by a
surface irony. I would suggest that the following—from *Féerie I*—
is a fair instance of the same atmosphere in his post-war manner.
There is an underlying rancour all through this book, and here
the tone is apparently flippant too, but, none the less, the central
idea in this passage which emerges at its end is sincere, and
emphasizes his life-long involvement with the ordinary life of
his time. Some explanation of this text is needed. He is talking
about St Malo, a town very dear to him as a Breton, where he
had a house before the war. The opening reference is to Chateaubriand, whose tomb is on the islet of *le Grand Bé*, accessible on
foot and at low-tide from the town itself. Not for Céline the
romantic isolation of René: he would wish his tomb to be within
the walls of the old city, in touch with the life that goes on there:

Je veux même plus de la tombe à René! son trou au Bé . . . ça me
serait offert! . . . je veux un mausolée pour moi-même, illuminé de
jour et nuit à l'endroit où vous voyez je veux dire, où le Cinéma a
lieu l'été, où toutes les familles viennent en choeur et les amoureux

et les alcooliques, où les petits chiens font plein de pipis sous les consoles, les guéridons, les adultes plutôt contre le kiosque, où quatre films fonctionnent à la fois, que les têtes tournent après, dévissent . . . vsss! vsss! toupillent! . . . que les terrasses font plein de bruit de cous, plus les exclamations de passions . . . je veux tout entendre de mon cercueil! . . . Je veux pas être inhumé hors-murs! (p. 230)

(I don't even want a tomb like René's! his hole on the Bé . . . if it were offered me! . . . I want a mausoleum all of my own, lit up day and night in the place you know, I mean where they have cinema in the summer, where all the families go en masse and the lovers and the alcoholics, where the little dogs piss under the tables, the marble-topped cafe tables, and the adults against the kiosk usually, where four films go on at once, and all the heads swivel round after them, unscrew . . . vsss! vsss! spin round! . . . and the café terraces are full of the sound of turning necks, with passionate exclamations on top . . . from my coffin I want to hear all that! . . . I don't want an extra-mural burial!)

There is one further comment that needs to be made before concluding on the subject of the style of Céline. It is with regard to the way in which the use of three dots as a device of punctuation changes over the years.

In *Voyage*, the device is employed for the most part in a conventional way. That is to say it occurs mainly in passages of direct speech or· in those sections of the first-person narrative which are reflective. It is used alongside other forms of punctuation and is by no means always combined with exclamation mark or question mark. It tends to suggest pause, reflection, uncompleted thought. Here is a typical example, which comes from a whole section in inverted commas representing the secret unspoken thoughts of nurses in a military hospital:

Il nous faut des excitants à nous, rien que des excitants . . . Vous serez vite oubliés, petits soldats . . . Soyez gentils, crevez bien vite . . . Et que la guerre finisse et qu'on puisse se marier avec un de vos aimables officiers. (p. 88)

(We need stimulants we do, just stimulants . . . You'll soon be forgotten, you sweet little soldiers . . . Be good, get yourselves killed quick . . . And let the war finish quick too, so that we can each marry one of your nice officers.)

The main narrative and descriptive sections of *Voyage* are virtually

devoid of the three dots, but they are also virtually without colons
and semicolons too: Céline seems to need merely comma, full
stop, exclamation mark and question mark. Indeed, the three dots
take over some of the functions of the colon and the semicolon.
(One could easily use a colon after *soldats* in the passage just
quoted.)

By *Mort à crédit*, four years later, there has been a definite
increase in the use of the three dots, and an even greater increase
in the use of the exclamation mark. More important, the three
dots are beginning to lose, in many cases, the element of pause or
reflection:

> Ah! vous en allez pas comme ça! . . . qu'elle me fait contrariée . . .
> Remontez donc un peu là-haut! . . . J'ai juste deux mots à vous dire.
> (p. 667)
>
> (Hey! don't go off like that! . . . is what she said crossly . . . Come up
> here again for a moment . . . I've something to say to you.)

Yet there are still extensive sections of this novel which have
fairly conventional punctuation, though still without colons or
semicolons.

In *Bagatelles*, one year later, the three dots have taken over as
the principal device of punctuation, usually associated with the
exclamation mark, and for the most part the original effect of
pause has gone. Instead, as I suggested briefly earlier in this
chapter (see above, p. 89), they serve to break up continuous
passages of narrative into sense blocks and rhythmical blocks,
diminishing the need for linking conjunctions and relative
pronouns, and reinforcing the sense of informal 'spoken' dis-
course. The process is developed in the subsequent novels—
though the two pamphlets, *L'Ecole des cadavres* and *Les Beaux
Draps*, perhaps because of their argumentative content, do con-
serve a good deal of conventional punctuation. A glance back at
the extracts quoted above from the later works will show
numerous examples of this.[23]

Céline was an extremely professional and meticulous stylist
who evolved his highly personal handling of the French language
gradually over a period of years and directly in relation to the

---

[23] Céline seems to have inserted the definitive punctuation at a late state in com-
position. This certainly emerges from examination of facsimiles of the MSS.,
Entretiens avec le Professeur Y, which I have been able to consult through the courtesy
of M. Jean-Pierre Dauphin.

subject matter of his novels. Molière is quite right of course when he tells Oronte that in literary creation 'Le temps ne fait rien à l'affaire' ('the time (you took) is of no importance'), but it is also right to stress that all the evidence we have shows that every word, every comma, every set of three dots in Céline is the result of a deliberate decision by the author. So what? one may feel inclined to say. The answer to that is that reflection on such decisions is chastening: there usually is a good reason, and one that serves the overall effect of the passage. The only two persons who—to my knowledge—have so far done any serious work on the manuscripts of Céline (MM. Jean-Pierre Dauphin and Henri Godard) are categorical: the finished product that we read is the result of four to five times as much manuscript in long hand. M. Godard, in his preface to the second Pléiade volume of the novels says (p. xxxv) of *D'un Château l'autre* that there are at least four preliminary versions of the definitive text, each of them over 1000 MS. pages:

> Pages inlassablement, jusqu'à la dernière mise au net, raturées, corrigées; tours de phrase ou mots successivement essayés, rejetés, modifiés jusqu'à ce qu'ils réalisent exactement une certaine ligne, à la fois musicale et stylistique: si paradoxal que le rapprochement doive paraître à certains, il n'est qu'un écrivain auquel on soit tenté de comparer le travail et l'exigence que révèlent les manuscrits de Céline, c'est Flaubert.

> (Until the final version, pages tirelessly crossed out, corrected; turns of phrase tried, rejected, modified successively until they bring off exactly a certain line, both musical and stylistic: even if the comparison may seem paradoxical to some, there is only one author with whom one is tempted to compare the labour and the exigencies revealed by the manuscripts of Céline, and that is Flaubert.)

My only quarrel with this remark is the suggestion at the end of something paradoxical about this comparison. It is both apt and obvious, and M. Godard need not have been afraid to say so. Both Flaubert and Céline were impressionists in their different ways, and both knew that if you want to be a better novelist than, say, Champfleury or Sartre, you have to work at your style.

CHAPTER FOUR

From *Mea Culpa* to *Les Beaux Draps*

One of the results of the general approval of *Voyage* by the left in France, was the translation of the novel into Russian by Elsa Triolet and Louis Aragon.[1] Since the royalties from this were not exportable from the Soviet Union, Céline decided in 1936 to go and spend his royalties on the spot. He spent some two months in Russia—August and September 1936—and then in December published (Denoël et Steele) a short pamphlet entitled *Mea Culpa*. Of this he said (allegedly) to Robert Poulet:

> Il en résulta un petit livre, où je donnais mon impression sur le 'paradis des prolétaires', publication qui me brouilla définitivement avec ces messieurs.[2]

> (The result was a little book, in which I gave my impressions about the 'workers' paradise', a publication which set me at loggerheads with these gentlemen for good and all.)

True, *Mea Culpa* marks the end of any tenderness for Céline on the part of the PCF and French communist critics. However, from the outset, communist opinion had expressed reserves about *Voyage*, and quite rightly too. Paul Nizan, reviewing it in *L'Humanité* (9 December 1932), had said:

> Céline n'est pas parmi nous: impossible d'accepter sa profonde anarchie, son mépris, sa répulsion générale qui n'exceptent le prolétariat. Cette révolte pure peut le mener n'importe où: parmi nous, ou nulle part.

> (Céline is not one of us: impossible to accept his profound anarchy, his scorn, his overall hatred which do not except the proletariat.

---

[1] Over which 'translation' Céline had no control (see Robert Poulet, *Mon ami Bardamu: entretiens familiers avec L. F. Céline* (Plon, Paris, 1971, pp. 92–3). Céline had no time for Aragon from the start, and by 1934 is already describing him as a 'supercon' ('magisterial cunt'). (Letter to Elie Faure, *Cahiers de l'Herne*, p. 74.)

[2] Poulet, op. cit., p. 93.

This pure revolt may lead him anywhere, with us, against us or nowhere.)

Trotsky too (in 1933) had made a similar point:

> *Voyage au bout de la nuit*, roman du pessimisme, a été dicté par l'effroi devant la vie et par la lassitude qu'elle occasionne plus que par la révolte. Une révolte active est liée à l'espoir. Dans le livre de Céline, il n'y a pas d'espoir.[3]

> (*Voyage au bout de la nuit*, novel of pessimism, has been dictated rather by a fear of life and weariness life provokes than by revolt. Active revolt is inseparable from hope. In Céline's book there is no hope.)

And the Soviet critic Anissimov, who wrote the preface to the Russian edition of *Voyage* (reproduced in French in *Cahiers de l'Herne*, pp. 452–6) makes precisely the same points at some length:

> Nous voyons combien est stérile l'emphase du livre de Céline. Ce livre est frappé d'une auto-destruction maladive. C'est la rançon que l'artiste, qui n'a pas trouvé en lui-même le courage nécessaire pour aller de l'autre côté des barricades, doit payer au capitalisme dont il est issu.

> (We see how sterile is the declamatory manner of Céline's book. The book is stricken by an unhealthy self-destruction. This is the price which the artist who has not found in himself the courage to cross to the other side of the barricade, must pay to the capitalist society of which he is a product.)

(Mercifully, Céline was not one to listen to such twaddle. Otherwise his subsequent works would have turned out like Zola's *Travail*.)

What prevented Céline from espousing official communism is abundantly clear, and not only from *Mea Culpa*. He sees communism as an entirely vulgar trick appealing to the materialist instinct in man. No difference between communism and most religions, except in degree—bread for all in an after-life, or bread for all after the *next* five-year plan.

> Les Pères de l'Eglise, eux, ils connaissaient leur boulot. Ils promettaient le bonheur mais pour l'autre monde.[4]

> (The Fathers of the Church, they knew their job. They promised happiness, but in the next world.)

---

[3] Quoted in *Cahiers de l'Herne*, p. 434.
[4] *Mea Culpa* (Denoël et Steele, Paris, 1936), p. 7.

By appealing to human materialistic instincts, the Soviet brand of communism has betrayed the true nature of communism. A mode of life based on an ideal of brotherhood, of sacrifice of self for the common good, is what communism should really be:

Ce qui séduit dans le communisme, l'immense avantage à vrai dire, c'est qu'il va nous démasquer l'homme enfin.[5]

(What is attractive in communism, its great advantage if truth be told, is that it sets out to unmask man at last.)

Freed from the bondage of capitalist exploitation, man needs a new set of ideals—a fourth dimension:

Il faut qu'on la découvre vite la quatrième dimension! la véritable dimension! Celle du sentiment fraternel, celle de l'identité d'autrui. Il peut plus accabler personne . . . Y a plus d'exploiteurs à buter.[6]

(What needs to be discovered quickly is the fourth dimension! the real dimension! That of brotherly affection, that of the identity of other people. He [the worker] can't destroy anyone else . . . there are no more exploiters to bump off.)

But instead, Soviet communism has substituted the *imposture* of a selfish pursuit of happiness:

La grande prétention au bonheur, voilà l'énorme imposture! C'est elle qui complique toute la vie! Qui rend les gens si venimeux, crapules, imbuvables. Y a pas de bonheur dans l'existence, y a que des malheurs plus ou moins grands, plus ou moins tardifs, éclatants, secrets, différés, sournois . . . 'C'est avec des gens heureux qu'on fait les meilleurs damnés'.[7]

(The great claim to happiness, that's the monstrous imposture! That's what makes life so difficult! Which makes people so poisonous, disgusting, intolerable. There is no happiness in this existence, merely misfortunes more or less great, early or late, startling, secret, postponed, underhand . . . 'It's out of happy people that the best damned are made.')

A genuine communism would accept the *facts* about the human condition and, while not seeking to deceive by illusory promises of happiness, would foster the spirit of cooperation and fraternity among men—'Le communisme par-dessus tout, même plus que les richesses, c'est toutes les peines à partager'[8] ('Communism

[5] Quoted by André Pulicani, *Cahiers de l'Herne*, p. 224.
[6] *Mea Culpa*, p. 20.
[7] ibid., p. 18.
[8] ibid., p. 20.

above all, is much more the sharing of all troubles than the sharing of wealth').

The assault against communism as he saw it in operation in Soviet Russia is continued at times in *Bagatelles pour un massacre* and *L'Ecole des cadavres*, and in one way the central theme of *Les Beaux Draps* is connected with it too, being an attack on materialism and an exposition of an Utopian egalitarian social system. The most impressive text is perhaps that of *Bagatelles* (pp. 76–80), concerning a visit he made in 1936 to a large hospital in Leningrad for the treatment of venereal disease:

> . . . ce dépotoir gigantesque, dit des 'maladies vénériennes', s'annonce bel et bien comme un hôpital de premier ordre, populaire et d'enseignement, s.v.p.! (. . .) J'ai servi dans la cavalerie pendant des années, jamais, j'en suis sûr, aucun vétérinaire de régiment n'aurait permis, même pour un soir, l'hébergement d'un escadron dans un casernement-taudis, déjeté pareil. (. . .) Et tout cela, n'oublions jamais, après vingt ans de tonitruants défis, d'injurieuses considérations pour tous les autres systèmes capitalistes, si rétrogrades . . . d'Hymnes au progrès social inouï . . . à la rénovation U.R.S.S. coopératrice! réalisatrice de bonheur! et de liberté, du pouvoir 'des masses pour les masses'! . . . le déluge enfin des plans abracadabrants, tous plus pharamineux, bouleversatiles les uns que les autres. (pp. 76–7)

> (. . . this terrible sewage dump, described as 'for veneral diseases' is supposed to be indeed a first class hospital, for the people and a teaching hospital into the bargain! (. . .) I served in the cavalry for years, and never I'm quite sure, would my regiment vet have allowed the squadron to be put up, not even for a single night in such a broken-down slum-barrack. (. . .) And all that, don't forget, after twenty years of thundering challenges and insulting observations about all the other so backward capitalist systems. Hymns to unheard of social progress, to cooperating Soviet renovation! bringer of happiness! and of freedom, and of power 'of the masses for the masses'! and then the deluge of hair-raising plans, each one more fantastic, more overturning than the last.)

There follows a quite horrifying detailed description of this hospital, the dirt, the misery:

> . . . quels débris! quel grandgousien chiot moisi. (. . .) je n'ai jamais ressenti d'étouffoir plus dégradant, plus écrasant, que cette abominable misère russe. (pp. 77–8)

> (. . . what a shambles! what a gargantuan mildewed shit-house!

(. . .) I've never experienced a more degrading, more overwhelming black hole than this abominable Russian destitution.)

the miserably underpaid nurses:

> . . . elles semblaient encore plus déchues, navrées, perclues, fondantes de misère que tous les malades hospitalisés. (p. 78)

> (. . . they seemed more abject, upset, paralysed, dissolving in misery than all the patients in the hospital.)

the total lack of even the simplest surgical instruments:

> Pas un broc, un trépied, une sonde, pas le moindre bistouri, la plus courante pince à griffes, de cette répugnante quincaille rien qui ne date au moins des Tzars . . . (p. 79)

> (Not a water-jug, not a tripod, not a probe, not the least lancet, or the most simple surgical clip, in all that repulsive ironmongery nothing that didn't date from the time of the Tzars . . .)

the complete impossibility of any sort of surgical cleanliness. The whole passage is punctuated by the insistent assurance from the accompanying Russian gynaecologist that 'Ici, confrère, tout va très bien' ('Here, colleague, everything is going fine'). Why, why should all this be so, asks Céline. The answer lies in figures. He is allowed to examine the account books, and concludes that to achieve even a mediocre standard of efficiency and propriety (nothing Scandinavian, he says, merely French) the budget for this hospital needs to be increased ten-fold. The end of the chapter generalizes the attack:

> Toutes les organisations administratives russes souffrent, sont accablées, condamnées à la même grotesque pénurie, aux mêmes similaires balivernes en hommes, en matières, en 'fonds' . . . Toutes sauf les théâtres, la police, les militaires, les commissaires, la Propagande . . . à la même mégoterie crasseuse, à la même contraction au 1/10 du budget normal. (p. 80)

> (All the Russian administrative organisations suffer from, are weighed down by, condemned to the same grotesque penury, to the same similar absurdities in men, in materials, in 'funds' . . . All except the theatres, the police, the armed forces, the commissars, the propaganda services . . . to the same sordid skinflintery, to the same contraction to 1/10 of a normal budget.)

This indictment is very revealing about the nature of Céline's 'political' writings. The description of the conditions in the hospital is vivid, terrifying and emotionally charged to the utmost, and at the same time full of practical details, including some statistics towards the end. His polemical point is well and truly made. However, *without* giving the evidence, he is then prepared to say that *all* Russian administrations (except those mentioned) suffer from the same grotesquely inadequate financial support. He may have been right, but he does not prove his case. This weakness for sweeping statements is of course a feature of polemic anyway—we only have to think of the content of party political broadcasts at election time—but it invalidates much of what he says as serious political material: we shall find many examples of it in his works of this period. We might almost throw back at Céline the epigraph—attributed to Lenin—which he places immediately after the section just considered:

> Le Mensonge n'est pas seulement un moyen qu'il est permis d'employer, mais c'est le moyen le plus éprouvé de la lutte bolchévique.
>
> (The lie is not only a permissible means, but it is the best tried means in the Bolshevik struggle.)

No one can state with certainty what were Céline's motives in publishing *Mea Culpa*, but it is possible to have a good guess. The title suggests that he is confessing the sin of having been associated with the left. It is certainly true that the left had tried to claim him as one of them—albeit with qualification as has been seen—after the appearance of *Voyage*. In *Mort à crédit* the chances of seeing some sort of political commitment were not very great, except that in the most general way the struggles of the young Ferdinand can be seen as those of any under-privileged youth in a capitalist society. But the whole second part of the book—from the appearance of Courtial des Pereires onwards—is devoid of any real political sense. Perhaps this is why the book had so muted a reception on the left. Céline was not yet to be written off, but he was not yet in the fold. And he had no intention of entering it. Nor did he seek to win support on the opposite flank either. Even if the most fervent praise for *Voyage* had come from a right-wing source—Léon Daudet in *L'Action Française*— Céline was not really a writer calculated to please in that area. *Mort à crédit* with its explicit sexual content and a vocabulary even less inhibited than that of *Voyage* was in no sense a work to appeal to the right: a few right-wing intellectuals—Rebatet and Brasillach, for instance—were able to see the aesthetic value of the novel, but for the essentially *bien-pensant* right-wing public, Céline was the reverse of acceptable. Only the left had to be dealt with therefore. *Mea Culpa* represents not only Céline's disgust at the monstrous lie he saw in Stalinist propaganda, but also his desire to have independence from the likes of the 'supercon' Aragon. It worked. When *Bagatelles* appeared in December 1937, Céline had no political allies and certainly no political commitment. He was soon to acquire allies, like it or not, but never to involve himself directly in political action: his intervention in the political scene was that of an isolated individual, deeply sincere if horribly misguided.

If one were to excise from *Bagatelles* its anti-semitic content, then it would clearly stand as a masterpiece of anguished polemic, to which many would only be too happy to subscribe. It is expert Céline, very funny in places, full of extraordinary linguistic fireworks, animated by a genuine sense of terror inspired by the knowledge that another World War was only months away. If only, one wants to say, he had not decided to lay responsibility for the holocaust he foresaw upon 'Les Juifs . . .' Why? Why? There are reasons; none of them sufficient to acquit him, but they do enable us to understand the situation with some degree of detachment. What is dangerous and insidious about racial and chauvinistic attitudes, whether they come from, say, Enoch Powell, Colonel Ghadafi, President Amin, Rev. Ian Paisley, the IRA or some illiterate *pied-noir*, is that they are always emotional. Racial prejudice, unfortunately, exists. It would be nice if it did not. But it is no good saying that anyone who subscribes to it ought to be shot, unless of course it is proposed thereby to solve for a while the problem of over-population in the world. In England we are perhaps too often unaware of the extent to which we are actually disliked in Europe: too many of us still secretly believe, as the old joke has it, that niggers begin in Calais, and that the Continental hotel-keeper is sure to cheat us if he can. . . . Interesting to remember that Gaullism, that extraordinary nineteenth-century phenomenon, a mixture of Bonapartism and Boulenger, now fortunately dying, acquired a certain extra credibility with parts of the French electorate by being anti-British. We ought to ask ourselves why. . . . There are good reasons, which are none of my business here. All this is to suggest that we must judge Céline's anti-semitism with a degree of humility: it is far too over-simplified to hold him responsible

for Dachau and condemn him out of hand as a result. He con-
tributed, certainly, but so, unwittingly no doubt, did Neville
Chamberlain and his Cabinet and all those totally sincere people
who gathered at the airport to cheer him when he returned from
Munich in 1938.

So let us try to approach this still explosive material with an
appropriate measure of cynicism. Perhaps the best key to *Bagatelles*
is found in its very first page—the one analysed in some detail in
the chapter on language (see above, pp. 98–9). We find there an
early statement by Céline—almost the first—on the subject of his
literary manner, and it is couched in inimitable terms: contempt
for the accepted principles of 'good' writing, and even more for
the fashionable literary scene and the servitude imposed by the
media upon a successful writer. Even if here we are involved in
aesthetics and not in politics, the essential tone of the book is
shown in this short passage. Sarcasm, often bitter, directed at
anyone or anything which could be regarded as forming part of
what—much later—we have come to call the 'Establishment',
together with an extraordinary profusion of language, richer in
its inventiveness and daring than anything in *Voyage* or *Mort à
crédit*, a deep and founded scorn and hatred for the press of the
time, and an irrepressible fund of scabrous humour—these are
all constant ingredients of the book. *Bagatelles* is in fact—as a
few contemporary critics did see—a work of genius in a number
of respects. What of course destroys it, and the word is not too
strong, is the omnipresent, infantile anti-semitic obsession, which
will shortly be illustrated at some length. It is fair to say that
both in *Bagatelles* and the later *Ecole des cadavres* the word *Juif*
becomes after a while a kind of synonym for 'Establishment
figure'. Attacking the political figures, the leaders of society and
public opinion of the late Third Republic has become a popular
activity in France ever since the days of Pétain, and Céline's
error (in terms of popular esteem) was to attribute the disastrous
state of affairs in French public life before the Second World War
exclusively to the Jews. Without that absurd analysis, much of
what he says in *Bagatelles* could stand (and, for that matter,
could apply quite nicely to the Fifth Republic too . . .). There are
splendid pages, totally applicable today, about the corruption of
life by the media (press, cinema, radio and advertising). There
are denunciations of the evils of pollution of the environment by
industry, there is a prolonged attack on the intellectual futility

of the arts in France in the thirties (including a series of contemptuous references to surrealism as the incarnation of what he calls 'l'art robot'). Both the bourgeoisie and the proletariat of France are castigated for a purely materialistic outlook on life, much of it fostered by alcoholism.

Why, however, should he suddenly decide to hold the Jews responsible for all this? It does not seem likely that we shall ever really know the full truth about it. Céline gives plenty of hints, but as we know, he took a delight in deforming the truth about his own views on many occasions. Various acquaintances of his have come along with specific anecdotal reasons, all or some of which may or may not contain some truth. All I can try to do here is to indicate some of the relevant factors.

The anti-semitic obsession first becomes a dominant theme in 1937 in *Bagatelles*, but it is present in a mild, comic form in his early play *L'Eglise* (1933), especially in the third act, set at the League of Nations in Geneva. In *Voyage* and *Mort à crédit* there are virtually no traces of it, but its presence even in a comic form in *L'Eglise* is probably significant.

It must be remembered that anti-semitism has been endemic in certain levels of French society for a long time. There is no need here to trace it down the ages: it is sufficient perhaps to point to the *Affaire Dreyfus* at the turn of the last century. The phenomenon is not confined to one social class: the aristocratic right has long been affected by it, but so, more importantly, has the immense body of *petits commerçants*, and to some extent part of the urban proletariat. It is only fair to add that it is not only anti-semitism that affects these groups, but a more general xenophobia. (If, in the last decade, the figure of the *Nord-Africain* has rather taken the place of *le Juif* as object of obloquy amongst these semiliterate strata, it is because of the painful process of de-colonization.)

Now Louis-Ferdinand Destouches was of what can certainly be called *petit bourgeois* stock. Even if the account of Ferdinand's childhood is far from a realistic piece of autobiography, it is still close enough in *broad* outline to the atmosphere in which Céline grew up, an atmosphere in which both chauvinism and xenophobia had long flourished in France. At one time or another Céline is to be found expressing not only anti-semitic views, but also anti-British, anti-American, anti-Russian and anti-Danish views.

It is also important to remember that in the thirties in France there grew up an 'intellectual' anti-semitism on the extreme right. *L'Action Française*, which was an influential paper between the two wars, turned to anti-semitism in the mid-thirties, and *Je Suis Partout* (an openly fascist paper founded in 1930, which became one of the most odious collaborationist papers during the German occupation) took up the same cause in 1934. A number of well-known names are to be found amongst the contributors to *Je Suis Partout* between 1934 and 1939: Pierre Gaxotte, Robert Brasillach, Thierry Maulnier, André Bellessort, Henri de Montherlant, Drieu la Rochelle, Henri Troyat, Georges Pitoëff, Marcel Jouhandeau, Henri Massis, Robert Poulet, Lucien Rebatet, Max Favalelli and Jacques Perret are some of them. An even longer list could be derived from the pages of *L'Action Française* but this had a certain degree of responsible independence at times, and its guiding spirit, Charles Maurras, though anti-semitic was not pro-Nazi, whereas *Je Suis Partout* was overtly and positively a fascist journal. Many reasons have been proposed for the growth of anti-semitism at this time—among them the Stavisky scandal of 1934, the beginnings of Nazi anti-semitic propaganda, and, perhaps most important, the increase in the Jewish population in France during the first half of the twentieth century, especially of course after the beginning of the Nazi persecution of the Jews.[9] Further impetus to the whole movement was given when Léon Blum became Prime Minister at the head of the Front Populaire government of 1936.

All this goes to show that in the years immediately before the Second World War, quite a number of 'intelligent' people were willing to be associated with periodicals which can only be described as of a highly compromising kind. Two more examples must suffice. *Candide*, another right-wing paper, had three of the *Je Suis Partout* team (Cousteau, Laubreaux and Gaxotte) as contributors in 1938, and also Montherlant and Mauriac. In 1937 and 1938 a series of lectures were announced in *Je Suis Partout* ('Les conférences de *Je Suis Partout*'): among the promised lecturers were Claudel, Montherlant, Ghéon, Tixier-Vignancour,

---

[9] According to Jacqueline Morand, *Les idées politiques de Louis-Ferdinand Céline* (Pichon et Durand-Auzias, Paris, 1972), p. 48, about 88,000 at the end of the nineteenth century, 200,000 in 1933 and 280,000 in 1939. (This book contains an excellent review of the whole topic.) Céline himself (*Bagatelles*, p. 149) says 90,000 in 1914 and 400,000 in 1936.

Chadourne, Maurras, Bonnard, Abetz (with Montherlant presiding) and Marinetti.

If we accept first that the milieu in which Céline grew up—in the years following the *Affaire Dreyfus*—was one in which anti-semitism was quite common,[10] if we add that he acquired a supreme contempt for the atmosphere of the League of Nations in Geneva during the twenties, where he was

> . . . secrétaire technique d'un Juif, un des potentats de la maison (. . .). Les places notables, les vrais nougats sont occupés, là comme ailleurs, par les Juifs et les 'maçons'. . . Faut jamais confondre, Ecole Normale, Oxford, Polytechnique, les beaux Inspecteurs des Finances, etc. Enfin l'Aristocratie . . .[11]

> (. . . technical secretary to a Jew, one of the big shots in the place (. . .). The really important posts, the really soft jobs are held, there as elsewhere by Jews and 'free-masons' . . . Don't get it wrong: Ecole Normale, Oxford, Polytechnic, the splendid Treasury officials etc., the Aristocracy in fact . . .)

if we accept as true one or more of the following: that a Jewish financial adviser had defrauded him of part of his royalties on *Voyage* and *Mort à crédit*; that he was forced to resign his post at the clinic in Clichy (in early 1938, after the publication of *Bagatelles* but before that of *L'Ecole des cadavres*) as a result of the appointment by the communist municipality of Clichy of a Lithuanian Jew called Ldouc[12] as head of the clinic; that his mistress, the American dancer Elizabeth Craig (to whom *Voyage* is dedicated) married a Jewish lawyer in America in 1934,[13] then at least we can discern emotional reasons for the definitive anti-semitic explosion in the years 1937–8. It would be hard to see any political conviction in any of it. The only political content in his thought up to *Bagatelles* which is at all relevant is an increasing disgust with the left, which reached its culmination in *Mea Culpa*,

---

[10] There are references in *Mort à crédit* to the anti-Jewish feelings of Ferdinand's father (e.g. p. 630): but Ferdinand says of this 'Il déconnait à pleine bourre' ('He was talking out of his arse') and 'Il traquait partout ses dadas' ('He always pursued his absurd obsessions').

[11] *Bagatelles* pp. 65–6. We are also told (ibid., p. 127) 'N'est-il pas amusant à ce propos d'observer que les jeunes Juifs des meilleures familles (Juifs français compris) se rendent le plus souvent à Oxford pour achever leurs études. "Finishing touch!".'
(It's amusing to note, isn't it? that young Jews of good family (French Jews included) usually go to Oxford to complete their studies.')

[12] See Robert Poulet, *Mon ami Bardamu*, pp. 91–2.

[13] See Henri Mahé, *La Brinquebaille avec Céline* (Table Ronde, Paris, 1969), pp. 90–103.

and which is connected with his anti-semitism in one respect in that he regards the Soviet Union as Jewish-dominated, and Stalin as 'franchement youtre'[14] ('straight Yid') as well as merely

> . . . un bourreau, d'énorme envergure certes, tout dégoulinant de tripes conjurées, un barbe-bleue pour maréchaux, un épouvantail formidable, indispensable au folk-lore russe.[15]

> (. . . an executioner, on a huge scale, true, dripping with conspirators' guts, a Blue-beard for Field Marshals, a tremendous scarecrow, essential for Russian folk-lore.)

This disillusionment with the left is confirmed in a letter to his friend, the (Jewish) writer Elie Faure (undated, but of early 1934 in all probability), where the following statements occur:

> Je suis anarchiste depuis toujours, je n'ai jamais voté (. . .) Je ne crois pas aux hommes (. . .) Je n'ai rien de commun avec tous ces châtrés—qui vocifèrent leurs suppositions balourdes et ne comprennent rien. Vous voyez-vous penser et travailler sous la férule du supercon Aragon par exemple? (. . .) Le complexe d'infériorité de tous ces messieurs est palpable. Leur haine de tout ce qui les dépasse, de tout de qu'ils ne comprennent pas, visible. Ils sont aussi avides de rabaisser, de détruire, de salir, d'émonder le principe même de la vie que les plus bas curés du Moyen-Age. Ils me fusilleront peut-être les uns ou les autres. Les nazis m'exècrent autant que les socialistes et les comminards itou. (. . .) Ils s'entendent tous quand il s'agit de me vomir. Tout est permis sauf de *douter de l'homme*.[16]

> (I've always been an anarchist, I've never voted (. . .) I don't believe in mankind (. . .) I've nothing in common with all these eunuchs— who bawl out their lumpish notions and don't understand a thing. Can you see yourself thinking and working under the sway of that magisterial cunt Aragon for instance? (. . .) The inferiority complex of all these gentlemen is obvious. Their hatred for everything that is bigger than they, that they don't understand, is crystal clear. They are as avid to denigrate, destroy, soil, cut down the very essence of life as ever were the stupidest priests of the Middle Ages. They'll shoot me perhaps, one lot or the other. The Nazis hate me as much as the Socialists and the commies the same. (. . .) They are all agreed when it's a question of execrating me. All is allowed except *lack of faith in mankind*.)

[14] *Bagatelles*, p. 37.

[15] ibid., p. 36. The turn of phrase 'un barbe-bleue pour maréchaux' was to become a favourite of his (see below, p. 141 on St Peter). He was later to describe Hitler as 'mage pour le Brandenbourg' ('A prophet for Brandenburg').

[16] Quoted in *Cahiers de l'Herne*, p. 74.

And also to Elie Faure he writes thus on 2 March 1935:

> Le malheur en tout ceci est *qu'il n'y a pas de 'peuple'* au sens touchant où vous l'entendez, il n'y a que les exploiteurs et les exploités, et chaque exploité ne demande qu'à devenir exploiteur. Il ne comprend pas autre chose. Le prolétariat héroïque égalitaire *n'existe pas.* C'est un *songe creux*, une faribole, d'où l'inutilité absolue, écoeurante de toutes ces imageries imbéciles: le prolétaire à cotte bleue, le héros de demain—et le méchant capitaliste à chaîne d'or. Ils sont aussi fumiers l'un que l'autre. Le prolétaire est un bourgeois qui n'a pas réussi. Rien de touchant à tout cela: une larmoyerie gâteuse et fourbe.[17]

(The sad thing is that *there is no 'people'* in the touching way you use the word, there are simply exploiters and exploited, and each one who's exploited dreams only of becoming an exploiter. He doesn't understand anything else. The heroic, egalitarian proletariat *does not exist*. It's a *pipe-dream*, a nonsense, hence the uselessness, absolute and sickening of all these derisory images: the blue-overalled worker, hero of tomorrow—the wicked capitalist with gold watch-chain. One is as big a shit as the other. The worker is a failed bourgeois. Nothing touching about that: senile and dishonest tear-jerking!)

These are important texts from a time when Céline, now the famous author of *Voyage*, was finding it necessary to formulate for himself his political standpoint as a result of the pressures upon him. They show us a man whose mistrust of political solutions to human misery is total and absolute. This mistrust was no doubt not new: it is implicit in the opening pages of *Semmelweis* (1924) and can be seen also in *Voyage* at times. It was never to alter.

In 1937—rather before many of his contemporaries—he had become convinced that another European war was on the way. Whatever else we can say about Céline's views, it is certainly clear that he always believed that war was the greatest possible evil and stupidity. All he wrote, from *Voyage* to *Rigodon*, bears this out. At the same time, his pacifism was mixed with patriotism and with the xenophobia already noted. He was genuinely proud to have been awarded the Médaille Militaire for bravery in 1914, and he volunteered for active service at the outbreak of war in 1939 (at the age of forty-five). What a curious—yet not unduly

[17] ibid., p. 75.

contradictory—set of views he seems to have held at the time of writing *Bagatelles*!

There is a minimal structure to *Bagatelles*, in that most of it is allegedly framed in conversations between Ferdinand (sometimes in this work referred to as Céline directly) and three friends, two of them doctors—his cousin, Gustin Sabayote, and Léo Gutman (a Jew)—and the third a painter, Popol. The opening conversation (with Gutman) is largely about ballet, and includes the transcription of two scenarii (*La Naissance d'une fée* and *Voyou Paul, brave Virginie*) which were later to be published again in *Ballets sans musique, sans personne, sans rien* (Gallimard 1959). The refusal of these two works, first by the Opéra, and then by the organizing committee of the 1937 Exhibition, is the pretext for the full open declaration of anti-semitism:

> J'en aurai jamais des danseuses alors? . . . J'en aurai jamais! Tu l'avoues! C'est tout pour les youtres (. . .) Ah! tu vas voir l'antisémitisme! (. . .) Ah! tu vas voir la révolte! . . . le réveil des indigènes! . . . (p. 31)
>
> (What no ballerinas for me, ever? . . . I'll never have any! You admit it! They're only for the Yids! (. . .) Just you wait for the antisemitism! (. . .) Just you wait for the revolt . . . the awakening of the natives! . . .)

And the work ends with yet another ballet scenario (*Van Bagaden*, also republished in the 1959 volume), ostensibly prepared for the Leningrad ballet, but never performed. But the body of the work is an almost uninterrupted monologue from Céline, during which a number of main themes are developed, but which does not have a close knit argumentative pattern.

There are three principal themes in the work. First an assault on communism along the lines already sketched in *Mea Culpa*, directed against its materialism and lack of true brotherhood and egalitarianism, with now the added nuances that the USSR is Jewish-controlled, and that communism and fascism are equally useless. Secondly, a generalized attack on the present state of France, both bourgeoisie and proletariat, again for selfish materialism fostered by the Jews who have infiltrated French society and who control the media. Thirdly—and of course the justification of the whole work in Céline's view—the warning that international Jewry is planning another war in order to bring about the self-destruction of the Aryan masses of Western

Europe, who are too stupid to realize what is in store for them: in order to prevent this catastrophe it is no use thinking of either Russia or England as allies since they are Jewish controlled and part of the plot—the only solution is an understanding with Germany. All this needs now to be illustrated by quotation in order to give also an impression of the polemical virtuosity as well as of the monumental naivety in places.

After being exposed to Ferdinand's first outburst, Gustin protests, and receives an answer worth noting:

> 'Mais t'es antisémite ma vache! C'est vilain! C'est un préjugé! . . .'
>
> 'Je n'ai rien de spécial contre les Juifs en tant que juifs, je veux dire simplement truands comme tout le monde, bipèdes à la quête de leur soupe . . . Ils me gênent pas du tout. Un Juif ça vaut peut-être un Breton, sur le tas, à l'égalité, un Auvergnat, un franc-canaque, un "enfant de Marie" . . . C'est possible . . . Mais c'est contre le racisme juif que je me révolte, que je suis méchant, que je bouille, ça jusqu'au tréfonds de mon benouze! . . .' (p. 49)

> ('But you bastard, you're an antisemite! That's nasty! It's a prejudice!'
>
> 'I've nothing particular against the Jews as jews, I mean just as poor sods like the rest of us, bipeds looking for food . . . They don't worry me at all. A Jew, he's probably as good as a Breton, on the whole, all things being equal, as an Auvergnat, a free-mason, a good little Catholic . . . Maybe . . . But it's Jewish racialism that I won't take, where I became nasty, where I boil with rage right down to the seat of my pants! . . .')

This is both explosive and insidious stuff. It seeks to provide a slight alibi in the opening section and then to provide a justification. One can certainly turn the racialist argument back on him as can be seen in many passages in *Bagatelles*:

> Le Juif est un nègre, la race sémite n'existe pas, c'est une invention de franc-maçon, le Juif n'est que le produit d'un croisement de nègres et de barbares asiates. (p. 121)

> (The Jew is a negro, the semitic race doesn't exist, it's a masonic invention, the Jew is no more than the product of a cross between negroes and Asian barbarians.)

or again:

> Ce qui nous gêne le plus dans les Juifs, quand on examine la situation, c'est leur arrogance, leur perpetuelle martyrologo-dervicherie, leur sale tam-tam. (p. 127)

(What exasperates most about the Jews, when one looks at the situation, is their arrogance, their perpetual dervish-martyr complex, their obscene noisy publicity.)

There is also a kind of incantation (pp. 181–2) which contains his essential view (expressed, of course, many years before the foundation of the State of Israel):

... Si l'on refoulait tous les Juifs, qu'on les renvoie
En Palestine avec leurs caïds franc-maçons—puisqu'ils s'adorent—
Nous cesserions d'être 'Intouchables'.
Au pays des Emirs négrites ...
Nous n'aurions ni guerre, ni faillite ...
Avant longtemps ... longtemps ... longtemps ...
Et nous aurions beaucoup de places vides ... immédiatement
Tout de suite ... les meilleurs en vérité ...

(... If one threw out all the Jews, sent them back
To Palestine with their masonic bosses—since they love each other—
We'd cease to be the 'Untouchables'.
In the land of negroid Emirs ...
We'd have neither war nor bankruptcy ...
For a long ... long ... long ... time
And there'd be lots of jobs going ... immediately
At once ... the best if you want to know ...)

Examination of the text surrounding the above passages justifies a summary of his viewpoint along the following lines. He is saying 'I've nothing against Jews as such,[18] but I am against their arrogant pretensions which do of course explain why they have been persecuted down the ages as they are so fond of reminding us. And in their own surroundings they are, no doubt, very nice people, but they have no business here in France holding down all the best jobs.' Céline's 'mistake' as a polemist was to imagine that such arguments would appeal to any but a tiny minority of literate persons. And *Bagatelles* was far too sophisticated and difficult to be read by the semiliterates who would have agreed with him, and who have their counterparts in England now on the extreme right.[19]

I have already described some of Céline's attitude to communism in connection with *Mea Culpa*. One further set of

[18] He does not, however, indulge in the ultimate hypocrisy of saying 'Some of my best friends are Jews.'
[19] Though we might have to admit that the combined efforts of Arab propaganda and Israeli policies *might* find him an audience again nowadays in some quarters.

illustrations is useful, because it provides a link forward to the
third pamphlet, *Les Beaux Draps*, as will be seen later. He is all
for a *genuine* communism of an egalitarian kind: he knows from
experience what social inequality means. The following passages
are all extracted from a torrential section of text which is very
representative of the overall tone of the book.

> . . . je suis pas réactionnaire! pas pour un poil! une minute! pas
> fasciste! (. . .) Mais pas du tout! mais moi je veux bien qu'on
> partage! Mais moi je n'ai jamais demandé mieux! Là! mes quatre
> sous sur la table! (. . .) Je veux bien tout remettre sur la table. Si l'on
> partage 'absolument'. (. . .) Je me sens communiste de toutes
> fibres! de tous les os! de toute barbarque! et ce n'est pas le cas pour
> bezef! (pp. 54–5)

> (. . . I'm not a reactionary! In no way! not for a moment! not a
> fascist! (. . .) Not at all! I'm all in favour, me, of sharing! I've never
> wanted anything else! There! My four halfpennies on the table!
> (. . .) I'll put all I have on the table. If there's a *total* share-out. (. . .)
> I feel myself communist in every fibre, in all my bones! in my flesh!
> and that's not true of the majority!)

That is the kind of communism he gladly adopts, but what
passes for communism is very different, and is, according to him,
a Jewish invention.

> Ce qu'on appelle communisme dans les milieux bien avancés, c'est la
> grande assurance nougat, le parasitisme le plus perfectionné des
> âges garanti admirablement par le servage absolu du prolétariat
> mondial . . . l'Universelle des Esclaves . . . par le système bolché-
> vique, farci superfasciste, boulonnage international, le plus grand
> coffre-fort blindé qu'on aura jamais conçu, rivé compartimenté,
> soudé au brasier de nos tripes pour la plus grande gloire d'Israel, la
> défense suprême des éternels youtres pillages, l'apothéose tyrannique
> des délires sémites! . . . (p. 55)

> (What's called communism in intellectual circles is merely a syrupy
> kind of insurance policy, the most impeccable parasitism ever down
> the ages, solidly guaranteed by the total servitude of the worldwide
> proletariat . . . the Slaves Commercial Union . . . devised by the
> Bolchevik system, stuffed, hyper-fascist, international riveting, the
> greatest armour-plated strong-box ever imagined, bolted, compart-
> mentalized, soldered in the brazier of our guts for the greater glory
> of Israel, the supreme defence of sempiternal yiddish robberies, the
> tyrannical apotheosis of semitic delirium! . . .)

He also feels it necessary to underline his own situation with respect to all this:

Rappelons un peu les événements: Monsieur Gide en était encore à se demander tout éperdu de réticences, de sinueux scrupules, de fragilités syntaxiques, s'il fallait ou ne fallait pas enculer le petit Bédouin, que déjà depuis belle lurette le *Voyage* avait fait des siennes . . . J'ai pas attendu mes 80 ans pour la découvrir l'inégalité sociale. A 14 ans, j'étais fixé une bonne fois pour toutes. J'avais dégusté la chose. (p. 55)[20]

(Let's get the chronology right. Monsieur Gide was still at the stage of asking himself, all reverent with hesitations, with sinuous scruples, with syntactical delicacy, whether or not it was a good idea to bugger his young Bedouin, when *Voyage* had already long ago had its effects . . . I haven't waited till I was 80 to discover social inequality. At 14 I was fully aware for good and all. I'd tasted it.)

There is an interesting passage near the end of the book which denotes his non-engagement with political parties, his contempt for right and left alike. He seeks to emphasize here that if the new war comes, the sufferer will be, of course, as usual, the ordinary man:

Quand ça deviendra trop compliqué, Thorez s'en ira au Caucase [he was roughly right], Blum à Washington [here he was very wrong] (s'ils ne sont pas butés) chargés de missions très complexes, toi t'iras voir dans les Ardennes, te rendre compte un petit peu, de l'imitation des oiseaux par les balles si furtives . . . si bien piaulantes au vent . . . des vrais rossignols, je t'assure . . . qui viendront picorer ta tête! . . .
    Ferdinand, quand c'est la bataille, le fascisme vaut le communisme, . . . Dans la prochaine Walkyrie, tu peux le croire très fermement, que ça soye Hitler qui remporte ou son cousin Staline . . . ça sera pareil au même . . . la façon qu'on sera têtards, nous (p. 191)

(When it becomes too difficult, Thorez will go off to the Caucasus, Blum to Washington (if they are not bumped off) entrusted with

<hr/>

[20] Gide bore him no grudge, and indeed was one of the few critics to see the literary qualities of *Bagatelles*. In his article about it (*La Nouvelle Revue Française*, April, 1938, reproduced in *Cahiers de l'Herne* pp. 468–70) he says, for instance, 'Et Ferdinand de s'emporter jusqu'au plus étourdissant lyrisme; ses griefs s'étalent et sa hargne, pour le plus grand amusement du lecteur' ('And Ferdinand proceeds to indulge in the most astonishing lyricism; his grudges emerge and his bitterness, to the greatest amusement of the reader'). Perhaps a pedantic note is reasonable here. The 'hesitations' of Gide alluded to here date back to the 1890s (see *Si le grain ne meurt*, pub. 1926), and when Gide began his communist flirtation—c. 1930—he was sixty-one and not eighty . . . Céline is behaving like a journalist here in fact!

highly complex missions, and you, you'll go off to the Ardennes to find out a little bit about how furtive bullets can imitate birds . . . chirping away so nicely in the wind . . . real nightingales, honestly . . . which will come and peck your head!

Ferdinand, when it comes down to battle, fascism is the same as communism . . . In the next version of the *Walkyrie* you can be dead sure of one thing, whether it's Hitler who wins or his cousin Stalin . . . . it will amount to the same thing . . . we'll be the twits just the same . . .)

Of course a communist would tend to say that anyone who could equate Hitler and Stalin in 1937 was nothing more than a fascist. Maybe. But the point is here that Céline has already—at length and with great bitterness—made known his views on Stalin and the USSR, and regards Hitler as no better. Hardly the words of a pro-Nazi, one may reasonably feel.

There is little difficulty in finding passages in *Bagatelles* on other topics—such as the consumer society and corruption by the media—which can command acceptance nowadays. It is in fact astonishing that anyone could have written with such acumen and foresight in 1937—if we disregard the *explanation* of the phenomena given by Céline, which is, of course, that of Jewish influence and policy. Here he is describing—with the aid of a typically coarse opening gambit[21]—the process of subjection of the public to the forces of 'standardization':

On encule un millimètre, le premier centimètre c'est le plus dur, le plus coûteux . . . pour les suivants ça va tout seul! Tous les pédérastes nous l'affirment. N'importe quel trou du cul peut devenir, bien enculé de publicité, un immense n'importe quoi. (. . .) La publicité, pour bien donner tout son effet magique, ne doit être gênée, retenue, divertie par rien. Elle doit pouvoir affirmer, sacrer, vociférer, mégaphoniser les pires sottises, n'importe quelle himalayesque, décervelante, tonitruante fantasmagorie . . . à propos d'automobiles, de stars, de brosses à dents, d'écrivains, de chanteuses légères, de ceintures herniaires, sans que personne ne tique . . . ne s'élève au parterre, la plus minuscule naïve objection. Il faut que le parterre demeure en tout temps parfaitement hypnotisé de connerie. (pp. 123–4)

[21] It is noticeable that Céline uses—flippantly and derisively—references to sodomy very frequently in *Bagatelles*. There's no real suggestion anywhere that he was homosexual, though he certainly found the subject of homosexuality of some physiological interest. In *Bagatelles* he finds it convenient to provoke laughter on the subject (cf. above, p. 99).

(You get your prick in one millimetre, the first centimetre is the hardest, the most costly . . . thereafter there's no problem! Every pederast will tell us this. Absolutely any arse hole can become, well buggered by advertising, an immense whatever you like. (. . .) Advertising, in order to render its full magical effect, must not be troubled, hindered, diverted by anything. It must be allowed to assert, consecrate, vociferate, trumpet abroad the worst stupidities, no matter what Himalayan, brainless, thundering phantasmagoria on the subject of cars, stars, tooth-brushes, writers, female pop singers, rupture trusses, without anyone batting an eyelid, or making from the theatre pit the tiniest simplest protest. The pit must remain permanently and totally hypnotized by stupid rubbish.)

Not only is this an attitude that applies with even greater force to our situation today—we have the added joy of television commercials—but it is an attitude that separates him absolutely from fascist techniques which depend so greatly on slogans and brain-washing propaganda.

More effective as far as the masses are concerned than this enslavement by propaganda (which has its principal effect on the bourgeoisie), is alcohol. The consumption of alcohol in France is higher than in any other country in the world—he produces statistics to show this—and the political power of the alcohol lobby is immense. All this of course he attributes to the 'Jewish' plan for 'standardization' in mediocrity:

C'est très simple, aucun nordique, aucun nègre, aucun sauvage, aucun civilisé non plus n'approche et de très loin, le Français, pour la rapidité, la capacité de pompage vinassier. Seule la France pourrait battre ses propres records de vinasse, ses descentes de picton. Ce sont d'ailleurs à peu près les seuls records qu'elle puisse battre. (. . .) Le Roi Bistrot, possède, lui aussi, tous les droits, par accord politique absolument intangible, à l'immunité complète, au silence total, à tous les encouragements, pour l'exercice de son formidable trafic d'empoisonneur et d'assassin. (pp. 92–3)

(It's quite simple, no northerner, no negro, no savage, nor no civilized being either, can get anywhere near at all to the Frenchmen in the matter of speed and capacity of knocking back wine. Only France could break its own records for wine-bibbing, for putting down plonk. They are, moreover, about the only records they can break. The Café is king, and he possesses, he too, full powers, by quite untouchable political agreement, complete immunity, in total silence, and with every encouragement to carry on his terrific trade of poisoner and assassin.)

France still leads the field in this respect, and indeed has a mighty alcoholism problem. And it is not so long ago—*pace* Céline—that a French Prime Minister, Pierre Mendès-France, was overthrown partly because he was Jewish and partly because he dared to make the mildest of modifications to the licensing laws. . . .

One of the key causes of the decadence of the arts in France and of the absence of *emotional* response from the public (this for Céline is of paramount importance) is the system of secondary education—part of the Jewish drive for standardization of course. Listen to him on the effect of a *lycée* education on children:

> Ils entrent dans l'enseignement secondaire, comme les petites chinoises dans les brodequins rétrécis, ils en sortent émotivement monstrueux, amputés, sadiques, frigides, frivoles et retors . . . (. . .) Ils resteront affublés, ravis, pénétrés, solennels encuistrés de toutes leurs membrures, convaincus, exaltés de supériorité, babilleux de latino-bobarderie, soufflés de vide gréco-romain, de cette 'humanité' bouffonne, cette fausse humilité, cette fantastique friperie gratuite prétentieux roucoulis de formules, abrutissant tambourin d'axiomes maniée, brandie d'âge en âge, pour l'abrutissement des jeunes, par la pire clique parasiteuse, phrasuleuse, sournoise, retranchée, politicarde, théorique vermoulue, profiteuse, inextirpable, retorse, incompétante énucoïde, désastrogène, de l'Univers: le Corps stupide enseignant . . . (p. 106)[22]

> (They go into secondary education like little Chinese girls into shortened shoes; and then come out emotionally monstrous, amputated, sadistic, frigid, frivolous and twisted . . . (. . .) They will remain dressed up, delighted, absorbed, pedantically solemn to the marrow, convinced, supremely self-satisfied, bubbling over with latino-pedantry, inflated with Greco-Roman vacuousness, with this risible 'humanist' pose, this bogus humility, this gratuitous fantastic frippery, pretentious warbling of formulae, deadening battery of axioms—handled, brandished down the ages for the dulling of the young, by the worst possible, parasitical, phrase-making, sly, constricted, politico-intriguing, theorizingly worm-eaten, self-interested, unremovable, crafty, incompetent, eunuchoid, disaster-producing clique in the whole Universe, the teaching stupid profession.)

Céline would no doubt have been surprised at the kind of ally that statement would have brought him in May 1968.

This kind of non-education—and for him the rot started in the Renaissance—has produced in the twentieth century a non-

[22] See above, p. 102.

literature written in what he calls (at various times) 'le style du Bachot', 'le style de Voltaire', 'le style d'Anatole France': a style full of ingenious finesse but drained of all emotional force. However, it is all that Jewish artists are capable of:

> Il faut qu'ils suppléent, qu'ils trichent, qu'ils pillent sans cesse, qu'ils sucent les voisins, les autochtones pour se soutenir . . . les Juifs manquent désastreusement d'émotion directe, spontanée . . . Ils parlent au lieu d'éprouver . . . Ils raisonnent avant de sentir . . . Au strict, ils n'éprouvent rien . . . Ils se vantent. (p. 47)

> (They have to deputize, fiddle, pillage all the time, suck their neighbours, the native inhabitants in order to maintain themselves . . . The Jews are disastrously lacking in direct, spontaneous emotion . . . They talk instead of experiencing . . . They reason before feeling . . . In truth, they don't feel anything . . . They boast about themselves.)

This line of thought brings with it a whole series of resounding condemnations of French authors down the ages from the Renaissance onwards:

> Depuis la Renaissance l'on tend à travailler de plus en plus passionnément pour l'avènement du Royaume des Sciences et du Robot social. (p. 108)

> (Since the Renaissance there's been a tendency to work more and more passionately for the coming of the Kingdom of the Sciences and of the Social Robot.)

Amongst 'Jewish' writers condemned are Montaigne, Racine, Stendhal, Zola and 'Proust-Proust'. (p. 81) Racine indeed comes in for special treatment—

> Racine? Quel emberlificoté tremblotant exhibitionniste! Quel obscène, farfouilleux pâmoisant chiot! Au demi-quart juif d'ailleurs! . . . (p. 136)

> (Racine? What a complicated quivering exhibitionist! Obscene, rummaging, swooning puppy! And one-eighth Jewish too! . . .)

—and for a special reason, which he has given often enough, namely the *obscenity* of the literature of love. He makes this point with particular insistence on the same page:

> Ecrire pourtant de cul, de bite, de merde, en soi n'est rien d'obscène, ni vulgaire. La vulgarité commence, Messieurs, Mesdames, au sentiment, toute la vulgarité, toute l'obscénité! Les écrivains, comme les écrivaines, pareillement enfiotés de nos jours, enjuivés

domestiques jusqu'aux ventricules depuis la Renaissance (. . .) en ont plein les babines ces croulants dégénérés maniérieux cochons de leur 'Amour'! . . . (p. 136)

(Writing of arse, prick, shit is in no way obscene in itself nor vulgar either. Vulgarity begins, ladies and gentlemen, with sentiment, full vulgarity, full obscenity. Writers (male and female) all equally sodomized nowadays, hebraised, domesticated to the core, ever since the Renaissance (. . .) these degenerate, affected, dirty-minded wrecks have their chaps slavering with their 'Love'! . . .)

It should, perhaps, be added that he does not spare contemporary English and American writers either—Virginia Woolf, Faulkner, Dos Passos, Sinclair Lewis and D. H. Lawrence (see above, p. 106 note 22) are among those dismissed.

A particularly eloquent attack is launched against Hollywood. On the subject of the Jewish-dominated pre-war film industry he is quite tireless, and I suppose some people would be willing to concede his point on this in part. For him Hollywood has replaced Buenos Aires in the white slave trade: European starlets —'des plus belles, des plus désirables petites Aryennes bien suceuses' (p. 138) ('the prettiest, most desirable little Aryan girls expert at sucking you off')—are shown rushing to the casting couches of Jewish film magnates. Hollywood has triumphed too: there is no lack of 'standardized' disciples. I am going to use the next quotation in an unorthodox way. The reader of *Bagatelles* is frequently struck by the extent to which Céline's ferocity is defensible, *except* with regard to the anti-Jewish obsession. I omit certain words in this passage, and replace them by the letters x and y, giving the key in footnote. Without the omitted words there is an attack on the media, violent indeed, but certainly arguable: read it again, though, with the words inserted. . . .[23]

. . . la foule (x) rapplique frémissante, elle déleste de tout son pognon, pour mieux sauter, elle engage tout pour mieux jouir (y), se vautrer (y), se pourrir (y), sa tête, sa viande, son âme et toute sa connerie. Elle se donne. Elle se damne. La foule (x) ne croit plus que les affiches des politiciens et des cinémas (y), les journaux et comptes rendus de films, et les critiques d'art, tous (y). (p. 118)

(. . . the mob arrives all agog, unloads all its money so as to be able to jump better, it pledges the lot so as to have more pleasure, to wallow in it, to rot, head, flesh, soul and all its stupidity. It gives itself, it damns itself. The mob only believes politicians' proclama-

[23] for x read 'aryenne': for y 'juif' or 'juifs'.

tions and cinema posters, newspapers and film reviews, and the art critics, all of them.)

His contemptuous conclusion to this section—devoid of racialist epithets—shows him to be in the grand tradition of polemical writings:

> Jamais domestiques, jamais esclaves ne furent en vérité si totalement, intimement asservis, invertis corps et âmes, d'une façon si dévotieuse, si suppliante.
> Rome? En comparaison? . . . Mais un empire du petit bonheur! une Thélème philosophique! Le Moyen Age? . . . L'Inquisition? . . . Berquinades! Epoques libres! d'intense débraillé! d'effréné libre arbitre! Le duc d'Albe? Pizarro? Cromwell? Des artistes! (p. 118)
> (Never were servants, never were slaves in truth so totally, so intimately subjugated, perverted body and soul, in so devout and imploring a manner.
> Rome? In comparison? A happy-go-lucky empire! a philosophical Thélème! The Middle Ages? . . . The Inquisition? . . . Children's tales! Epochs of liberty! of extreme relaxation! of unbridled free will! The Duke of Alba? Pizarro? Cromwell? Artists all of them!)

The final main theme running through *Bagatelles* is the threat of oncoming war. It probably caused the book to be written, and was also given by Céline after the war as the reason for his antisemitic writings.[24]

It is as clear as daylight that his analysis of affairs was wrong— even leaving aside his obsessions about a plot by international Jewry to destroy the 'Aryans' of Western Europe. No alliance with Germany could have averted war from the moment Hitler came to power in 1933. (The Russians when they signed their pact with Nazi Germany in 1939 were under no illusions about this.) But it must be emphasized that at least up to the German invasion of Czechoslovakia in March 1939, a very large section of public opinion in both France and England supported a policy of trying to reach an understanding with the Axis powers of Germany and Italy. This policy of 'appeasement' led to the Munich agreement, and was only abandoned in March 1939. It was supported in both countries by people of differing views: the largest number were probably those who thought that there *must* be a way of peaceful co-existence with Nazi Germany. They were wrong. There were also those—quite numerous on the

[24] See Zbinden interview (Radio Lausanne); reproduced Pléïade, vol. II. pp. 936–45.

right—who thought of Hitler as a bulwark against Stalinist communism. He was, indeed, but he brought a terror infinitely more sinister and infinitely more barbarous. And then there were the few—and they *were* very few—who were genuinely pro-Nazi and pro-fascist. My contention is that Céline, despite anti-semitism, was most certainly not amongst these few—though they of course promptly hailed him as a recruit—and that he did have as his principal motive pacifism, which is not one of the fascist virtues. There are, as will be seen, dangerous and even incriminating statements on this whole issue in *Bagatelles* and even more in *L'Ecole des cadavres* in the following year (1938), but they are much more an indication of his political ignorance than of informed adherence to Nazism. (He admitted this ignorance in later years.)[25] Politically uncommitted and isolated as he was in the years before the war, and contemptuously suspicious of the French press, he had no access to real political information. One may reasonably say that in that case he was excessively foolish to write as he did, and indeed guilty. What needs to be established on the evidence is the extent and nature of his guilt. Much depends on what can be established about his conduct during the German occupation of France, but there is some material in *Bagatelles* to be looked at first.

According to Céline, the left in France—or at least its political leaders of the Front Populaire, especially Léon Blum—naturally want an alliance with the Jewish-dominated Soviet Union. The Jewish City of London and the equally Jewish bankers of the USA are anxious for the destruction of Germany, which under Hitler is threatening their control. But of course, a war between Germany and other European states will suit them nicely. Céline rejects any thought of an alliance with Stalin's Russia: his illusions about Russia (if ever he had any) had been as completely shattered as those of Gide. As for England as an ally:

L'Angleterre alliée? mes burnes! (. . .) Un an pour mobiliser . . .
encore un an pour instruire . . . Nous serons déjà tous asticots quand
débarqueront dans les Flandres les premiers invertis d'Oxford . . .
la jolie Home Fleet du Whisky se répandra sur l'Atlantique
expectante . . . Les Juifs sont rois dans la Cité n'oublions jamais . . .
l'une de leurs suprêmes citadelles avec Wall Street et Moscou . . .
(p. 60)

[25] See again Zbinden interview (Radio Lausanne); reproduced Pléïade, vol. II, pp. 936–45; see also above, p. 24, note 4 (quotation from this interview).

(England as an ally? Balls! (. . .) One year to mobilize . . . another for training . . . We'll all be already maggots when the first Oxford inverts will be landing in Flanders . . . the beautiful whisky Home Fleet will spread itself about the expectant Atlantic . . . We must never forget that the Jews reign in the City . . . one of their supreme citadels along with Wall Street and Moscow!)

He was not quite right about all this (even taking 'Oxford' to stand as a symbol for the English privileged classes . . .) but this kind of line had often been taken about British *land* participation in the 1914–18 war. And, despite the introduction of conscription in Britain (after Munich) for the first time ever in peacetime, the British contingent in France in 1939–40 was but a fraction of the size of the French army. This was helpful to the Vichy government later.

The war that Céline sees coming is desired by Jewry:

La guerre pour la bourgeoisie c'était deja bien fumier, mais la guerre maintenant pour les Juifs! Je peux pas trouver d'adjectifs qui soient vraiment assez glaireux, assez myriakilogrammiques en chiasse, en carie de charogne verdoyeuse pour vous représenter ce que cela signifie. (p. 58)

(War for the bourgeoisie was already revolting enough, but war for the Jews now! I can't find any adjectives that are really sufficiently phlegm-covered, sufficiently myriakilogrammically full of shit, of green decay of corpses to describe to you what that means.)

The traitor class is the bourgeoisie, ignobly pro-Jewish or Jewish dominated:

Je me demande toujours ce qui est le plus dégueulasse, une merde de Juif bien aplatie, ou un bourgeois français tout debout . . . lequel qu'est plus infect davantage? Je peux vraiment pas décider. (p. 60)

(I always ask myself which is the most disgusting, a shit of a Jew cringing away, or a French bourgeois on his feet . . . which is really more foul? I can't honestly make up my mind.)

It is always going to be possible to appeal to the war-like instincts of the ordinary Frenchmen, especially as their women are only too glad to see them off at the Gare de l'Est:

Vous pouvez partir tranquilles . . . vous serez remplacés dans vos boulots promptement, dans vos maisons et dans vos lits . . . (. . .) la femme, surtout la Française, raffole des crépus, des Abyssins, ils vous ont des bites surprenantes! . . . (. . .) Cocus des tranchées,

pauvre viande 'kachère'! vous ne serez pas oubliés! vous serez
pompés, happés, déglutis, fondus dans la Victoire juive... On vous
arrangera en pensions pour les veuves bien consentantes!...
(p. 60)

(You can go off without worry... you'll be promptly replaced in
your jobs, your homes and in your beds... (...) Women, especially
Frenchwomen, admire men with fuzzy hair, Abyssinians, my dear,
they have surprising cocks!... (...) Trench cuckolds, poor
Kosher meat, you won't be forgotten! You'll be sucked up, snatched
up, swallowed up, absorbed into the Jewish Victory... There'll be
pension arrangements for the willing widows!...)

If Céline were dictator he would pass a law consisting of three
simple clauses: (1) All male Jews from seventeen to sixty to be
attached at the outbreak of war to front-line infantry units. None
of these conscripts to rise above the rank of captain. (2) No other
employment than first-line infantryman to be permitted to any
Jew in wartime. (3) Any breach of these enactments punishable
by death. He goes on to explain all this by saying:

Mon petit décret, voyez-vous, de mobilisation du juif, de son
affectation très stricte, n'est pas une petite rigolade... Bien compris,
bien admis, bien assimilé par nos youtres, il peut donner des
résultats dont vous serez grandement surpris, tout à fait précieux,
providentiels, nous évitant, quel miracle, de participer, à toute
viande, au plus grandiose charnier des âges... qui ne demande qu'à
fonctionner... qui hurle déjà devant nos portes. (p. 63)

(My little law, mind you, about mobilization of the Jew, his strict
posting, it's not at all a joke... Well understood, well accepted,
well assimilated by our jewboys, it can give results (which would
surprise you a lot) of a most valuable providential kind, preventing
us, what a miracle, from taking part, with all our flesh, in the
vastest slaughter of all time... which is only too ready to get
going... which is screaming already at our doors.)

This is, of course, an old, charming and Utopian notion—here
applied to the Jews—but more usually directed at politicians:
would heads of state and their civil service and diplomatic
advisers be so willing to engage their countries in war if the
immediate consequences for the whole lot of them was front-line
infantry service in the ranks? The 'if' is too big for there to be
any reasonable answer, but the question retains its propaganda
value. And Céline gives his version of the idea—predictably—in
effective slogan form ' "Un Juif par créneau"... telle est ma

devise pour la guerre prochaine' (p. 63) (' "One Jew per battle-
ment" . . . that's my slogan for the next war').

But as Céline is not dictator, and since his law will never be
passed the conclusion is:

En définitive, Français 'Cocoricos',[26] vous partirez à la guerre, à
l'heure choisie par M. le Baron de Rothschild, votre seigneur et
maître absolu . . . à l'heure fixée, en plein accord, avec ses cousins
souverains de Londres, de New-York et Moscou. C'est lui, M. de
Rothschild, qui signera votre Decret de Mobilisation Générale, par
la personne interposée, par la plume tremblotante de son pantin-
larbin-ministre. (p. 177)

(In fact, 'cock-a-doodle-doo' Frenchmen, you'll go off to war at the
moment chosen by M. le baron de Rothschild, your lord and
absolute master . . . at the hour fixed, in full accord with his
sovereign cousins in London, New York and Moscow. It's M. de
Rothschild, he, who will sign your decree of General Mobilization,
via the intermediary, via the quivering pen of his puppet-lackey-
minister.)

Now we are very conscious in this day and age of the feeling
that we have little or no control over our destinies in this area—
even under a beautiful system of parliamentary democracy—that
the really important decisions are probably not even taken by the
politicians, so why bother to elect them? . . . How skilfully does
Céline exploit this regrettable feeling!

He only needs to add one further notion—that which came out
in 1938 in the form of 'Why die for Czechoslovakia?' or in 1939
as 'Why die for Danzig?' Near the end of the volume he expounds
this in very succinct form, and at the same time ties it in with
his anti-semitism and his reasons for wanting an alliance with
Germany. This section of *Bagatelles* (pp. 192-3) contains by far
the most compromising material in the book: the summary
which follows gives a run-down of the 'ideas' therein together
with the most damaging remarks. He would not mind at all if
Hitler attacked Russia. The number of Russian victims would not
be greater than those liquidated by Stalin in peacetime. So let him
take the Ukraine, Czechoslovakia and Romania too if he wants,
so long as he leaves us in peace.

Moi je voudrais bien faire une alliance avec Hitler. Pourquoi pas? Il a
rien dit contre les Bretons, contre les Flamands . . . Rien du tout . . .

[26] = chauvinist.

Il a dit seulement sur les Juifs . . . il les aime pas les Juifs . . . Moi non plus . . . J'aime pas les nègres hors de chez eux . . . C'est tout. (. . .) Je veux pas faire la guerre pour Hitler, moi je le dis, mais je ne veux pas la faire contre lui, pour les Juifs . . .

(I'd very much like to make an alliance with Hitler. Why not? He's said nothing against the Bretons, against the Flemish . . . Nothing at all . . . He's only said things about the Jews . . . He doesn't like the Jews . . . Nor do I . . . I don't like negroes away from their own country . . . that's all. (. . .) I don't want to go to war for Hitler, no, I don't, but I don't want to go to war against him, for the Jews . . .)

To the objection that an alliance with Hitler would be dangerous because of the superior strength of Germany he replies that Hitler would be fully occupied for years in coping with his conquests in Eastern Europe. Moreover even if that were not so 'Deux millions de boches campés sur nos territoires pourront jamais etre pires, plus ravageurs, plus infamants que tous ces Juifs dont nous crevons' ('Two million Boches camped in our territory will never possibly be worse, more predatory, more shameful than all these Jews who are destroying us'). He would prefer twelve Hitlers to one Blum—'Hitler encore je pourrais le comprendre, tandis que Blum c'est inutile' ('Hitler I could still understand, whereas with Blum it's not worth trying.').

At this point his interlocutor—here Gustin—asks him if he wants to kill all the Jews. The answer is no, but that if there is a war they should be among the victims. Expanding on this, he is led to make what is perhaps the most crude statement of the whole work:

> . . . un seul ongle de pied pourri, de n'importe quel vinasseux ahuri truand d'Aryen, vautré dans son dégueulage, vaut encore cent mille fois plus, et cent mille fois davantage et de n'importe quelle façon à n'importe quel moment, que cent vingt-cinq mille Einsteins, debout, tout dérétinisants d'effarante gloire rayonnante . . .[27]
>
> (. . . a single nail off the stinking foot of no matter what wine-sodden, dazed Aryan tramp, wallowing in his vomit, is worth a hundred thousand times more, and one hundred thousand times more again in any way you like and at any moment, than one hundred and twenty-five thousand Einsteins upright, all dazzling with startling radiant glory.)

No wonder certain contemporaries wondered whether Céline was

[27] This because of Einstein's openly professed Zionism.

not trying to ridicule anti-semitism! Gide in his NRF article in
April 1938 already referred to (see above, p. 90) came very close
to the truth when he said:

> Céline excelle dans l'invective. Il l'accroche à n'importe quoi. La
> juiverie n'est ici qu'un prétexte qu'il a choisi le plus épais possible,
> le plus trivial, le plus reconnu, celui qui se moque le plus volontiers
> des nuances, qui permet les jugements les plus sommaires, les
> exagérations les plus énormes, le moindre souci de l'équité, le plus
> intempérant laisser-aller de la plume. Et Céline n'est jamais meilleur
> que lorsqu'il est le moins mesuré. C'est un créateur. Il parle des
> Juifs, dans *Bagatelles*, tout comme il parlait, dans *Mort à crédit*, des
> asticots que sa force évocatrice venait de créer.[28]

> (Céline excels at invective. He hangs it on to anything. Jewry is here
> no more than a pretext, chosen by him as the most stupid possible,
> the most vulgar, the best known, that which most willingly derides
> subtleties, which allows the most summary judgements, the most
> enormous exaggerations, the least concern for equity, the most
> intemperate insouciance of the pen. And Céline is never better
> than when he is the least measured. He is a creator. He talks about
> the Jews in *Bagatelles*, just in the way he talked in *Mort à crédit* about
> the maggots that his evocative power had created.)

I think Gide is quite right about the deliberate and provocative
exaggerations of Céline's invective: they should not be taken too
literally. But, I fear, he is wrong when he takes anti-semitism to
be merely a kind of pretext for Céline—it was more than that.
Indeed, long after Céline had dropped his anti-semitism, he holds
on to certain 'scientific' notions about race, still for polemical
reasons, in order to demonstrate that the supremacy of the white
man is over and that the future lies with the Chinese. . . .[29]

This point of view is beginning to emerge in *Bagatelles*—though
here only used against the French—and it is with some remarks
about this that I conclude on the subject of this book. What
Céline probably wished to leave as the major impression at the
end of the work was neither the desirability of anti-semitism, nor
the fear of coming war, nor the need for an alliance with Germany
to prevent that war, but rather his demonstration of the decadence
and hypocrisy of the France of the period. The final sequences of
Bagatelles are a kind of pendant to the opening section, where

[28] Gide goes on to quote part of the passage in *Mort à crédit*—p. 1009—about the
asticots at Blême-le-Petit.

[29] See, for example, *Rigodon*; see also below, pp. 224 and 233.

there is what he calls a 'Baedeker' evocation of his stay in Leningrad, and also a final ballet scenario (pp. 200–226). The author
takes formal leave of his public on p. 200—'. . . Grande révérence
. . . Grande féerie . . . Je vous salue! Votre serviteur! . . .' ('. . . Big
bow! . . . Big enchantment! . . . Greetings! Your humble servant!
. . .')—immediately after a last conversation with his Jewish friend
Gutman (Gide in the article just quoted considers this dialogue to
be 'des mieux réussis'). Gutman suggests to Ferdinand that he is
on a very dangerous tack, that he will only make enemies for
himself—and that he has gone about things in quite the wrong
way. Instead of attacking and insulting his fellow countrymen, he
should handle them as the Jews do, much more tactfully. 'Regarde
un peu les indigènes, les Juifs ne les contrarient jamais eux . . .'
('Look at the natives a bit, the Jews never upset them at all . . .')
It is not necessary to do so because the natural French instinct
down the ages has been to adore their conquerors, to present
their arses for willing penetration—beginning with the Romans:

> Ils s'en congratulent encore à 18 siècles de distance! . . . Toute la
> Sorbonne en jubile! . . . Ils en font tout leur bachot de cette
> merveilleuse enculade! . . . (p. 197)

> (They are still congratulating themselves about it 18 centuries later!
> . . . The entire Sorbonne exults over it! They construct their entire
> *bachot* examination out of this wonderful sodomization! . . .)

This being so, they can surely make do for now with a Jewish
prick instead:

> Le paf de youtre c'est bas, j'admets! dans la série animale, mais
> enfin quand même, ça bouge . . . Ça vaut bien une bite d'Empereur
> mort? . . . (. . .) Puisque c'est le destin des Français de se faire miser
> dans le cours des âges . . . puisqu'ils passent d'un siècle à l'autre . . .
> d'une bite d'étrusque sur une bite maure . . . sur un polard de
> ritain . . . Une youtre gaule ou une saxonne? . . . Ça fait pas beaucoup
> de différence! (p. 197)

> (A Yiddish cock is pretty low I admit! in the animal kingdom, but
> at least it moves . . . It's better than the prick of a dead emperor?
> . . . (. . .) Since it's the destiny of the French down the ages to have
> it up themselves . . . since they pass from one century to the next
> . . . from an Etruscan prick onto a Moorish prick . . . onto an
> Italian tool . . . a Jewish rod or a Saxon? Doesn't make much
> difference!)

With this Ferdinand agrees. More than that, he underlines the

same point, and gives—for the first time—his view of the future
for the French:

> A présent, en pleine décadence, faut se faire étreindre par des
> larvaires . . . se contenter de ce qui reste . . . (. . .) Mais plus on se
> fait foutre . . . plus on demande . . . Et puis voilà qu'on leur promet
> aux Français, des bourreaux tartares! . . . (. . .) Des tortureurs
> impitoyables! . . . (. . .) Et puis des Mongols! . . . encore plus
> haineux! . . . plus bridés! . . . Qui croquent la terre et les vermines
> . . . Ah! comme ils vont nous traverser! . . . Et puis d'autres, plus
> chinois encore! plus jaunes! . . . plus verts . . . (. . .) C'est la vie des
> anges par le pot! . . . Ils nous tuent . . . Voilà comme ils disent les
> Français! (pp. 198-9)

> (At present, in full period of decadence, the only thing to do is to
> be screwed by a few grubs . . . make do with what's available . . .
> (. . .) But the more you get fucked . . . the more you want . . . Well,
> here's what is promised for the French. Tartar executioners! . . .
> (. . .) pitiless torturers! . . . (. . .) And then some Mongols . . . even
> more full of hatred . . . more constricted! . . . Who eat soil and
> vermin . . . Ah! How hard they're going to ram it up us! . . . And
> then others, still more Chinese looking! yellower! . . . tougher! . . .
> (. . .) Paradise via the arse! . . . They're killing us . . . That's what the
> French are saying.)

The whole of this uproarious passage is well sustained . . .
Céline was not homosexual, and the choice here of the image of
sodomy is part of the triumphant sarcasm of his final address to
his compatriots in 1937, an image of the humiliation which he
thought they deserved. Being cruel to be kind? A kind of political
suicide? Ultimate washing of hands? Elements of all three. There
is at present no proposal to reprint *Bagatelles* (or the other two
pamphlets). It is easy to see why. But it is totally wrong. No one
can fully understand Céline without some knowledge of these
works.

I have dealt with *Bagatelles* at some length because it is out of
print and virtually inaccessible to most readers, because it is an
essential text for the understanding of Céline, and because, despite
the disagreeable and sometimes even disgraceful material to be
found in it, it is for the most part magnificently written and
deserves the description given by Charles Plisnier in a review of
it in 1938:

> Eh bien! vu ainsi—purement et simplement sous l'angle littéraire—

Bagatelles pour un massacre est un chef d'oeuvre de la plus haute classe. Un chef d'oeuvre et un tour de force.[30]

(Well, seen thus—from a purely and simply literary stand point—*Bagatelles pour un massacre* is a masterpiece of the highest order. A masterpiece and a virtuoso turn.)

I can deal much more briefly with *L'Ecole des cadavres*, written in the same vein and taking up the same themes—with, if anything, greater violence—and confine myself to outlining the relatively few new ideas it contains. It was published in November 1938, some six weeks after Munich. It has a short five-page introductory dialogue (between Céline and a siren found swimming the Seine near Courbevoie), but otherwise it is an entirely straightforward piece of statement by Céline. The tone is more constantly anti-semitic, there are few digressions, and the whole work is immensely repetitive. It was written in a hurry and shows all the signs of this: the vocabulary has all the author's usual verve, but the incidence of three dots and of exclamation marks is reduced, which suggests that there was not much time for stylistic tinkering. It is Céline's one real incursion into what one might call journalism, and it is by a very considerable distance his feeblest and least interesting book. Frankly, real devotion to the author is required if one is to fight one's way through the 300-odd pages. There are passages which take some of the ideas of *Bagatelles* further, and a few others where new lines appear. Mercifully it will not take long to cover them.

The maintenance of the anti-semitic tone does not require illustration. The attack on the Soviet Union and its materialistic distortion are repeated, and linked with them is a passage on the absence of any real sense of the class struggle among the French proletariat:

La conscience de classe est une foutaise, une démagogique convention. Chaque ouvrier ne demande qu'à sortir de sa classe ouvrière, qu'à devenir bourgeois, le plus vite possible (. . .) Le prolétaire, le militant le plus ardent, il a envie de partager avec son frère damné de classe, à peu près comme le gagnant à la loterie nationale il a envie de partager avec tous ceux qui ont perdu. Il veut bien partager la merde ce prolétaire, mais pas le gâteau. (. . .) Pas plus de communisme véritable dans les classes prolétaires que de pâquerettes au Sahara . . . (pp. 129–30)

[30] In *L'Indépendance Belge* (19 March 1938).

(Awareness of class is a load of rubbish, a demagogic convention. Every worker asks nothing more than to get out of his working class, to become middle class, as soon as possible (. . .) The proletarian, the most ardent militant, has about as much desire to share with his luckless brother worker as has the winner in the national lottery to share with those who have lost. He's willing to share the shit, the worker is, but not the cake. (. . .) No more real communism in the proletariat than there are daisies in the Sahara.)

This gives him a lead into a discussion of what communism should really be, which is both a development of notions briefly sketched in *Bagatelles* and a prefiguration of the principal theme of *Les Beaux Draps*:

Le communisme est avant tout vocation poétique. (. . .) On ne devient pas communiste. Il faut naître communiste, ou renoncer à le devenir jamais. Le communisme est une qualité d'âme. Un état d'âme qui ne peut s'acquérir. Rien ne peut modifier, atténuer, exalter le ton, la valeur, la joie d'une âme. Propagandes, éducations, violences, intérêt, souffrances, et même le fameux Amour n'atteignent pas l'âme. L'âme s'en fout. (. . .) Le Communisme doit être folie, avant tout, par dessus tout, Poésie. (pp. 130–32)

(Communism is above all a poetical vocation. (. . .). You don't become a communist. You must be born a communist, or give up the idea of ever becoming one. Communism is a quality of the soul. A spiritual state which can't be acquired. Nothing can modify, attenuate, exalt the tone, the value, the joy of a soul. Propaganda methods, educational systems, violences, self-interest, sufferings, not even the famous Love can reach the soul. The soul doesn't give a damn (. . .) Communism must be a kind of extravagance, above all and before all, Poetry.)

This is a cry of idealistic hope, written at a time and in a context which make it surprising. By Céline. A destructive, nihilistic, despairing, embittered Céline. This is a very important text, and it has never been commented on since it was written. It would not be very significant if it were isolated, but there is the evidence of *Les Beaux Draps* three years later to show that it was not. This may help a lot in explaining the various stances adopted by Céline. The note of hope is at once contrasted with statements about communism as actually exemplified in the Soviet Union:

Le Communisme sans poète, à la juive, à la scientifique, à la raison raisonnante, marxiste, à l'administrative, (. . .) n'est plus qu'un très emmerdant procédé de tyrannie prosaïque, absolument sans essor, une imposture juive satrapique absolument atroce, immangeable, inhumaine, une très dégueulasse forcerie d'esclaves, une infernale gageure, un remède pire que le mal. (pp. 132-3)

(Communism without the poet, in the Jewish, scientific, rational reasoning, marxist, administrative manner, (. . .) is no more than a most infuriating process of prosaic tyranny, absolutely without inspiration, a Jewish satrap-like imposture, absolutely atrocious, uneatable, inhuman, a very revolting hot-house for slaves, a hellish gamble, a cure worse than the ill.)

Not surprisingly the attacks against England become numerous and specific in L'Ecole des cadavres. After Munich the British attitude to Hitler did begin to harden, rather more obviously than it did in France. The House of Lords is Jewish. The Intelligence Service—Jewish-controlled, of course—is, with the backing of the Jewish City of London, behind all the war-mongering preparations for holocaust. The poor French do not realize that all their activities have been forecast, arranged, manipulated years ahead by the British Intelligence Service (pp. 151-2). The English Court is even regarded as a significant political force:

La Cité, 'l'Intelligence', la Cour juive anglaise sont parfaitement responsables, depuis Cromwell, de toutes nos faillites, de toutes nos débacles, en tous genres. (p. 154)

(The City, 'the Intelligence Service' the Jewish English Court, are completely responsible, ever since Cromwell's day, for all our bankruptcies, all our collapses, of every kind.)

The imminence of a royal visit to France gives rise to this fascinating passage:

Quand vous descendez hurler vos faveurs sur le passage de Georges VI, demi-juif, de sa reine Bowen-Lyon [sic] la juive, mandatés par Chamberlain demi-juif, Eden demi-juif, Hoare-Belisha (Horeb Elisha parfaitement juif), (. . .) vous pouvez sûrement vous vanter d'avoir merveilleusement passé votre après-midi. (p. 160)

(When you go into the streets to shout your approval at the passing by of George VI (half-Jewish) of his queen Bowen-Lyon [sic] the Jewess, mandated by Chamberlain (half-Jewish), Eden (half-Jewish), Hoare Belisha (Horeb Elisha completely Jewish), (. . .) you can certainly pride yourself on having spent your afternoon wonderfully.)

One cannot help feeling that his admiration for the skill and power of 'l'Intelligence Service' is just a trifle exaggerated. . . . If our pre-war ministers in the thirties had been a little better informed, then perhaps they would not have made such an almighty hash of things. One feels, too, that Céline has no very precise idea of the political significance of the British monarchy, the House of Lords and what he calls the 'Court'. But he is not alone among Frenchmen in that. It's a pity, however, to have to bring him down to the intellectual level of, say, *France-Dimanche* today.

But not only George VI and Queen Elizabeth are Jewish: there is also 'la juive Simpson' (p. 200), and—delightful revelation —Pope Pius XI and his Secretary of State (soon to become the pro-fascist Pope Pius XII):

> Rien de plus juif que le Pape actuel. De son nom véritable Isaac Ratisch. (Achille Ratti.) (...) Le Vatican est un Ghetto. Le Secrétaire d'Etat Pacelli, aussi juif que le Pape. (p. 266)

> (Nothing more Jewish than the present Pope. His real name Isaac Ratisch. (Achille Ratti.) (...) The Vatican is a Ghetto. Pacelli, the Secretary of State, as Jewish as the Pope.)

A little further on we have one of the rare references (in all Céline) to Christianity:

> La religion christianique? La judéo-talmudo-communiste? Un gang! Les Apôtres? Tous Juifs! Tous gangsters! Le premier gang? L'Eglise! Pierre? Un Al Capone du Cantique! Un Trotzky pour moujiks romains! L'Evangile? Un code de racket . . . L'Eglise catholique? Un arnaquage aux bonnes paroles consolantes, la plus splendide des rackets qui ait jamais été montée en n'importe quelle epoque pour l'embéroutage des Aryens. On ne fera jamais mieux! (...) La nouvelle variété du genre, le stratagème 'communiste', c'est de 'l'à genoux' aussi pour tout le monde, bien sûr, forcément, mais ça vaudra jamais l'autre, l'évangélique! (p. 271)

> (The Christian religion? The judaeo-talmudo communistic one? A gang! The apostles? All Jews! All gangsters! The first gang? The Church! Peter? A chanting Al Capone! A Trotsky for Roman moujiks! The Gospels? Rule-book for racketeers . . . The Catholic Church? Skilful dressing up of words of consolation, the most splendid racket ever set up in any epoch for the misleading of Aryans. No one will ever do better! (...) The new variety in this field, the 'communist' stratagem, that has 'down on your knees' too, for everybody, of course, inevitably, but it's nothing like so good as the other, the evangelical one.)

What on earth can Céline have thought was going to be the effect of all this material—and on whom? Even in the wildest pages of *Bagatelles* there is a discernible degree of aesthetic control of material that is often lacking in the second pamphlet: it is as though, exasperated by the relative lack of response to his earlier outburst, and even more aware of the approach of war, he writes not only hastily but petulantly and without any real attempt at persuasion. The Munich agreement (mocked by him—pp. 169-70—not unreasonably as being merely a postponement of war by an unprepared England) which at least seemed to demonstrate to public opinion the desire of the Western powers to come to terms with the Axis, severely weakened some of the propositions (one cannot call them arguments) of *Bagatelles*, and it may well be that this constrained him to repeat the propositions even more loudly and crudely in *L'Ecole des cadavres*, as well as to intensify the anti-British tone.

There are also in this second pamphlet a number of very compromising remarks about Hitler. They are couched, however, in such general and puerile terms—rather like the comments on England—that it is hardly possible to consider them as statements that accept Nazi *philosophy*. The passages which follow are the most extreme examples in the work:

Qui a fait le plus pour l'ouvrier? c'est pas Staline, c'est Hitler. (p. 107)

(Who has done most for the worker? Not Stalin, it's Hitler.)

Quel est le véritable ami du peuple? Le Fascisme.
Qui a fait le plus pour l'ouvrier? L'U.R.S.S. ou Hitler? C'est Hitler.
Y a que regarder sans merde rouge plein les yeux.
Qui a fait le plus pour le petit commerçant? C'est pas Thorez, c'est Hitler!
Qui nous préserve de la guerre? C'est Hitler!
Les communistes (juifs ou enjuivés), ne pensent qu'à nous envoyer à la bute, à nous faire crever en Croisades.
Hitler est un bon éleveur de peuples, il est du côté de la vie, il est soucieux de la vie des peuples, et même de la nôtre. C'est un Aryen.
(p. 140)

(What is the true friend of the people? Fascism.
Who has done the most for the worker? The USSR or Hitler? It's Hitler.
You've only got to look without your eyes being full of red shit.
Who has done most for the small tradesman? It's not Thorez, it's Hitler.

Who has protected us from war? It's Hitler.

The communists (Jews or Jewish influenced) simply want to send us to the slaughter, to kill us in crusades.

Hitler is a good breeder of peoples, even of ours. He is an Aryan.)

Leaving aside the fact that he may have been right about the *petit commerçant* social group in France, always reactionary, from César Birotteau to Poujade, it is painful to write out, type up and cause to be printed such sorry material. I only do so because it does help support my contention that Céline was politically an ignoramus, and also because it is desirable that what he actually said should be *known*.

Towards the end of the book he reiterates emphatically his desire for a full military alliance with Germany, to preserve the peace of Europe, to destroy the influence of Britain in Europe and to extirpate the Jewish plague. France and Germany had been separate for 1100 years—since the Treaty of Verdun in 843—so let them now join together to form (with Italy and Spain) the 'Confédération des Etats Aryens d'Europe' (p. 284). Moreover, the *important* part of France (roughly north of the Loire) is of Germanic origin: he regards the *méridionaux* as an inferior brand of Frenchmen. . . .

> Moi je veux qu'on fasse une alliance avec l'Allemagne et tout de suite, et pas une petite alliance, précaire, pour rire, fragile, palliative! quelque pis-aller! Pas du tout! Mais non! Mais non! . . . Une vraie alliance, solide, colossale, à chaux et à sable! A la vie! A la mort! (p. 283)[31]

[31] There is a judicious comment on Céline's advocacy of an alliance with Germany in Jacqueline Morand, *Les idées politiques de Louis-Ferdinand Céline*, p. 130: 'Le point sur lequel il convient d'insister c'est que Céline prêche l'alliance franco-allemande en 1937-8, époque de Munich, époque où la plupart des quotidiens et hebdomadaires (à l'exception de la presse communiste), où les actualités cinémato-graphiques (. . .) sont envahis par ces élans de fraternité franco-allemande et par les proclamations farouchement pacifistes des hommes politiques au pouvoir. Réclamer l'alliance franco-allemande en 1937-8 comme le fit Céline, c'était reprendre un thème très communément développé par les autorités officielles et très répandu dans l'opinion publique.'

('The point which ought to be stressed is that Céline is preaching a Franco-German alliance in 1937-8, time of Munich, time when the majority of daily and weekly papers (except for the communist press), when cinema news programmes (. . .) are all full of surges of Franco-German friendship and of the timidly pacifist proclamations by the politicians in power. To demand a Franco-German alliance in 1937-8, as did Céline, was to take up a theme very frequently expounded by the official authorities and very widespread in public opinion.') But of course he had rather special reasons. . . . .

La France n'est latine que par hasard, par raccroc, par défaites, en réalité elle est Celte, Germanique pour les trois quarts. Le latinisme plaît beaucoup aux méridionaux franc-maçons. Le latinisme c'est tout près de la Grèce. La Grèce c'est déjà de l'Orient. L'Orient c'est en plein la Loge. La Loge c'est déjà du juif. Le Juif c'est déjà du nègre. Ainsi soit-il. (p. 284)

(What I want is that there should be an alliance with Germany and at once too, and not a little, feeble, laughable, fragile, palliative one! a last resort! Not at all! No! No! . . . a real alliance, solid, colossal, firmly cemented! For life! and death!

France is only a Latin country by chance, by accident, by defeats, in reality France is three-quarters Celtic and Germanic. Latin culture is much liked by our meridional free-masons. It is near to Greece. Greece is already Oriental. The Orient is fully masonic. Masonry is already Jewish. The Jew is already negro. So be it.)

In *L'Ecole des cadavres* there are frequent references to contemporary political figures. The most interesting are those to figures of the extreme right—his views on the extreme left have already been seen—such as Maurras, Doriot, Colonel de la Roque and Pétain. Maurras he treats as a hypocrite, a 'lycéen enragé' (p. 253) ('angry schoolboy') and his style as 'Liquoreux, ânânonnant, tendancieux faux-témoin, juif' (p. 189) ('Syrupy, st-stammering, tendentiously false-witness, Jewish'). Doriot's ideas are dismissed in the following terms 'Nous sommes en pleine loufoquerie, en plein crânouillage loufoque creux, venteux, bien français! Cocorico!' (p. 258) ('We are here in full absurdity, in full absurd, hollow, windy boasting, very French! Cock-a-doodle-doo!'). De la Roque is nicknamed 'Colonel Ghetto' and said to be 'aux gages de la même racket israélite que Messieurs Blum, Cachin, Thorez, Verdier, Lebrun' (p. 123) ('in the pay of the same Jewish racket as MM. Blum, etc.'). Pétain is dealt with on several occasions as a war-monger, and as such in the service of Jewry: in one passage (pp. 165–6), he is made to speak with a Central European Jewish accent—'Moi Bedain'—giving his listeners a rendezvous with death in a few months' time—'Je vous retrouve aux Nécropoles! Je veux que ca soit le plus gigantesque cimetière! mon cimetière Bedain!' ('We will meet again at the Necropolises! I want it to be the most gigantic cemetery! My Bedain cemetery!'). It is no surprise therefore to find that the extreme right (which had greeted *Bagatelles* with delight) remained virtually silent on *L'Ecole des cadavres*. Ferdinand had become too compromising even for them. Or, more truly, he had attacked them too! His isolation at the outbreak of war was total: no one—from extreme left to extreme right—was with him, and this was probably what he wanted. He says as much in what is rather a fine passage right at the end of the book. He is scornfully denying the allegation that he had been paid by Hitler to write it:

Réfléchissez un petit peu que je gagne avec mes livres, mes romans, tout simplement dix fois plus d'argent qu'il m'en faut pour vivre. (. . .) Je l'ouvre comme je veux, où je veux, ma grande gueule, quand je veux. Ne vous cassez pas le haricot. Ce que j'écris je le pense, tout seul, et nul ne me paye pour le penser, ne me stimule. Personne, ou presque personne ne peut se vanter d'en faire autant, de se payer ce luxe. (. . .) A 71 ans j'emmerderai encore les juifs, et les maçons, et les éditeurs, et Hitler s'il me provoque. Qu'on se le dise. Je dois être, je crois bien, l'homme le moins achetable du monde.[32] [He continues in what is to become a familiar vein in his post-war writings]
    Voilà Ferdinand, au poil. Il faudra le tuer. Je ne vois pas d'autre moyen. Le malheur, c'est que les gens vous jugent toujours d'après leurs propres tendances, et qu'ils sont presque tous à vendre, n'importe quel jour, par tous les temps. Même les plus riches, les plus superbes. Ils n'arrêtent pas de s'offrir. En fait, leur vie n'est qu'un putanat perpétuel plus ou moins décoratif, plus ou moins chichiteux, somptueux, prétentieux. (. . .) Cessez de me juger d'après vous-mêmes, à votre mesure. (. . .) Ne vous touchez plus dans les coins. (pp. 299–300)

(But think a little about what I earn from my books, my novels, in simple terms ten times more money than I need to live (. . .) I open it when I want, where I want, my big mouth. Don't you worry. What I write I believe, all by myself and no one pays me to believe it, no one inspires me to do so. Nobody, or practically nobody, can claim as much, can afford this luxury. (. . .) At the age of 71 I'll still be annoying the Jews, the Free-masons, and the publishers, and Hitler too if he provokes me—let that sink in. I must be, so far as I can tell, the least bribable man in the world.
    There is Ferdinand, stark naked. He'll have to be killed. I don't see any other way out. The trouble is that people always judge you by their own inclinations, and that they are nearly all for sale, on any day, at any time. Even the richest, the proudest. They never stop offering themselves. In fact, their existence is just one ceaseless whoredom, more or less decorative, more or less affected, sumptuous, pretentious (. . .) Kindly stop judging me in terms of yourselves, by

[32] No one has produced evidence to counter this (see below, p. 238).

your standards (. . .) And stop touching yourselves up over in the corner there.)

When the war came in 1939, the Céline 'Médaille Militaire de 1914' overcame the pacifist Céline. Turned down for active service in the army on medical grounds, he became doctor on a ship that was torpedoed by the Germans. In other words, patriotic feelings overcame the alleged pro-Nazi sympathies.

In 1945 what was to count against Céline in terms of the law, was not what opinions he may or may not have held before the war, nor even during the opening months of the war, but what he was alleged to have done or written 'entre le 16 juin 1940 et la date de la Libération, en temps de guerre', that is to say during the period of the German occupation of France.

Now whatever judgement about Céline in 1937–8 you may have formed from the foregoing pages—and I have tried to quote typical passages at some length to enable some judgement to be made—it is likely to be modified by consideration of the wartime years. New works published by Céline during the period were: (1) *Les Beaux Draps* (Nouvelles Editions Françaises, Paris, 1941) (2) A short preface to the history of Bezons by his friend Albert Serrouille, *Bezons à travers les âges* (Denoël et Steele, Paris, 1944) and (3) *Guignol's Band I* (Denoël, Paris 1944). Only the first of these has any significance in the present context. The preface to Serrouille's book has, not surprisingly, no political significance at all, and *Guignol's Band I*—apart from an opening description of the German bombardment of Orléans in 1940—is set in London during the First World War.

Les Beaux Draps, however, the third of the pamphlets, is important. It is, as the title suggests, partly an opportunity for Céline to say to his compatriots 'I told you so—just look what a mess we're in now!' It is shorter than the first two pamphlets[33] and only takes some of their familiar themes. The tone is for the most part very different, and the last third of the book is not in the polemical manner at all. The anti-semitism is still there, but less prominently and much less aggressively. The pro-German tone of 1937–8 has disappeared: there are virtually no references to the Germans or Hitler. There is a substantial opening section

[33] *Bagatelles* has roughly 110,000 words; *L'Ecole des cadavres* 85,000; *Les Beaux Draps* 45,000.

devoted to the defeat of France, in which the ex-soldier of 1914 pours his contempt upon the French army of 1940 for running away from the enemy. (This could later be used by his enemies as evidence of his being 'un mauvais Français'.) But the main point of the book—and its novelty—is the development of his views about what a regenerated France should be like. Jews have no place in it, of course. At the centre of his ideas are two basic principles: first, the concept of the nation as a family, inter-dependent and conscious of the needs of all the members of the family, and secondly—much space is devoted to this—the insistence on equality of incomes within the national 'family'—what he calls, in fact, 'du communisme Labiche, du communisme petit bourgeois' (p. 137). This is, indeed, a formal working out of the opinions already noted in the earlier pamphlets on equality and 'true' communism. Not a very compromising work, though it does contain sentences, which, isolated from their context, were used against him at the time of his trial in 1950. The last twenty pages or so of the book—on which no one to my know-ledge has ever made significant comment—are in part a moving evocation of the miseries of the poor during the rigours of winter in occupied Paris, and in part a very extraordinary fantasy provoked by this. A few examples will suffice to show the overall tone of the book.

The only 'sinister' anti-semitic phrase in *Les Beaux Draps* is this:

> Bouffer du juif ça suffit pas, je le dis bien, ça tourne en rond, en rigolade, une façon de battre du tambour si on saisit pas leurs ficelles, qu'on leur étrangle pas avec. (p. 115)
>
> (Attacking [lit. eating] Jews isn't enough, I have to say, it becomes futile, a joke, merely a kind of publicity stunt, if you don't get hold of the strings they pull and strangle them with them.)

Read out in isolation I suppose that could sound like incitement to the extermination of the Jews. But the context of the sentence makes it innocent enough. He is being heavily ironical at the expense of the Vichy press, which was beginning to indulge in anti-semitic propaganda, and the remark is flippant. He is recognizing in this passage that the mass of the French people regards anti-semitism as a bourgeois device to deflect hostility on to the Jews. This does not please Céline, but he sees that it is the case. Moreover, this is the *only* remark written by Céline that could conceivably bear a more grave interpretation. Much more

typical of the mood in *Les Beaux Draps* is his wry forecast for
New York. We have already seen that for him from Jew to
Negro is but one step—what he foresees has the kind of poetic
justice that might appeal to James Baldwin:

> Dans cent ans les blancs habiteront à New York un quartier réservé:
> les nègres iront voir au Nouvel-Harlem les 'pâles' danser la polka.
> (p. 33)

> (In a hundred years the whites will live in a special area of New
> York: the negroes will go to New Harlem to watch the 'pale-skins'
> dance the polka.)

The other 'incriminating' sentence in *Les Beaux Draps* (by
'incriminating' I mean here, used against him at the trial in 1950)
is this statement about attitudes towards the Germans: 'c'est
comme pour devenir pro-allemand j'attends pas que la Commandatur pavoise au Crillon' (p. 156) ('The fact is that I don't
wait until the German Commandatur has its flag on the Hotel
Crillon to become pro-German'). Once again context is important.
It is totally honourable. He is attacking what had better (in
Célinian terms) be described as political arse-licking. He is
hostile to those who seek to curry favour with the occupying
power by denouncing their compatriots and he makes the specific
point—which I have never seen quoted in his defence—that
however hostile he may have felt towards Blum, Mandel and
other similar political figures, he would not dream of attacking
them when they were down, i.e. imprisoned in this case by the
Vichy government. The sense of his original remark comes out
quite simply in its context: he is implying that there was some
point in being pro-German *before* the war, but not since the
defeat. How clear could one expect anyone to be in Paris in 1941
and still get published? As Jacqueline Morand very properly says
in her examination of this phrase and that about the Jews:

> De toutes façons, il semble bien que ces deux seules phrases soient
> insuffisantes pour faire des *Beaux Draps* un pamphlet collaboration-
> iste (personne d'ailleurs ne l'a réellement soutenu).[34]

> (In any case, it surely seems that these two sentences alone are not
> enough to make *Les Beaux Draps* into a collaborationist pamphlet
> (no one really maintained this moreover).)

However, they were used in the 1950 trial.

[34] Jacqueline Morand, *Les idées politiques de Louis-Ferdinand Céline*, p. 131.

On the subject of the 1940 defeat we find a very recognizable Céline. His bitterness and his irony on the subject (discernible in the post-war works too) are expressed in his best and most attacking manner, as the following passage shows:

> Croyez-moi si vous voulez, on pouvait pas aller si vite, on a bien fait tout ce qu'on a pu, pour rattraper l'Armée Française, des routes et des routes, des zigs zags, des traits en bolide, toujours elle nous a fait du poivre, jamais elle s'est fait rattraper, l'Armée Française. Y avait du vertige dans ses roues. O la retraite à moteur! Oh! la prudence pavoisée! Oh! les gendarmes redevenus hommes! à la grelottine sauve- qui-peut! J'ai vu des tanks de 40 tonnes bousculer nos orphelins, nous bazarder dans les colzas pour foncer plus vite au couvert, la foire au cul, orageante ferraille à panique . . . (pp. 11–12)

> (Believe me if you will, one couldn't go fast enough, we did our best certainly to catch up with the French army, road after road, zig-zags, straight stretches like a flash, it always managed to give us tough marches, never let us catch it up, the French army. Its wheels were dizzy. Oh! motorized retreat! Oh! what gleeful prudence! Oh! to see gendarmes becoming ordinary men again! quivering free for all! I've seen 40 ton tanks pushing past our orphans, thrusting us into the rape fields so as to run faster under cover, shitting themselves with fear, roaring, panicking ironmongery!)

A passage like this might be thought a good defence against an accusation of fascism: A fascist army must, *ipso facto*, even in defeat, be glorious (like the Italians on the Greco-Albanian border). But it could not, and did not, commend itself to those— such as both Pétain and de Gaulle—who needed to maintain intact the notion of the honour of the French army.

Before discussing the positive elements in *Les Beaux Draps*, the blueprint for a new society, it is well to remember the position taken by successive Vichy governments under Pétain from 1940 onwards. Pétain's position was, of course, an impossible one, and the man himself of a very limited intelligence in international affairs, but there was one ingenious psychological device that emerged from the confusion and muddle-headedness of Vichy. Confronted with the disaster of 1940—a military disaster without parallel for centuries—what could a Maréchal de France (even if not directly concerned with the activities of the French army in 1939–40) invent to boost morale and cover up the inglorious retreat? Merely to hold Third Republic politicians responsible was not sufficient (and untrue—the officer class in 1939 bears a heavy responsibility), though it was a major leitmotif, culminating in the embarrassment of the Riom trials. Sackcloth and ashes were deemed to be the fashionable garb. (De Gaulle could say with reason in 1940 that France had lost a battle but not the war, and partly thanks to him this turned out to be true.) Vichy had to accept that as far as they were concerned, France had lost the war: the meeting between Pétain and Hitler at Montoire was a tacit acceptance of this. The line had therefore to be that purification of a nation can emerge from defeat. 'Renouveau national' —from a state too awful to be described—is a constant theme in Vichy literature. One feels that if they had dared, some of them would have liked to draw the parallel between the defeat of France in 1940 and Voltaire's Lisbon earthquake and attribute both to the wrath of God. . . . Anyway, national revival was to be achieved in part by substituting for the 'Liberté, Égalité, Fraternité' of the Republican tradition, the new device of 'Famille, Travail, Patrie'. If the Vichy regime had any positive quality at all it was in the pathetic father-figure of the elderly Pétain, trying hard, despite the remoteness of his temperament conditioned by nearly sixty years of stultifying military life, to behave like a human being, receiving countless delegations of peasants, workers, school-children and *tutti quanti*.[35] As has just been seen, Céline had expressed scathing views about him in *L'Ecole des cadavres*: indeed, no one less likely to appeal to him could be imagined than this incarnation of the officer-class for which he never showed any tenderness at all. What specific evidence there is on this suggests that he regarded Vichy—like Soviet communism— as an imposture.[36] None the less the phrase 'renouveau national' was in the air, and Céline's plan for this was published at an opportune moment.[37]

The main proposals made in *Les Beaux Draps* are as follows. The first and most important, without which the others could not have effect, is the establishment of equality of income through-

[35] It makes one think of De Gaulle's predilection for 'bains de foule': indeed there are curious similarities between the two men.

[36] Rebatet (in *Cahiers de l'Herne* p. 233) quotes him as saying in late 1940 'Vichy, c'est de l'inexistant, de la fumée, de l'ombre' ('Vichy doesn't exist, it's smoke, shadow').

[37] In early 1942 the police seized copies of *Les Beaux Draps* in Toulouse (which was of course in Vichy-controlled France), probably because of the blistering comments on the French army.

out society. Income—not to exceed 100 francs (1941) per day per person—to be based on what is necessary to provide for the basic needs of each human being, and *not* on the kind of work performed nor on the degree of responsibility exercised by him. (The sum of 100 per day would be increased according to the number of children in a family up to a maximum of 300 francs.) Linked with this is the creation of an extensive system of social security, giving protection against illness, unemployment and old age, this financed out of the sums in excess of 100 francs per day retained by the state. Limited rights of property would be allowed: everyone to have the right to own a house and up to 500 square metres of garden, transmissible to his heirs. An extensive programme of nationalization would be necessary to ensure the maintenance of employment in this egalitarian community. Thirty-five hours per week would be the maximum that anyone should be required to work in shop or factory. Farming would be collectivized. Once this state of social equality were reached, there would be some chance of effecting psychological changes in the attitude of human beings to each other. The absence of 'class' difference due to disparity of incomes would make possible the concept of the nation as a *family* whose members care for one another. The only proposal about government is that there should be a 'father' of the national family, a dictator, who would be paid 200 francs a day as a special favour.

To bring about these essential psychological changes, two other steps would be taken, first a total reform of the educational system, and then, linked with this, a positive encouragement of the fine arts. His strictures on the 'corps stupide enseignant' have been seen above in *Bagatelles*: here the most memorable phrase is 'O pions fabricants de Déserts!' (p. 163)[38] ('O "pions", creators of deserts!') The attack on traditional education is continued with vigour. It stultifies the development of the personality of the child, and, worse, it destroys the liveliness and joyfulness of childhood and produces bored and lifeless pedants instead:

> Regardez les petits enfants, les premières années . . . ils sont tout charme, tout poésie, tout espiègle guilleterie . . . A partir de dix, douze ans, finie la magie de primesaut! mués louches sournois butés cancres, petits drôles plus approchables, assommants, pervers grimaciers, garçons et filles, ragoteux, crispés, stupides, comme papa

[38] *Pion*. No real English equivalent. 'Student-teacher' is as near as we can get.

maman. Une faillite! Presque parfaits vieillards à l'âge de douze ans!
Une culbute des étoiles en nos décombres et nos fanges! Un désastre
de féerie. (pp. 159–60)

(Just look at small children, in the early years . . . they're full of
charm, of poetry, of naughty gaiety . . . From 10 or 12 years onwards,
an end to this spontaneous magic! changed into nasty, sly, obstinate
dunces, unapproachable little rogues, infuriating, perversely
grimacing, boys and girls, tale-telling, tense, stupid like daddy and
mummy. A total failure! Almost perfect old men at the age of
twelve! Stars plunging into our ruins and our mud! Enchantment
brought to disaster!)

The solution is that 'L'école doit devenir magique ou disparaître,
bagne figé' (p. 178) ('School must become an enchantment or
disappear, fossilized prison'). It is by being based on the lessons
of the fine arts that school can become 'magique'. What must be
fostered in the child are discrimination, excitement and passion,
the only qualities which are truly useful in life. (This is all totally
in line with his insistence on the prime importance of the expression and transmission of *emotion* in art.) Physical education has an
essential place too:

Que le corps reprenne goût de vivre, retrouve son plaisir, son
rythme, sa verve déchue, les enchantements de son essor . . . L'esprit
suivra bien! . . . (p. 175)

(Let the body recover the taste for life, rediscover its pleasure, its
rhythm, its lost verve, the enchantments of its inspiration . . . The
mind will surely follow on! . . .)

This programme is going to require teachers with a gift for
conveying enthusiasm: they must be

Gens au cours du merveilleux, de l'art d'échauffer la vie, non la
refroidir, de choyer les enthousiasmes, non les raplatir, l'enthou-
siasme le 'Dieu en nous', aux désirs de la Beauté devancer couleurs
et harpes, hommes à recueillir les féeries qui prennent source à
l'enfance. Si la France doit reprendre l'âme, cette âme jaillira de
l'école. (pp. 177–8)

(People aware of the beauty of existence, of the art of warming life,
not of chilling it, of encouraging enthusiasms, not of quelling them,
the enthusiasm which is 'God within us', bringing colours and harps
to every impulsion towards beauty, men able to gather together the
enchantments which have their source in childhood. If France is
ever to recover its soul, that soul will spring from the schools.)

This outline is enough to show how very different *Les Beaux Draps* is from the earlier 'political' texts by Céline. For any reader who had not detected in *Semmelweis*, *Voyage* and *Mort à crédit* the clear indications of an underlying warmth of human understanding, the tone of the positive section of the book would come as a puzzling surprise. For any reader who had read the ballet scenarii and who had seen the enormous importance of fantasy in the novels, it would come as no surprise, but rather as a precious confirmation in direct statement of some of the most meaningful attitudes of Céline. Even if it is only too easy to dismiss the egalitarian proposals as sentimental unrealizable nonsense which provides further evidence of the author's political naivety, it should be remembered that the discontent with our present form of society in Western Europe and in the USA which emerged so strongly in the sixties and early seventies is based on the very reproaches that Céline directed against it in all three pamphlets. Apart from the residual anti-semitic tone, there is nothing in *Les Beaux Draps* that is 'collaborationist' or pro-Nazi.

It ends with a moving description of the plight of the poor and elderly during the hard winter of 1940–41, as seen by Céline amongst his patients at Bezons (pp. 205-17). He almost always writes well when his compassion is aroused, and these pages are no exception. They lead into a lyrical meditation on destiny and death, inspired first by the blinding confusion of whirling snow-flakes, and which takes up the contrast between human cruelty and human gaiety so central to the whole book (pp. 217-22). *Les Beaux Draps* is a very curious and very revealing work. It is scandalous that it has not been reprinted.

Finally, the evidence about Céline's other activities during the German occupation of France must be considered. It should be said at the outset that despite his pre-war pamphlets, despite the undoubted anti-semitism, despite the pro-German sentiments voiced before the war, there is *no* evidence of collaboration with Germans during the war that has been substantiated. There was a journey to Berlin in 1942 with a French delegation of doctors to visit hospitals there. There was his presence in Paris at the showing organized by the German authorities of a film on the subject of typhus. There were constant contacts with German medical colleagues and with Dr Karl Epting, whom he knew before the war, who was a literary critic and the author of the only critical study of Céline published in Germany before the end of the war. Epting states[39] that the only requests Céline ever made to the German occupation authorities were for allocations of paper for the printing of his books, and copious requests for medical supplies for his clinic at Bezons. Céline himself adds that he made five applications (all refused) for permission to visit St Malo where he had a house, and that he made one (unsuccessful) plea on behalf of a mental defective condemned to death by the military court of Quimper. No one has produced evidence which counters the following categorical assertion he made in his defence from prison in Copenhagen on 6 November 1946:

> Je n'ai jamais mis un pied à l'Ambassade d'Allemagne, ni avant, ni pendant l'occupation. Je n'ai jamais appartenu à aucune des nombreuses sociétés franco-allemandes—culturelles, littéraires, médicales etc. Je n'ai jamais appartenu de ma vie à rien du tout, sauf à l'Armée française et glorieusement.[40]

> (I've never set foot in the German Embassy, neither before nor during the occupation. Nor have I belonged to any of the numerous Franco-German societies—cultural, literary, medical, etc. I've never belonged to anything in my life, except to the French army, and to that with honour.)

The question as to whether he undertook any journalistic activity during the Occupation or not, is more complicated. Here it is not easy to establish the exact truth. His own statement on this matter in 1946 is categorical again:

> ... je n'ai jamais de ma vie écrit dans un journal, ni parlé à la radio, ni tenu une conférence. Tout le monde à Paris sait que je suis l'antijournalisme, l'antiradio, l'antipublicisme en personne. Je suis probablement le seul écrivain français de renom demeuré strictement, jalousement, farouchement *écrivain* et rien qu'*écrivain*, sans aucun compromis.[41]

> (... never in my life have I written in a newspaper, nor spoken on the radio, nor given a lecture. Everyone in Paris knows that I am anti-journalism, anti-radio, anti-publicity incarnate. I'm probably the only French writer of repute to have remained strictly jealously, purely a writer and nothing but a writer, without any compromise.)

[39] *Cahiers de l'Herne*, pp. 240–43.
[40] ibid., p. 483.
[41] ibid.

Now this is technically exact. Careful and exhaustive examination of the French press during the Occupation has failed to reveal anything by Céline that could be called an article. It looks as though he was determined not to receive payment for journalistic activity. But there are, however, a number of *letters* addressed to acquaintances in the world of journalism which did appear, and various alleged interviews with him were reported. Only one of these was acknowledged by him to have taken place. There have been unearthed, so far, thirty-four appearances of Céline's name with attribution of statements to him, spread over the period January 1941 to April 1944—forty months—and dispersed among twelve different newspapers or periodicals. This figure should be reduced to twenty-five in point of fact, since five of the entries are merely reprints of extracts from existing works by Céline, three are repeats of material elsewhere in the list, and one is a formal letter authenticating the one interview which he acknowledged having given. And of these twenty-five, quite a number are of doubtful authenticity, and several are trivial bits of gossip. The number of *significant* texts—assuming all are authentic—does not exceed sixteen. And Céline fiercely contested the authenticity of a number of these. Even if we decide not to believe him, sixteen disparate pieces—mostly repeating things he had already said in print before—over a period of nearly three and a half years hardly amount to extensive involvement with the collaborationist press. Céline's fame, his known anti-semitism and his pro-German stance before the war made him a very desirable name to be able to use in such a press, and it is quite clear that had he so wished, he could have had the choice of a number of papers in which to be a regular contributor. A lot of well-known gentlemen did so contribute. Céline, in his 'defence' of 1946, mentions some of them:

Pendant l'Occupation d'autres auteurs français bien connus, tels La Varende, H. Bordeaux, Guitry, Montherlant, Simenon, Giono, Chadourne, Ed. Jaloux, MacOrlan, Pierre Hamp etc., ont fourni sans cesse une amusante ou grave copie aux journaux de la collaboration et même aux Revues franco-allemandes. Ils ne s'en portent pas plus mal aujourd'hui. Ils se promènent librement à Paris.[42]

(During the Occupation other well known writers, such as La Varende, H. Bordeaux, Guitry, Montherlant, Simenon, Giono,

[42] ibid., p. 484.

Chadourne, Ed. Jaloux, MacOrlan, Pierre Hamp, etc., provided constantly flippant or serious material to the collaborationist newspapers and even to the Franco-German periodicals. They are no worse off nowadays. They can walk around freely in Paris.)

This a modest list. If one looks merely at two of the nastier papers of the period—*Je Suis Partout* in Paris, and *L'Emancipation Nationale* in Lyon—one finds contributions (articles, *inédits* of various kinds) from the following: Morvan Lebesque, Jean Anouilh, Marcel Aymé, Jean Sarment, Jean de Baroncelli, René Barjavel, Jean Ajalbert, Charles Dullin, André Billy, Maurice Bardèche, André Thérive, Ramon Fernandez and Jacques Boulenger. These form a nice mixture of novelists, dramatists, journalists, critics and academics. The purpose of mentioning these names is *not* to besmirch reputations: clearly writers had to publish where they could during the Occupation (though many presumably jibbed at appearing in the two papers just mentioned). It is simply to point out that 'ils ne s'en portent plus mal', whereas Céline was bitterly attacked for collaboration. There is no doubt whatsoever that such a charge could have been brought with very much more justification against others than him.

When the sixteen-odd 'contributions' by Céline are examined, the dominant impression is that 90 per cent of the material is to be found already in the three pamphlets. Any competent— and unscrupulous—journalist could produce such texts, making only minor modifications of date and slight changes of reference. Whether this happened, in fact, or whether Céline himself *did* produce this material, is not particularly important in view of the fact that it had all been published before. There are, however, one or two new themes. One that is probably genuine Céline (because it also forms a major part of the interview which he did acknowledge having given) is a bitter attack on war-profiteers and the black market, notably on the prospering peasantry.[43] He suggested that most of these sharks were at one and the same time well in with the Germans (otherwise they could not make such fantastic profits), and pretended Gaullist sympathizers. This, of course, was described at the Liberation as libel against the Resistance. Another theme linked with this is disgust at those traitors—it is the word he uses—who were making money out of economic collaboration with the Germans:

[43] *Je Suis Partout* (29 October 1943). The piece is headed 'Céline nous écrit'.

La guerre 39 est une affaire mirifique pour trente millions de Français. Dix millions sont *victimes* à plaindre, pas davantage! Les autres ne sont que grimaciers, égoistes, cabotins et putains. Ils jouent la résistance mais pleurent intimément pour que la guerre dure! (. . .) A quand la liste intégrale et nominative de tous ceux qui ont gagné quelque chose avec les Allemands? Là voilà, la vraie liste des *collaborateurs efficients*, pas les idéalistes et spéculateurs en pensées gratuites. Qu'on nous foute la paix avec les traîtres. TRAÎTRES alors, D'ABORD, tous ceux qui ont gagné un CENTIME avec les Allemands![44]

(The war of 1939 is marvellously good business for 30 million Frenchmen. Ten millions are *victims* who deserve pity, not more. The others are merely posturers, egoists, ham actors, whores. They pretend to be of the resistance but deep down they wish for the continuation of the war. (. . .) When may we hope for the full name by name list of those who have profited in one way or another from the Germans? That is the real list of *effective collaborators* not the idealists and the speculators in abstract ideas. Enough of this balls about traitors. TRAITORS indeed, FIRST OF ALL, all those who've got one CENTIME out of the Germans!)

One group of texts, and one alone, is compromising. On 21 November 1941, *L'Emancipation Nationale*, a pro-Doriot paper, published an interview with Céline entitled 'Propos receuillis par Ivan M. Sicard'. (Substantial sections of this were reprinted later—31 March 1943—in Doriot's own paper *Le Cri du Peuple*.) Céline denied vehemently having ever written or dictated the key incriminating words, or anything like them. What were they? In answer to a question by the interviewer about the newly formed 'Légion anti-bolchévique' in which Doriot served for a while and which fought with the Germans on the Eastern Front, Céline is alleged to have said:

. . . Et Doriot s'est comporté comme il a toujours fait. C'est un homme. Et oui il n'y a rien à dire. Il faut travailler, militer avec Doriot. Vous avez raison. Chacun de notre côté, il faut accomplir ce que nous pouvons. Cette Légion si calomniée, si critiquée, c'est la preuve de la vie. J'aurais aimé partir avec Doriot là-bas, mais je suis plutôt un homme de mer, un Breton. Ça m'aurait plu d'aller sur un navire m'expliquer avec les Russes.

(. . . And Doriot has behaved as he always has. He's a man. Well, yes, there's no more to say. We must work and militate with Doriot. You are right. Each of us independently, we must do what we can.

This legion which has been so calumniated, so criticized, is the proof of life. I'd have liked to go off there with Doriot, but I'm a man of the sea, a Breton. I'd have liked to go off on a ship and have a little argument with the Russians.)

Now this is a very extraordinary text in more than one way. It provides the *only* example known of Céline giving positive approval to any politician and—more surprising still—suggesting adherence to Doriot's party. He had been contemptuous enough about Doriot in *L'Ecole des cadavres* for this to seem unlikely. His denial[45] is very categorical: of the compromising passage he says 'Je n'ai jamais écrit ni dicté ces lignes ni rien de semblable, c'est un faux, une invention' ('I have never written nor dictated these lines, nor anything of the kind, it's a forgery, an invention'), and then goes on to say that he met Doriot three times in all, on each occasion at a dinner-party given by a medical colleague of his, 'le Dr Bécart, 37 bis Bd Verthier,' that he disliked Doriot and his entourage intensely. It is certainly true that Doriot was a loudmouthed, vulgar and highly self-seeking individual, whom one would have expected to be absolute anathema to Céline. There is, however, another alleged text which should be mentioned. This appeared in *Les Cahiers de l'Emancipation Nationale* (March 1942), and was headed 'Lettre à Jacques Doriot', purporting to come from Céline, and expressing the same kind of approval and support.

It is really not easy to decide on this one. Doriot was an odious crook and Sicard was editor of *L'Emancipation Nationale*, which, as I have already said, was one of the nastiest collaborationist papers: both texts could well be forgeries as Céline maintained. On the other hand, as Doriot was dead (killed in an Allied air-raid in Germany), Céline was pretty safe in his denial, and obviously needed to make it in 1946. His detestation of Russian communism *may* have led him to commit himself to support for the Doriot faction, but I cannot help regarding it as out of character.[46]

Another reason for regarding the Sicard interview as a piece of journalistic 'collage' is that bits of it sound like genuine Céline and other bits are adaptations of bits of the pamphlets. This,

[45] *Cahiers de l'Herne*, p. 485.
[46] *Cf.* Album Céline (ed. Jean-Pierre Dauphin and Jacques Boudillet (Bibliothèque de la Pléïade, Paris, 1977), p. 170 '. . . Ephémère est son intéret pour Jacques Doriot. . . .'

for instance, represents what we know of his attitude to the Jewish question in 1941 quite accurately.

Voyez-vous, je suis un vieux médecin et un Breton . . . En voilà un qui vient me dire: 'Docteur j'ai mal à la gorge', il faut qu'il n'ait plus mal. 'Docteur, je pe peux pas pisser', je le fais pisser. C'est mon métier. La France était malade, elle est malade. Qu'est-ce qu'elle avait? Le Juif, bien sûr et d'abord. Mais l'antijudaïsme n'est pas un système en soi, il faut partir d'un système. C'est un des aspects du boulot mais il ne faut pas rester sur ce dada, ça ne sert à rien . . . (. . .) Je ne suis pas bon pour jouer de la musique, de la petite musique anti-juives.

(Well now, I'm an elderly doctor and a Breton . . . Let's say someone comes to me and says 'Doctor, I've got a sore throat', well he mustn't have one any more. 'Doctor, I can't piss!' I make him piss. It's my job. France was ill, still is. What was wrong with her? Jews, of course and first of all. But anti-judaism isn't a system by itself, one must start by having a system. It's one of the aspects of the job, but there's no point in sticking just to this obsession, . . . (. . .) I'm not on to play tunes, little anti-Jewish tunes.)

On the other hand, a passage a little further on, 'Pour devenir collaborationniste je n'ai pas attendu que la Commandatur passe au Crillon', looks like an adaptation of a passage already quoted above from *Les Beaux Draps* (see above, p. 166). I have no difficulty in imagining Sicard seizing on the original sentence in *Les Beaux Draps*, altering it syntactically to fit his new context, *and* replacing the word *pro-allemand* (innocent enough pre-war) with the compromising *collaborationniste*, and the more emotive *pavoise* with the neutral *passe*, but I really cannot conclude either way on this.

All that Céline would admit after the war was that a certain number of letters had indeed been written by him to specific individuals and that some of them had been published, sometimes in suspiciously altered form. This is almost certainly true, but it does not entirely let him off the hook. If as a well-known writer you write a long letter to the editor of a newspaper—even if it is a personal letter to someone you know—and this letter contains your general opinions about certain issues of the day, you must be pretty ignorant about journalists if you feel surprise when your letter is prominently published. At least, if it happens to you once, you need not be so naïve as to repeat the performance if you really do *not* want your views published.

The overall conclusion must be that Céline *did* on occasion
allow his known views (from the pamphlets) to be published in
this oblique manner, but that he did not perform as an active
collaborating journalist. He insists vehemently too that he never
sought nor received any money in connection with journalism[47] and
that he never received any money at all from any German source.
The cynical would no doubt say that of course he had to maintain
this line. But it is up to the cynic to prove it in that case, and there
has never been one shred of evidence of this sort forthcoming.

Two final testimonies must be called upon before I try to sum
up the main lines of this examination of a controversial, obscure
and little-known period of Céline's literary career. The first is
from a writer of exceptional talent, both novelist and critic,
Lucien Rebatet, an avowed fascist and for years a regular
member of the editorial team of *Je Suis Partout*. The second is
from an opposite source: Robert Chamfleury, active member
of the Resistance movement, and the tenant of the flat immediately
below that of Céline (rue Girardon, Montmartre) throughout the
period of the Occupation. Both these testimonies were published
in *Cahiers de l'Herne*, and both, it must be said, were written many
years after the events they describe.

First, two passages from Rebatet's article 'D'un Céline
l'autre'. In the first he relates a conversation in Paris in October
1940, in which Céline is alleged to have said:

'. . . Ce qu'il y a de vrai, c'est que les Fritz ont perdu la guerre.'
Je le regardais stupéfait. Que lui était arrivé? Nous étions le 12 ou
le 15 octobre 1940. Les gaullistes les plus effrénés de l'Hôtel du Parc
[at Vichy] auraient ete sidérés par un tel propos, Churchill lui-même.
'Sans blague, Louis? Qu'est-ce qui te fait croire ça?' 'Ils ont paumé,
et nous avec. Une armée qui n'apporte pas une revolution avec elle
dans les guerres comme celle-là, elle est cuite. Tordus, les Frizous.'

('. . . There's one thing certain, the Fritz have lost the war.' I looked
at him, stupefied. What had happened to him? It was the 12th or
15th October 1940. Even the most fanatical Gaullists at the Hotel du
Parc would have been shattered by such a remark, Churchill himself too. 'Really, Louis? What makes you believe that?' 'They've
lost, and us with them. An army that doesn't bring with it a
revolution in a war of this kind, it's had it. Screwed up, the Boches.')

[47] The desire to be able to say this truly may well explain the device of writing
'letters'. It is extremely characteristic of him *not* to want payment from any
newspaper.

This is certainly what Céline thought *after* the war about the Germans: it is remarkable that it should be attested as early as 1940 by a witness who on this issue is hardly suspect. It may be that Rebatet has got the date wrong: such views expressed in 1944 at Sigmaringen (where they also met) would be less surprising. But Rebatet seems very certain, and one can see that if such were Céline's views from late 1940 onwards, his conduct with regard to the collaborationist press becomes understandable.

A little further on Rebatet writes:

> Quant au rôle politique de Louis-Ferdinand Céline durant l'occupation allemande, il avoisinait le néant. (...) Sauf peut-être sous une ou deux broutilles sans importance, aucun des journaux 'collaborateurs' ne put se targuer de la signature de Céline.[48]

> (As for Louis-Ferdinand Céline's political role during the German occupation, it was more or less nil. (...) Apart from one or two unimportant scraps, no 'collaborationist' newspaper could boast of having texts signed Celine.)

The whole of Rebatet's article is interesting: it has a substantial piece on Sigmaringen, where, if he is to be believed, Céline was openly and publicly derisive about the Germans.

The second witness is fascinating. In 1950, Roger Vailland (Prix Goncourt) published in *La Tribune des Nations* (13 January) an article entitled 'Nous n'épargnerions plus Louis-Ferdinand Céline,'[49] ('We should no longer spare Louis-Ferdinand Céline'). This purported to give an account of a discussion taking place in 1943 in the fourth-floor flat, rue Girardon, belonging to Robert Chamfleury and his wife, Simone. A group of *résistants* consider assassinating the tenant of the flat above—Céline—and drop the idea because unanimity cannot be reached. Céline wrote a reply to this, years later, in *Crapouillot* (February 1958) of which Chamfleury totally approved. Chamfleury wrote an article in *Cahiers de l'Herne* entitled 'Céline ne nous a pas trahis' ('Céline did not betray us') in which he denies the truth of Vailland's story, and goes on to state that Céline was fully aware of what was going on in the flat underneath him, and said in fact:

> 'Vous en faites pas Chamfleury, je sais à peu pres tout ce que vous faites, vous et votre femme, mais ne craignez rien de ma part . . . je vous donne ma parole . . . et même si je peux vous aider!'

[48] *Cahiers de l'Herne*, pp. 228–39. The passages quoted are on p. 232.
[49] ibid., p. 247.

[Chamfleury continues]

'Mieux, un certain jour, je suis venu frapper à votre porte, accompagné d'un Résistant qui avait été torturé par la Gestapo. Vous avez ouvert, vous avez examiné la main de mon compagnon, et, sans poser aucune question, vous avez fait le pansement qu'il convenait, ayant parfaitement deviné l'origine de la blessure.'

('Don't worry, Chamfleury, I know perfectly well what you are doing, you and your wife, but don't have any fears about me . . . I give you my word . . . and indeed, if I can be of help . . !'

'More than this, one day I knocked on your door, with me was someone in the Resistance who'd been tortured by the Gestapo. You opened the door, you examined my companion's hand, and without asking any questions, you dressed the wound as needed, being completely aware of its origin.')

Elsewhere Chamfleury makes the point that it would have been possible for Céline to have denounced his neighbours to the authorities at any moment had he so wished, and that he, Chamfleury, would not be alive to write his article had Céline done so.[50]

This chapter is presented in a way which, I hope, will enable the reader to make up his own mind about the grim years 1938–44 in Céline's career. Elsewhere I have been more willing to make interpretative suggestions because the texts are available and you can read them for yourself and disagree (or agree) with me as a result. But the 'banned' pamphlets are hard to find, and until the French grow up and republish them, a whole essential section of Céline is denied to all those who cannot afford the time to track down these texts—or the money to pay for them.[51]

However, even with extensive quotation—which has been deliberate in this chapter—the entire evidence is subject to selection by me, even if I have been trying quite hard to be honest. This is why I am about to propose an interpretation of all the foregoing material none the less.

It is abundantly clear that Céline had anti-semitic views over a number of years. Whether these should be dated from 1928 (the beginnings of *L'Eglise*) or from 1937 (*Bagatelles*) is not of great importance. What matters is that by 1941 they were waning, and had disappeared by 1946. (In a communication in December 1949 to M. le Président Drappier—who was judge at his trial in 1950—Céline says about *Les Beaux Draps*:

> A l'époque ou cet ouvrage fut publié (1941) je ne savais *rien*, absolument *rien*, des déportations juives, ni d'aucune déportation. Je n'ai d'ailleurs appris ces atrocités qu'à la fin de la guerre. Je regrette mon ignorance (même remarque pour la réédition de *Bagatelles* et de *L'Ecole*)').[52]

> (At the time this book was published (1941) I knew *nothing*, absolutely *nothing* about the deportation of the Jews, nor about any deportations. Moreover, I only learnt about these atrocities after the war. I deplore my ignorance (same comment regarding the republication of *Bagatelles* and of *L'Ecole*)).

These views were not based on any serious thought: they were born of his milieu and of prejudice, and what little pretence there is in the pamphlets at documentation and the presentation of evidence is all derived from low-grade contemporary sources.[53] What gives this trivial material some force is of course its handling by Céline in *Bagatelles*: in *L'Ecole des cadavres* much the same material is handled with greater violence and much less efficacy.

By 1938 he had cut all the links with existing political groups. His anti-communism is not ideological but emotional, and partly triggered off by a desire to shrug off the attempts of the left to claim him as one of them. The allegation that he was a fascist or a Nazi stems in part from his anti-semitism and from his advocacy of an alliance with Germany around the time of Munich, which caused him to write certain sentences favourable to Hitler. But he does not subscribe to any recognizable fascist ideology other than the attack on Jewry, and indeed his strong anti-militarist and pacifist views run directly counter to fascism, as does his egalitarianism. The anti-British stance is linked also with the anti-semitism as well as provoked by a standard French nationalist line of thought which, since the days of Louis XIV at least, has always seen England as striving to keep the balance of power in Europe by encouraging war between the various nations therein.

While Céline continued to hold anti-semitic views after the beginning of the war, these were to diminish quite rapidly, and

---

[52] Unpublished text communicated to me by M. Jean-Pierre Dauphin.
[53] See, for example, article by Emmanuel Mounier in *Cahiers de l'Herne*, pp. 466–7.

give place to a kind of racialist thought which had no political consequences. (It is clear that after the war he was quite sure that the supremacy of the white man was over—he has been proved right about that after all—but he regretted it really, which presumably is not what one should properly think.) There is no admiration of the Germans during the wartime period, and indeed a lot of contempt and hostility. There is no evidence of collaboration with the occupying power, and there is a minimal participation in journalistic activity. There is instead the development of the positive notions on the transformation of French society (*Les Beaux Draps*) which are idealistic, revolutionary and unrealizable. There is no evidence that Céline profited financially in any way from the German occupation.

Why then, one may wonder, was he regarded with such tremendous hostility at the Liberation? The most obvious answer is that the revelation of what Nazi policy to the Jews had *really* been, the discovery of the real truth about Dachau and the other camps as they were overrun by the allied armies, and as the few survivors told their story, led to worldwide horror and indignation, and that, consequently, anyone who had advocated racial discrimination against the Jews was bound to be regarded with opprobrium.[54] Added to this was the fact that Céline and his wife fled from France in 1944 to Germany, *en route* for Denmark. He made no secret of his reasons for this—self-preservation. He had been listed—wrongly, I think—by the BBC as a notorious collaborator, and had received many threats from the Resistance movement. He is almost certainly right in thinking that he would have been shot out of hand in the first days of the Liberation had he remained in Paris. His flat was ransacked, his manuscripts destroyed or stolen, and later on his publisher, Denoël, *was* assassinated. It is to be remembered that the backbone of the civilian French Resistance (and all honour to them) was communist, and they had no reason to regard him as anything other than an absolute enemy. But an almost more important factor behind the ostracism he suffered for many years after 1945 was that there was *no* significant group of persons to defend him in France: he had deliberately severed all political ties and he had shot and wounded too many sacred cows. He often said himself

[54] This is understandable and just. As long as, for example, one may hold Dr Kissinger in the same opprobrium for the deaths in Chile after the fall of Allende. They were fewer, but he was much more directly responsible. . . .

in the post-war period that the unforgivable crime he had committed was really the writing of *Voyage*. . . .

A last example of prejudice—to show the climate even in 1950—was to be the horror expressed at the minimal sentences on Céline in the 1950 trial, by Madeleine Jacob in the paper *Libération* on 22 February 1950, where she castigates the court for the lenience extended to 'l'alcoolique' Céline. Anyone who had the very least information about him would have known that he was a non-smoking, non-drinking ascetic.

My conclusion is as follows. Anti-semitism? Guilty. Fascism or Nazism? Not guilty. Collaboration? Not guilty. Profiteering? Not guilty. It was both shameful and irresponsible for Sartre to write in his article 'Le Portrait d'un anti-sémite' in 1945[55] 'Si Céline a pu soutenir les thèses socialistes des nazis, c'est qu'il était payé' ('If Céline was able to support the socialist theories of the Nazis, it's because he was paid'). A minimal sense of honour would have required such an accusation to be supported by proof. Sartre never sought to justify his remark, and allowed it to be reprinted in 1954.[56] *Tartre* indeed, as Céline constantly named him thereafter.

Opinions must vary about Céline's defence of his anti-semitic period: He repeated after the war that it was to expose the warmongering tendencies of 'un certain clan juif' that he wrote *Bagatelles* and *L'Ecole des cadavres*. He wanted the removal of Jews from control in France—and their return to Palestine where possible—but always maintained (truthfully) that he never desired nor advocated any kind of persecution. It would have been a good thing if he had gone on record *clearly* and in print after the war as admitting that he had been wrong. He never did so unequivocally. And that we must accept as being in character. But he was a man of *honour*: he did not believe in kicking people when they were down (see above, p. 166). He devoted much of his life to kicking those on top, a proper and even likeable activity. . . .

CHAPTER FIVE

Guignol's Band I and *II*

Not long before the Allied landings in Normandy, Céline's first novel since *Mort à crédit* was published (Denoël) in April 1944. It is not surprising that it passed almost unnoticed at that point in time. Republished (Gallimard) in 1952, again it was virtually passed over in silence: Céline had been amnestied and had returned to France only in 1951, and the period of conspiracy of silence about him was still on. Lucien Rebatet, one of the most remarkable and talented of the extreme right authors, and who had a great admiration for Céline, wrote in the course of a fascinating article that when he read *Guignol's Band I* in 1944 he'd thought little of it, but reading it again many years later he'd seen his error:

> Quelques mois plus tôt, je n'avais vu dans son *Guignol's Band* qu'une caricature épileptique de sa manière (je l'ai relu ce printemps, un inénarrable chef-d'oeuvre, Céline a toujours eu dix, quinze ans d'avance sur nous). (p. 235)[1]
>
> (A few months earlier, I'd only seen in *Guignol's Band* an epileptic caricature in his usual manner (I've re-read it this spring, a riotously comic masterpiece. Celine has always been ten or fifteen years ahead of us).)

It appears that the second part of *Guignol's Band* was completed in 1944 in first version, before Céline left Paris for Germany. There is evidence that he revised it in Denmark between 1945 and 1947,[2] and, having done so, dropped the idea of a *third* part, and devoted himself instead to what was to become (see below, Chapter 8) *Féerie II, Normance*. What exactly happened to the various versions between 1947 and Céline's death in 1961 is not clear, but in 1964 *Guignol's Band II* was published (Gallimard), presented—and the text established—by Robert Poulet.[3]

---

[1] *Cahiers de l'Herne*, p. 235.
[2] See Jean-Pierre Dauphin and Jacques Boudillet, *Album Céline*, pp. 194 and 202.
[3] Not a critical text: we have no idea how accurate it is.

For the flimsiest of reasons—which may have had some commercial point in 1964—Poulet invented for this volume a title
of his own, '*Le Pont de Londres*'. There is no reason now to call
it anything other than *Guignol's Band II*: it is a continuation of the
first volume, and has links with it both plot-wise and with regard
to characters.

The main character of *Guignol's Band II* is introduced fifty
pages before the end of *Guignol's Band I*, and the first sentence of
the second volume follows on naturally from the end of the first.
Because of this, and because the two volumes were written
consecutively, I propose to disregard M. Poulet's false title and
also the fact that twenty years lies between the two publication
dates, and consider them as one long narrative—some 700 pages
in all.

Indeed, looked at thus, *Guignol's Band* is seen to have the same
fundamental structure as *Voyage* and *Mort à crédit*—namely a
long first part in which there are many characters and much minor
incident, followed by a second part where a new main character
'takes over' and the narrative acquires a much more definite
pattern. In *Guignol's Band* the new character is Sosthène de
Robiencourt who bears much resemblance to Courtial des
Pereires, both in temperament and habit of speech. He is
joined, however, by two other important characters, Colonel
O'Colloghan and his niece Virginia. Part II is mostly about
Ferdinand and these three characters: only occasionally do the
characters of Part I re-appear until an extensive sequence near
the end of the book where they again become of importance.

The novel opens with an evocation of the exodus of the French
population in 1940 before the advancing German armies, in
particular the bombardment of Orléans and the bridge there
over the Loire. But after less than twenty pages of this we are
transported to London—the London of the First World War—
where Céline himself indeed spent many months after being
invalided out of the army. In the chronology of Céline's life as
seen through the novels, *Guignol's Band* should be a massive
insert in *Voyage*, coming immediately before the African section
of that work.

As usual, of course, we are not in the domain of autobiography.
There is a strong and vividly observed atmosphere of wartime
England, and some amusing shots of the milieu of prostitutes
which Céline certainly knew well at the time, but the actual

incidents of the novel are a discreet mingling, in the usual
Célinian manner, of fact and fantasy. A recurrent theme is that of
London docks, the river, the sea-going ships, a topic that always
brings out in Céline a kind of romantic nostalgia. There are
several 'hallucinatory' sequences—one at least of uproarious
gaiety in Part II, where Sosthène, dressed as a Chinese mandarin,
causes a massive traffic jam in Piccadilly by performing a sensa-
tional dance to the despair of the pursuing police.

The most important thing of all about *Guignol's Band* is that it
is enormously light-hearted in tone except for the opening thirty
pages. The Ferdinand of this book is far from the bitter and
taciturn character of the first half of *Mort à crédit*, and stems much
more from the Ferdinand who found a kind of contentment
working for Courtial. And he has not yet acquired the serious
disillusion of Bardamu. I think this is not hard to explain. In
1915 Céline was invalided out of the army, admittedly with nasty
injuries that were to affect all his subsequent career, but also having
proved himself in battle and having won the Médaille Militaire
for outstanding bravery. For him the nightmare of war was over,
and most honourably. He was twenty-one. It must have seemed
that life was looking up for him. There is some testimony about
his life in England at this time from a friend, Georges Geoffroy,
who worked with him at the French Consulate in London and
who shared rooms with him in Gower Street for some months.
Geoffroy says many other things:

Nous avions ainsi l'occasion de voir—à côté de gens très bien—
beaucoup d'individus bizarres et douteux qui enchantaient Louis
Destouches, lequel aimait beaucoup observer les gens, faire leur
connaissance pour les écouter parler et les étudier ... Certain jours,
nous avions de l'argent, d'autres jours nous étions totalement
fauchés! Les choses s'arrangeaient toujours à Soho. Les maquereaux
français et leurs protégés étaient gentils pour nous, toujours prêts à
nous offrir à dîner.[4]

(We also had occasion to meet—apart from highly respectable
people—a good number of strange and suspect characters who
delighted Louis Destouches, who enjoyed observing people and
getting to know them, to listen to them talking and to study them ...
Sometimes we had money, at others we were completely broke!
There was always a way round this in Soho. The French pimps and

[4] *Cahiers de l'Herne*, p. 201. N.B. nothing should be read into 'protégés'. This
volume of *L'Herne* is grotesquely full of misprints.

their dependants were always good to us, always ready to give us a meal!)

Apart from this resource in Soho—much exploited especially in Part I—there was quite certainly for Céline an early love-affair in London,[5] and we now know that he contracted a first marriage there (see above, p. 34). At all events *Guignol's Band II* shows us—who would have thought it?—Ferdinand in love with the young Virginia, freely admitting it, talking about it incessantly, and making her pregnant. Not at all the standpoint of Bardamu at the very beginning of *Voyage*—'L'amour c'est l'infini mis à la portée des caniches'[6]—nor yet the Céline who in 1954 said to Marc Hanrez about love as a theme of literature:

C'est gentil, c'est agréable, mais je ne crois pas que cela mérite fort une littérature. Je la trouve grossière et lourde aussi, cette histoire 'Je t'aime'.[7]

(It's nice, it's pleasant, but I don't really think it's worth writing about. In fact, I find it vulgar and ponderous all this fuss about 'I love you'.)

He shows that attitude in his treatment of Madelon in *Voyage*, but in *Guignol's Band II* he makes a total exception. It is without question the warmest and most benign of all Céline's works, amusing, grotesque in places, tender for the most part, full of the enthusiasm of youth, and showing too Ferdinand's yearning for the sea, for travel to distant lands: a 'voyage' not to the end of the night but to a new life with his little Virginia. But that does not seem possible at one point, and Ferdinand is quite willing to leave for South America alone, so greatly does the sea attract him. This was the work that he was writing during the war— after *Bagatelles* and *Ecole des cadavres*—and it gives the directest possible lie to those critics who thought him played out after *Mort à crédit* as well as to those who only see in him nihilism and despair. . . .

The narrative structure of *Guignol's Band I* and *II* is, briefly, as follows.[8] After the introductory section on the bombardment of

[5] See *Mort à crédit*, p. 506; see also *Féerie pour une autre fois I*, pp. 143–5.

[6] Pléïade, vol. I, p. 12; see also above, p. 97.

[7] Marc Hanrez, *Céline*, p. 124.

[8] References are to the Gallimard edition—*Guignol's Band I* (1957), and *Guignol's Band II* (1964).

Orléans we are introduced to the London of 1915, where Ferdin-
and is seen in the milieu of *souteneurs* and prostitutes. He has had
an introduction to Cascade Farcy, a powerful figure in the
milieu, who is running a highly successful brothel in the West
End, and through him he meets a series of exotic characters all
more or less on the run from the police, notably Borokrom, an
East European chemist, Dr Clodovitz of the London Hospital,
and a series of (mostly French) prostitutes. There are two main
sequences in the book. First, a lengthy presentation of Cascade
and his set-up (pp. 32–140) which has as its most dramatic
moment a fight between two of the prostitutes in which one of
them is knifed in the buttocks and transported to hospital. Then
(pp. 141–222) comes a section involving Ferdinand, Borokrom
and an elderly, miserly pawnbroker named Van Claben and his
housekeeper, Delphine. In a very extraordinary passage (p. 187ff.)
in which they are all under the influence of drugged cigarettes,
Van Claben brings out a great quantity of gold coins (completely
out of character, as Ferdinand notes), which he is eventually
forced to swallow. In an attempt to up-end him and recover
the money, Ferdinand and Borokrom drop him down a flight of
stairs. His skull is fractured and he is killed. They decide to hide
him in the cellar and come back later with other members of the
milieu to recover the money. Borokrom shuts Ferdinand and
Delphine in the cellar and sets fire to the house with a bomb, but
they manage to escape and rejoin him. Ferdinand decides to leave
them and lie low for a while. Recounted in a few lines thus
baldly, this incident sounds grotesque and implausible, to say
the least. But it is written in the now familiar 'hallucinatory'
manner and the reader is carried along on a flood of effervescent
colloquialism (all in the historic present) and the notion of filling
a pawnbroker's belly with his own ill-gotten gold gives a
particular edge to the sequence. The consequences of all this
are seen late on in *Guignol's Band II*.

   The rest of the book (pp. 223–314) gradually sets up the main
lines for *Guignol's Band II*. Ferdinand keeps out of the way of
Cascade and company, since he believes (rightly) that Borokrom
will have placed the responsibility for Van Claben's death on
him. He goes eventually to the French Consulate and asks to be
sent back to the army, but is refused on medical grounds. However, he meets there a curious character dressed in Chinese
costume, who after a while gives Ferdinand his card, which reads

Hervé Sosthène de Robiencourt, Prospecteur Agréé des Mines, Explora-
teur des Aires Occultes, Ingénieur Initié. Sosthène, impresario and
stage magician, is a mystic too and an expert on the Far East.
They plan to travel together to Tibet. Sosthène's wife tells
Ferdinand about Sosthène's theatrical background, confirms that
he knows the East, but adds that since they have no money there
can be no question of a journey to Tibet. They look at the small
ads. in *The Times* and find that a Colonel J. F. C. O'Colloghan,
22 Willesden Mansions W.W.I., is seeking 'Gaz Masks Engineers'[9]
to perfect a new design of gas mask for submission to the War
Office. 'Very large profits expected'[10] continues the advertise-
ment. *Guignol's Band I* ends with Sosthène and Ferdinand jumping
on a No. 29 bus to call on the colonel.

Guignol's Band II carries straight on from there. There is a
crowd of applicants outside the colonel's home, but Sosthène and
Ferdinand manage to jump the queue, are received and taken on
by the colonel. The house is luxurious, the food and drink
copious and excellent—and, there is Virginia, the colonel's
fourteen-year-old niece . . . Ferdinand falls in love with her at
first sight, one page into the novel.

Thereafter the narrative has two threads, often interwoven,
for nearly 300 pages (pp. 8–297): first, the work done in the
colonel's laboratory by the colonel and Sosthène; second, the
love between Ferdinand and Virginia. The gas masks do not make
much progress and the laboratory is wrecked on one occasion
due to the effect of one of the gases on the two experimenters
who demolish it and all the equipment there in an almost maniacal
fury. But Ferdinand's love for Virginia does prosper: he is deeply
enamoured of her beauty, her grace and her teasing good humour.
On page 236 she tells him that she is pregnant: this both delights
him, and alarms him (in view of her age!). He will never leave
her: they will run away together far away, overseas. And Sosthène,
who no longer wants to run risks with poison gas, can come too.
The colonel has conveniently disappeared for some days, so the
three leave the house without trouble (p. 297).

The final section of the book (pp. 298–406) is the most inventive and remarkable. Ferdinand, helped by Prospero, a landlord
of a dock-side pub (visited before in *Guignol's Band I*) tries to get
a passage on a ship for all three of them. The captain will only

---

[9] In English in the text.
[10] In English in the text.

take him—as cook. At once he agrees, and begins to regard his
Virginia and Sosthène as tiresome encumbrances. But her gentleness and her tears affect him none the less and he pretends at
least that he will send for them both later . . . very soon . . . they
will go by luxury liner . . . not on a dirty old sailing ship like
him. But none of it is to be. They return to announce to Prospero
that Ferdinand is to sail that night to la Plata. Prospero says he
can't possibly leave that evening: it is St Ferdinand's day, his
name day, and Cascade and all his friends are coming to the pub
to have a party in his honour. And, punctuated by the explosions
caused by a Zeppelin raid, the party indeed takes place. In the
course of it Borokrom and Clodovitz arrive with a mysterious
package, rolled up in a tarpaulin: it is the body of Van Claben,
which Clodovitz has managed to remove from the London
Hospital mortuary. Cascade explains to Ferdinand that if you kill
someone you have to finish the job and get rid of the body: no
body, no trial. So Cascade and his friends have rounded things
off and the body is consigned to the Thames. The long night
passes, and Ferdinand's ship has sailed. He must remain in
London, helped by Cascade. He and Sosthène and Virginia set
off back into the city. Perhaps they will ring up the colonel and
try to explain things. . . . They are not sure. . . . They cross
London Bridge in the early morning: the wind is blowing fiercely,
it is very cold. . . . They need some hot coffee. . . . Sosthène and
Virginia have a new lease of life: they want to play hide and seek.
Ferdinand has great difficulty in getting them to move on. But
they do. And now he must take charge of them:

> . . . c'est moi le pitre maintenant. C'est un monde! Moi qu'ai le
> souci, la discrétion.[11]

> (. . . I'm the clown now. It's a whole existence! I've got the
> responsibility, the tactfulness.)

These are the final words.

Whatever else may be said about this long two-volume novel,
it should be clear from this rapid summary that while maintaining
many Célinian themes and remaining for a great deal of the time
at the social level he usually treats, it has an emotional climate
which is not that of the first two novels. It is not possible to
describe it as anarchical, destructive or even particularly pessimistic. This would seem to be one moment in the existence of

[11] See below, pp. 204 and 224.

Ferdinand/Bardamu when many options seem open, and when the realization that for him the supreme horror and absurdity of war is over and that he has somehow, by chance, escaped from almost certain death, causes him to be immensely receptive to the stimulus of a new and exotic milieu in another country. The things that make Ferdinand happy in *Guignol's Band*, despite constant reference to the pain he has suffered from his war wounds, are—perhaps in this order of importance:—the freedom of his mode of life in London, away from the Passage des Bérésinas, away from the nightmare of the trenches; the excitement of his love for Virginia, part of whose attraction is her extreme youth and childlike playfulness and simplicity; and then also the constantly recurring presence of London docks, the river, the ships loading for distant parts all over the world. At the age of forty-five to fifty, after two novels of a much blacker and more violent kind, and after the despairing wrath of the two pre-war pamphlets, Céline was somehow able to evoke with tenderness and humour the mood of Ferdinand at twenty-one. Perhaps, as he was writing *Casse-pipe* during the same period, it was the result of a reaction against the army setting and the brutality of war. At all events, *Guignol's Band I* and *II* form an important part of the narrative output of our author, under-discussed by critics so far and obscured by the silliness of Poulet's preface to his so-called '*Le Pont de Londres*'.

Stylistically the work has left behind the relatively traditional manner of parts of the two pre-war novels, and is mostly in the staccato exclamatory manner of the post-war works. A very great deal of the text is direct speech in the present tense, and those parts dealing with Cascade and his followers are by no means easy to follow without a reasonable knowledge of traditional *argot*. But the descriptive passages are more conventionally written and they are extremely evocative, familiar yet very literary. I should add that there are frequent short interpolations in English to be found in the text. Céline obviously knew English quite well—he must have spent overall a very considerable time in England—but the bits he uses in the text are frequently incorrect, or at least 'off' English. Now this may be deliberate, or it may be that he didn't mind. It would not have been difficult for him to get someone to correct them. The effect is curious for a reader on this side of the Channel, and oddly effective since it gives the impression of a young foreigner writing down bits of ordinary speech which he hasn't quite heard correctly—which is, after all, what was no doubt the case for Ferdinand.

For an English reader—especially if he be a Londoner—there is a further intriguing feature, the topography of the novel. In its course we are led around London quite considerably, from Piccadilly and Leicester Square out to Whitechapel, Wapping and Greenwich, to Waterloo station, to Willesden and Maida Vale. But although the author clearly knows his London well, he sometimes amuses himself by confusing the topography. For instance (*I*, p. 34), he states that Borokrom made a living by playing the piano in pubs from the 'Elephant' to the 'Castle', and places these two locations at either end of the Mile End Road. Or he will devise a 'direct' route for a car conveying the wounded whore mentioned above from the West End to the 'London Hospital' in the East End which is as follows (*I*, pp. 100–101) 'Tottenham . . . le Strand . . . Fleet Street, la Banque, Seven Sisters . . . après "l'Elephant",' ending up 'au bout du Mile End'. He is not imitating Chesterton's route to Brighton by way of Wigan Pier, but rather is deliberately using place-names to evoke an *atmosphere* without wanting the reader to suppose that he has a street-plan in front of him as he writes. After all, in *Mort à crédit* he places the Porte Brancion on the wrong side of Paris, near Clichy. It is as though he wanted to stress that he is not Balzac nor even less Zola.

Indeed, atmosphere is particularly important in *Guignol's Band*. The long section which presents the world of Cascade and his variegated band of prostitutes has a great deal of familiar direct speech made vigorous by the extensive use of three dots, as in this passage where Cascade is complaining how difficult life is— the police being awkward, losing at cards and on racing, only his whores being profitable:

> Ça va mal les hommes! Ça va mal! . . . Cascade par-ci! . . . Cascade par là! . . . On me veut! . . . On me cherche! . . . Je pue peut-être? . . . Tous les poulets qui me reniflent! . . . Celle-la qu'arrête pas de chialer! . . . A la manoche je perds comme cinquante! . . . Aux courses mes gayes foncent à reculons . . . Y a que les souris qui me radinent! . . . Là, je manque de rien! . . . Je dois convenir! . . .'
> (*I*, p. 70)
>
> ('Look fellows, things are pretty bad! Pretty bad! . . . Cascade, here! . . . Cascade, there! . . . I'm wanted . . . I'm being looked for! . . . Perhaps I smell? . . . All the coppers sniffing at me! . . . And that

girl who won't stop crying! . . . What I lose at cards is nobody's business! . . . At the races the horses I back all go in reverse . . . It's only the tarts who do my work for me! . . . There I can't complain! . . . I have to admit! . . .')

But the three dots can be used quite differently. In the many passages concerning Ferdinand's feelings for Virginia they help to suggest a kind of tender thoughtfulness, as here where Ferdinand is consoling her about her pregnancy:

> . . . je cherchais quelque chose . . . je la comprenais bien . . . Ah! . . . elle avait vraiment de la peine . . . Ah! je voulais la consoler . . . Elle voyait bien moi aussi que je me fendais le coeur . . . je savais pas le dire en anglais . . . que ça me fendait le coeur . . . je l'aimais bien . . . voila! . . . je l'aimais bien toute petite là sur mon épaule! . . . (*II*, p. 240)

> (I tried to find something to say . . . I understood her completely . . . Ah! . . . She was really unhappy . . . Ah! I wanted to console her . . . she could see perfectly well that it was breaking my heart too . . . I couldn't say it in English . . . that it was breaking my heart . . . I was very fond of her . . . that's it! . . . I was very fond of her, so small she was, as she leant on my shoulder!)

The hallucinatory manner is found on numerous occasions in *Guignol's Band*, and nowhere perhaps more strikingly than where Sosthène's performance in Piccadilly Circus is treated in a vein of exuberant fantasy. He chooses to demonstrate his mystical power—or rather that of Goa, a deity who possesses him in trance—in the middle of the traffic, and it is certainly effective . . . So is the vocabulary used by Céline throughout the episode (*II*, pp. 251–5), as this short passage shows:

> Il me montre les camions, les bus qui tremblotent tous devant lui, tous les moteurs qui suintent, fusent, giclent de plus pouvoir embrayer, grincent, démantibulent, foirent, dégueulent. Tout l'enorme troupeau pagayeux, les monstres fumasses, butés, domptés comme ça sur l'asphalte péteux. Ah! Ça fait horrible . . . de l'"Empire' jusqu'à la 'Royale', c'est un embouteillage infect, une anguille se ferait écraser, une puce ne retrouverait pas ses petits. (*II*, p. 252)

> (He showed me the lorries, the buses quivering before him, all of them, all the engines sweating, melting, spurting because they couldn't get into gear, grinding, falling apart, shitting, vomiting. The whole enormous shambolic flock, the smoking, obstinate

monsters, tamed like that on the crackling asphalt. Oh! Terrible
sight ... from the 'Empire' down to the 'Royal' a disgusting traffic
jam, an eel would be crushed, a flea wouldn't be able to find its
children therein.)

In sharp contrast are the passages which evoke the atmosphere
of Thames-side London. Two major ones are at the beginning
of Part I and near the end of Part II, surrounding the narrative,
as it were, carefully placed in position of emphasis. The first of
these is a particularly significant nostalgic 'invitation au voyage'.

Le ciel ... L'eau grise ... les rives mauves ... tout est caresses ...
et l'un dans l'autre, ne se commande ... doucement entraînés à
ronde, à lentes voltes et tourbillons, vous vous charmez toujours
plus loin vers d'autres songes ... tout à périr à beaux secrets, vers
d'autres mondes qui s'apprêtent en voiles et brumes à grands
dessins pâles et flous, parmi les mousses à la chuchote ... Me
suivez-vous? (I, p. 46)

(The sky ... the grey water ... the mauve banks ... all caressing ...
one leading into the other so none dominates ... gently drawn into
the dance, in slow turns and pirouettes. You become more and
more enticed towards other more distant dreams ... quite willing
to perish for noble secrets, towards other worlds which begin to
form in sails and mists in great pale vague patterns amongst the
whispering cabin-boys ... Do you follow me?)

From the later passage—very near to the end of the book—
comes this excerpt which gives the movement and excitement of
the day's work beginning in the docks: even if Ferdinand has by
now missed his chance to sail away to South America, the
emotion aroused in him by the spectacle of vessels preparing for
sea suggests that indeed his departure will not be long delayed:

Là alors on voit les bateaux ... tout le jeu des wharfs ... tout le
grand travail ... les mouillages ... les bordées ... le tintouin ...
tout le carrousel ... des cargos ... les gros ... les minces! ... les
effilés ... les camouflés ... les plates palanques ... tout ça hâle
barre entre les remous ... au coup de sifflet ... branle-bas aux
docks ... souque! file! amarre! ... les bouées dandinent ...
effrontés canots ... ô partout ... doublent, pivotent, claboussent ...
moussent ... dix, cent, mille ... tout éberlué ... il faut aimer ...
Moi ça me fascine ... je ne le cache pas ... je m'émerveille ...
(II, p. 403)

(There then, you see the ships ... all the activity of the wharfs ...
all the busy work ... coming alongside ... tacking ... the din ...

the whole carnival . . . cargo ships . . . big ones, small ones . . .
slender ones . . . camouflaged ones . . . flat-bottomed . . . all of them
working, steering amongst the eddies . . . at the sound of the
whistle . . . action stations at the docks . . . batten down! let go!
make fast! . . . the buoys caper . . . impertinent dinghies . . . oh,
everywhere . . . overtake, wheel round, raise spray . . . froth . . .
ten, a hundred, a thousand . . . astonishes one . . . You have to love
it . . . Me, it fascinates me . . . I can't pretend otherwise . . . I find
it marvellous . . !)

These representative extracts show that Céline's mature style is
capable of conveying a wide range of differing moods. *Guignol's
Band* has not yet received a great deal of critical attention, largely
because of the circumstances of its publication. Once the twenty-
year gap between the appearances of Parts I and II is forgotten
and once the work is looked at as a continuous narrative, its
unity of structure is seen to be most skilfully devised. It sets an
awkward problem for those who want to regard Céline as purely
destructive and pessimistic and for that reason alone it is a work
that must be taken into account in any overall assessment of him.
Humour, tenderness and nostalgia give it a very special flavour.

CHAPTER SIX

Casse-pipe

In 1948 Céline was far away in exile in Denmark. For the mass of the French public he was a presumed collaborator still awaiting trial. However, there were friends of his in France who were trying to defend him, notably the novelist Albert Paraz. In 1948 the periodical (published by Gallimard) called the *Cahiers de la Plëïade* contained (in its fifth number) extracts from a novel by Céline entitled *Casse-pipe*. Its editor (Jean Paulhan) showed courage in accepting a text by Céline so soon after the Liberation, and was guided—as he always was—by considerations of aesthetic integrity. Politically the text is completely innocuous, being the next stage after *Mort à crédit* in the life of Ferdinand—concerning his first experiences in a cavalry regiment before the First World War. Letters written by Céline from Denmark show that Paulhan's decision gave him much encouragement, and there is little doubt that Paulhan was later responsible for Gallimard (by far the largest and most influential publisher in France) taking on the works of Céline from 1952 onwards.[1]

There is reason to believe that *Casse-pipe* was begun and completed some time during the war and that the manuscript was in part destroyed or stolen by those who pillaged Céline's Montmartre flat at the moment of the liberation in 1944. Three blocks of text survive. First a substantial chunk published in 1949 by Chambriand and republished by Gallimard in 1952—running to 149 smallish pages of print in the Gallimard edition—which looked like being the opening pages of the novel. In 1958 Robert Poulet was able to publish as an appendix to his interesting, if naïve volume *Mon ami Bardamu: Entretiens familiers avec L. F. Céline* a further fifteen-page chapter given to him by Céline. And in the *Cahiers de l'Herne* (1963 and 1965, republished together 1972) there are two further fragments—some two pages in all.

[1] Céline later (1954) quarrelled with Paulhan.

Further indications about its content are given in Poulet's book (p. 105) in the form of an alleged statement by Céline.[2] This indicates that the book was going to deal with a group of soldiers under the command of a warrant-officer who, losing contact with their unit in the confusion of battle, without orders, without food, without any information about the course of the battle, become undisciplined marauders, and even break open the cash-box which is amongst their regimental baggage. The warrant-officer, at first powerless to stop all this, then a participant in it, eventually realizes the enormity of the military crimes committed and his own responsibility in it all, and leads his men into death at the fiercest point of the battlefield. This would certainly explain the title '*Casse-pipe*'.[3] The fragments we *have*, however, are set pre-war, and they are enough to indicate that the completed text would probably have been a major work. (It is not impossible that the manuscript may come to light at some stage if it was merely stolen in 1944 and not destroyed.)

About the material so far published it is possible to make a few remarks in support of the view that a completed *Casse-pipe* might have been a very important work. There are two attitudes detectable in Céline about the army (evidence comes from else-where in his works); the first is undeniably hostile, the second admiring. Officers are remote, inhuman, contemptuous and, often enough, incompetent, even if personally brave. Warrant-officers and NCOs are without exception shown as coarse, brutal, petty tyrants capable of the most odious malevolence. The ordinary soldier, victim of his superiors, is quickly turned into a cunning, treacherous, thieving animal. Yet, the army of 1914 held the German advance: unlike that of 1940 it did not run all the way from Dunkerque to the Pyrenees (cf. see above, p. 167). And, however degrading military existence was in those years (1912–14), it had its moments of splendour and excitement.

The atmosphere into which the narrator is plunged on arrival at barracks late at night as a volunteer is as much a shock to the

---

[2] Poulet's book, while being undoubtedly one of the more serious 'anecdotal' volumes about Céline, cannot be regarded with great confidence as a source of reliable information. Céline is alleged in the book to have said a number of things that are now known to be untrue—though that was probably Céline playing with his interviewer. . . . And the passage about *Casse-pipe* here summarized is palpably a rewriting by Poulet of what he could remember of their conversation.

[3] *Casse-pipes* (masc. invariable noun), is a slang word for 'war'. *Casser sa pipe* means to die, and Céline's singular *Casse-pipe* can be taken to mean 'slaughter'.

reader as it is to him. The sentry at the gate announces his arrival to the NCO on duty—in the guard-room:

—Brigadier! C'est l'engagé!
—Qu'il entre ce con-là! (p. 8)

('Corporal! It's the volunteer!'
'Tell the cunt to come in!')

There are twenty men in the guard-room, the smell is remarkable:

La viande, la pisse et la chique et la vesse que ça cognait, à toute violence, et puis le café triste refroidi, et puis un goût de crottin et puis encore quelque chose de fade comme du rat crevé plein les coins . . . (p. 9)

(What hit you good and hard was the smell of flesh, piss, quids of tobacco, silent fart, and then nasty cold coffee, and then a touch of horse-dung, and then also something insipid like dead rat all over the place.)

The 150-odd pages that make up this fragment simply describe the events of this first night. The guard goes out on patrol in the barracks in pouring rain, with the narrator tagging on behind still in civilian clothes. The corporal has forgotten the pass-word for the night, the patrol hides in one of the stables, they are found there by a furious warrant-officer. Some horses have got loose and are galloping around the barracks in the dark. The fragment ends with the sounding of reveille on a trumpet and the barracks coming suddenly to life. There is no pause, no let-up in the cascade of violent direct speech and action throughout the whole fragment. It is not an easy text to read if only because of the plethora of military slang, but it has a quite extraordinary impressionistic quality, some highly effective imagery and is written in the mature Célinian manner, with full use of the *trois points*, as in this passage at the very end of the fragment—the sounding of reveille:

Karvic a envoyé la fin, deux appels aigus . . . Tout au bout de son cuivre . . . Deux flèches vers les toits . . .
    Alors tout autour de nous il a sorti comme des yeux . . . des choses dans la brume . . . des mille fenêtres à vous regarder . . . des reflets, je crois . . . des reflets . . . Il faisait presque jour à présent . . .

ça pâlissait d'en haut . . . des toits . . . et tout le quartier . . . les
murs . . . la chaux . . . (p. 156)

(Karvic sent off the last bit, two sharp calls . . . right at the end of
his bugle . . . Two arrows towards the roofs . . .

And then, all round us, eyes seemed to emerge . . . objects in the
mist . . . looking at you from the thousand windows . . . reflections,
I think . . . reflections . . . By now it was about daylight . . . getting
paler up above . . . roofs . . . the whole district . . . walls . . . white-
wash . . .)

The chapter reproduced by Poulet does not add much. It
contains two vignettes of officers and a few rapid portraits of
other ranks, with the particular indication of how army life turns
ordinary soldiers into thieves, out of pure self-defence—the
English term is 'scroungers', perhaps—'C'est plus voleur qu'une
bordée de pies, plus canaille qu'un tréfond d'égout, c'est le vice
lui-même un homme de trois classes' ('A three-year conscript is
more thieving than a flock of magpies, more filthy than the
depths of a sewer, vice in person').

The short extracts in *Cahiers de l'Herne* deserve perhaps two
comments. The narrator has become an NCO, and in the first
extract he describes being in the annual parade along the Champs
Élysées on 14 July 1913. And there is a certain excitement about
the mass movement of so many men:

Ça fait un mouvement d'amplitude sept mille cavaliers au galop . . .
Faut entendre ça comme résonance. Faut voir aussi tout l'éventail,
les cuirassiers . . . le flot hérissé de dragons . . . la légère à tombeau
ouvert qui prend la corde à l'aile marchante. Il en mugit dans
l'avalanche le fol cavalé . . . jusqu'aux gradins ça carambole et ça
gronde. Voilà le travail! (p. 26)

(Seven thousand cavalrymen at the gallop make a good broad
movement . . . it makes a pretty good sound. It's worth seeing, too,
the whole fan-shaped deployment, of breast-plated horsemen . . .
the spiky flood of dragoons . . . the light cavalry at breakneck speed
cutting inside the marching flank. The whole mad cavalcade sounds
like a roaring avalanche . . . bouncing about and thundering over to
the spectator's stands. Good work!)

In the second—very brief—extract he reflects on the nature of
military discipline, how it brutalizes the soldier and isolates him
from real life:

Au coeur de la discipline tout ne doit être que tremblement! Merde!
Con ou chiant du soir au matin la recrue, et le dimanche, et vice-
versa. Voilà! Le vin blanc, l'aramon poisseux, un coup de racontar
cochon, ça suffit pour un 'russe', qu'il la boucle. Sans pétoche—
extraordinaire, le Haricot n'a plus de sens. Faut tout oublier, le
civil, la ville, la campagne, éponger tout ça . . . Pas de regrets. Rien
comme souvenir . . . (p. 26)

(Trembling should be at the heart of discipline! Shit! The recruit is
a cunt and a nuisance from dawn till dusk including Sundays and
vice-versa. Right! White wine, slimy plonk, the odd dirty story,
that's good enough for a recruit, let him keep his trap shut. If he's
not shit scared, the ordinary soldier makes no sense. Got to forget
everything, being a civilian, town, country, wife, all that out . . .
No regrets. No memories . . .)

His military experience—especially that of the wartime months
until he was wounded—left a great mark on Céline. The earliest
text we possess by him is a notebook kept when he was in
the army in 1912–13. Some of the despair it contains carries
on into *Casse-pipe*, and yet there is also present a realization
that the misery of military life has meant a challenge of self-
discovery:

Que de fois je suis remonté du pansage, et tout seul sur mon lit, pris
d'un immense désespoir, j'ai malgré mes dix sept ans pleuré comme
une première communiante (. . .) J'ai senti que les grands discours
que je tenais un mois plus tôt sur l'énergie juvénile n'étaient que
fanfaronnade et qu'au pied du mur je n'étais qu'un malheureux trans-
planté ayant perdu la moitié de ses facultés et ne se servant de celles qui
restent que pour constater le néant de cette énergie (. . .) je cache
un fond d'orgueil qui me fait peur à moi-même je veux dominer
non par pouvoir factice comme l'ascendant militaire mais je veux
que plus tard ou le plus tôt possible êntre un homme complet, le
serai-je jamais, aurai-je la fortune nécessaire pour avoir cette facilité
d'agir qui vous permet de vous éduquer.' (p. 11)

(How many times have I come up from the stables, and all alone on
my bed, seized by tremendous despair, have I—despite my seventeen
years of age—wept like a girl at first communion (. . .) I've felt that
all those fine speeches I made a month ago about the energy of youth
were just idle boastings, and that, let's face it, I was nothing but a
poor uprooted sod who's lost half his faculties and was only using
those he's still got to establish the nullity of that energy (. . .) I've a
lot of hidden pride deep down which makes me afraid of myself.
I want to dominate not through the bogus authority of superior

military rank but I want later on or rather as soon as possible to be a whole man, will I ever be, will I have the necessary luck to possess that ease of action which lets you educate yourself.)

It is sad that we have only fragments of *Casse-pipe*, a book that Céline was uniquely qualified to write.

CHAPTER SEVEN

Féerie pour une autre fois I and *II*

In 1952 and 1954 appeared the two parts of *Féerie pour une autre fois*, the second of them having the sub-title *Normance*. I propose to say less about these works than about any of the other novels. This is because in my view Part II (written before Part I) at least does not really come off. It may well be that I'm wrong about this: that later generations will be more perceptive, more receptive to what Céline seems to be trying to do. I find Part I uneven in tone and Part II monotonously over-written, and am inclined to consider both as products of the worst moments of Céline's life, being written at least in part during the years of comfortless exile in Denmark, and when he was struggling to find a new subject matter and to treat it in the stylistic manner that had first become clearly apparent in *Bagatelles* just before the war. Works of transition, perhaps, between the 'novels' up to and including *Guignol's Band I* and *II* (all of which had a 'fictional' narrator, Bardamu and Ferdinand, and all of which were set before 1932) and the 'chronicles' which are the great trilogy *D'un Château l'autre*, *Nord* and *Rigodon*, where Céline speaks in his own name and recounts his own experience (even if much modified for artistic reasons) in 1944–5 in Germany.

Féerie I is not a narrative work. Dedicated 'Aux animaux, aux malades, aux prisonniers' ('To animals, invalids and prisoners'), it is a long fiery meditation during which Céline, in writing—so he would have us believe—from his prison-cell in Denmark, reflects in particular upon the days in 1944 in Paris before he left for Germany and upon his present state awaiting a decision about his extradition. Some of it is touching (his memories of St Malo before the war for instance), some of it is amusing (the unforgettable depiction of the French diplomat in Copenhagen under the name of 'Gaëtan Serge d'Hortensia, l'Assesseur nègre de l'Ambassade, représentant l'union des Cinglés, diplomatiques,

politiques, coloniaux, et ectoplasmiques',[1] and a great deal of it
is a scornful defiance of his detractors and enemies written with
all the verve and grim humour of which he is capable. In some
respects *Féerie I* is quite a rewarding work, for the linguistic
fireworks are present in great quantity and the standpoint is
understandable. But a reader who does not know the circumstances well and who is not very informed about the state of
France in the immediate years after the Liberation of 1945, will
find it hard to follow in general and many of the contemporary
allusions will escape him.

In the chapter 'From *Mea Culpa* to *Les Beaux Draps*' there was
a good deal of information about the 'guilt' of Céline. He was
guilty of exploiting that nasty streak of anti-semitism that is,
alas, endemic in France, and he did not cease to mock the achievements of the French armies in 1940. If he had not fled in 1944 he
would either have been assassinated at the Liberation or over-
hastily judged in the purge trials of 1945-6. He categorically
maintained that, like most Europeans, he had no knowledge
during the war of the Nazi extermination camps. He considered himself innocent and a patriot. Indeed, as has been
suggested, had he been willing around 1946-7 to disavow publicly
his anti-semitism, things might have been different for him. But
it was not in his character to do so, and we can say no more of
that. He certainly disavowed it freely enough in private letters.
Instead, in works like *Féerie I* he counter-attacks his enemies,
pours out all the bitterness he feels about his imprisonment in
Denmark (at the request of the French government), reiterates
his contempt for the courageous pillagers of his flat in Paris,
who in 1940 had run, he says, from Bruges to Bayonne. Even
now, more than thirty years after the Liberation, this attitude
is not endearing and certainly didn't help much in 1952. *But*,
there is no doubt that he does all this very well: the polemist of
the *pamphlets* had not lost his touch for epic vituperation.

Although there is no real structure to *Féerie I*, the following
remarks about its contents may be of help to intending readers.
The book opens in Céline's Montmartre flat in early 1944 or
thereabouts. He has two visitors—an old friend, Clémence
Arlon, and her adolescent son, Pierre. Why have they come to
see him, from the far side of Paris? They won't say, indeed they
say practically nothing. The boy has his hand in his trouser pocket.

[1] See *Féerie I*, p. 51; see also above, p. 103.

A revolver? An erection? wonders Céline (see above, p. 110). He decides that they have come to look over the flat, waiting for him to be shot when the war is over. He is already getting warnings of this fate, from the BBC, by anonymous letters, from friends who are anxious for him. This first section lasts from p. 11 to p. 48. Thereafter we virtually lose sight of Clémence and Pierre, and Céline begins his long rumination in the past and on his present incarceration in Copenhagen. He knows that all his Montmartre possessions have been destroyed—including the manuscripts of *Casse-pipe*, *Guignol's Band* and *Le Roi Krogold* (p. 65)—and that he is reduced to penury, so what can he do? He's not going to give in. He is innocent. He must write. What? *Féerie!*

> Vous achetez *Féerie*! Le texte vous vexe? Ça vous regarde! C'est de moi que je ris, c'est moi le squelette à croûtes, lichens! Le marrant le sort où je suis chu! en cinquante ans de labeur féroce, inventions, conscience et honneur, héroïque, moi médaillé avant Petain, pilorisé par des pillards! outragé par des galopiauds, des Bruges Bayonne l'échalotte! 'Maillots-cacas'! Ah! (p. 52)[2]

> (You buy *Féerie*! The text annoys you? That's your business! I'm laughing at myself, I'm the skeleton with scabs, lichens! Comic the fate I've met! After 50 years of ferocious hard work, inventions, conscience and honour, heroic is what I am, decorated earlier than Petain, pilloried by pillagers! insulted by galloping cowards, the Bruges to Bayonne squadron! shit jerseys! Ah!)

This passage can stand as representative of the prevailing tone of the book, and it also gives us a clue to the meaning of the title. The old aggressive mockery of Ferdinand is there, with a new note of real personal bitterness. And he is now going to become a public entertainer—'C'est de moi que je ris' is an extension of the remark at the end of *Guignol's Band II*—'C'est moi le pitre maintenant' (see above, p. 190, and also below, p. 224). 'Programme chérie?' ('Programme, darling?') he asks on several occasions. 'Gloire à Ferdinand! Achetez-le *Féerie*! *Féerie*! Gloire et milliards à Ferdinand!' (p. 204) ('Honour Ferdinand! Buy it! *Féerie*! *Féerie*! Honour and billions for Ferdinand!') 'Achetez *Féerie*! achetez *Féerie*! le livre qui vous réjuvène l'âme, boyaute le boyau!' (p. 209)/('Buy *Féerie*! buy *Féerie*! the book that rejuvenates your soul, embowels the bowels!')

[2] The final allusion is to the '*Maillot jaune*'—yellow jersey—worn by the leading cyclist in the *Tour de France*.

A *Féerie* is an entertainment in which an element of magic or the supernatural seems included. The magic in *Féerie I* is essentially Céline's ironic fantasy about himself in this whole long central section of the work. Here he is in prison, in nasty inhuman conditions guarded by boring, ignorant Danes and pestered by the grotesque presence of the effeminate Hortensia outside his cell at irritating moments. Why is he there? Because he deprived people like Clémence and her son Pierre and all those courageous avenging pillagers of the spectacle of his public assassination.

He hints—and it must be admitted with some reason—that there were a good many public figures and writers whose wartime record was a lot less clean than his in terms of collaboration and who seem to be doing quite well. So he envisages a public ceremony in which, as a result of the splendours of *Féerie*, he should be totally vindicated and made triumphant. All this is written in an ironic manner that could not be taken by the French public of 1952, and quite understandably so. But Céline was *not* seriously seeking public rehabilitation at that juncture: he was holding on to a genuine belief in his own essential innocence. Let future centuries judge, he seems to imply. His personal view is that the last clean and decent moment in French history was the defence of Verdun in 1917 during the war in which he fought with honour and in which the French armies stood their ground.

All this of course is an attempt to *explain* not to *defend* his attitude. If you're fool enough to make a public intervention of a racialist kind as did Céline in 1937 and 1938—from whatever motives—then you must pay a certain price. I do think, however, that he was probably made to pay enough between 1945 and 1951, and that there were a substantial number of more guilty persons who never paid at all, and who even attained positions of public honour and dignity. And I also think that certain of those who most fiercely attacked Céline did so without just cause and without looking at the hard evidence. The Danish government was in a good position to judge dispassionately the evidence that *was* produced to justify extradition, and its verdict was that there was no case for extradition. That needs some countering.

So Céline does not ask forgiveness in *Féerie I*; he does not plead for mercy either, nor for rehabilitation. He wants a triumphant comic acceptance. Not the Panthéon:

Le lieu est impeccable mais triste, Panthéon . . . verrouillé, scellé, tcétéra . . . O cette solitude entre morts! Non! Flûte! Je veux du monde! (p. 232)

(An impeccable place, but sad, the Pantheon . . . locked, sealed, cetera, . . . Oh! that solitude amongst the dead! No! Never! I want company!)

If all this happens, he'll be back in Montmartre like a flash and back to his medical practice. He imagines his return there and his meeting with an old friend, Julot, who has been awarded the Légion d'Honneur for heroism and in compensation for losing both his legs (p. 234). From this point on, to the end of the volume (p. 327) Julot takes over the central role. . . . Once again we witness this pattern in Céline—Robinson, Courtial, Sosthène, and now Julot. (He is to be also in almost total control of the events of *Féerie II*, *Normance*.) He is a sculptor, embittered, jealous and lascivious, and Céline, in order to establish him, leaves his present fantasy and takes us back to wartime Montmartre, introduces the character of his own wife (here called Arlette), one of the victims of the libidinous Julot. We are back to the time before the end of the war, before Céline's flight to Germany and Denmark, and again we have the atmosphere of threats to his life, the receipt of little coffins sent through the post by the Resistance. The final pages see us back in the prison in Copenhagen: the Féerie is ended for the time being. . . .

If *Féerie I* is difficult but worth studying for its strident ironical gaiety and fantasy, *Féerie II* is more difficult, longer and a lot less worthwhile. Its 364 pages are largely an evocation of an Allied air-raid in Paris towards the end of the war. Its dedication to 'Pline L'Ancien' makes the parallel with the famous eruption of Vesuvius described by that author (and its second dedication to Gaston Gallimard sounds like a piece of semi-irony if one is to judge by the tone of the *Entretiens avec le Professeur Y*, published the following year), and is made explicit near the beginning of the book:

Ils achèteront plus tard mes livres, beaucoup plus tard, quand je serai mort, pour étudier ce que furent les premiers séismes de la fin, et de la vacherie du tronc des hommes, et les explosions des fonds d'âme . . . ils savaient pas, ils sauront! . . . un Déluge mal observé c'est toute une Ere entière pour rien . . . toute une humanité souffrante qu'a juste servi d'asticots! . . . Voilà le blasphème et le pire! Gloire à Pline. (p. 25)

(They'll buy my books later on, much later, when I'm dead, so as to find out what were the initial tremors of the end, and of the fundamental treachery of men, of the explosions of the depths of soul . . . they did not know, they will know! . . . A poorly observed Flood is a whole Era gone for nothing . . . an entire suffering humanity just used as maggots . . . That is blasphemy of the worst kind. All honour to Pliny!)

I think the best I can say for *Féerie II* is that it is perhaps an apprenticeship stylistically for the far more impressive *Rigodon*. The minimal bombardments of Paris pale beside the devastation of Germany in the last months of the war, and make a much less impressive subject, but they set Céline off into a mood of hallucinatory lyricism which frankly cannot be sustained over 400 pages. We watch the various inhabitants of the block of flats where Céline lives on the seventh floor with his wife, Lili (and their cat Bébert, who here makes an important entrance into French fiction), and are shown their reaction as the bombs fall.

As for Julot, he is eventually spotted perched on the windmill of the Moulin Rouge, apparently guiding and directing the Allied aircraft as they attack:

Jules là, tout seul, sur tout Paris! voyez l'insolence! Empereur des flammes entre les ailes du moulin à panaches! crépitantes! Je vous bafouille pas moi! Je vous dis vrai! . . . et la joie de ce tronc! le défi! il gigote dans sa caisse, trémousse! à l'autre houle! encore une autre! d'une rambarde l'autre! pivote! voilà! broum! une aile du moulin lui scierait la tête! . . . (p. 90)

(Jules there, all alone, above the whole of Paris! the insolence of it! Emperor of the flames between the sails of the feathered windmill! crackling! I'm not misleading you! I'm telling the truth! . . . And the joy of this torso! what defiance! he bounces about in his box, wriggles! another surge! and another! from one rail to another! pivots! there! broum! an arm of the mill might well saw off his head! . . .)

Various allegorical or symbolical interpretations of this work have been suggested. They may be true for their purveyors as far as I know, but I can't help remembering Céline's 'je ne suis pas un homme à *idéâs*'. Jules in this book is a bore, and so is Ferdinand, frankly: not even the undoubted vigour of the language can really compensate for this.

Three-quarters of the way through there is a flicker of hope for the patience of the courageous reader. Ferdinand, Lili (Bébert, of course, too) and another character called Ottavio make a hole in the wall of their ruined building and find themselves in an undamaged flat:

> . . . une grande pièce propre . . . rien d'esquinté! . . . et dans l'immeuble tout contre le nôtre! . . . pas la berlue! je vois parfaitement . . . une pièce intacte! . . . un salon même! . . . un vrai salon! . . . cette maison-là a pas souffert! Je le déclare . . . (p. 318)

> (. . . a big clean room . . . nothing damaged . . . and that is the building right next to ours! . . . not imagination! I see perfectly well . . . an intact room! . . . a drawing-room in fact, a real one! . . . this house hasn't suffered! I declare . . .)

There, silently seated at a table prepared for dinner, is Norbert:

> Il était là assis, songeur . . . le regard fixe . . . on pouvait croire qu'il nous regardait, il nous regardait pas . . . (p. 319)

> (He was sitting there, dreamily . . . fixed gaze . . . one could believe he was looking at us, he wasn't looking at us . . .)

Apart from the fact that Norbert seems very like the important participant in the action of the trilogy we are about to discuss next, the actor Le Vigan, there is no particular interest to be derived from the subsequent fifty pages of text. Norbert says much more than ' . . . "il ne s'est rien passé" ' ('. . . "nothing has happened" ') (how right he is, we may feel). ' "Il va se passer! Oui! Certes! *Il va! Il va se passer!*" ' (p. 324) (' "Something will! Yes! Certainly! It will! It will happen!" ') What is about to happen, it seems to Norbert, is the arrival of the Pope, Churchill and Roosevelt. So what? The whole sequence is as lively as late Ionesco and there is no other text by Céline which could conceivably be so described.

'*Achetez Féerie I*' by all means, but *Féerie II* is perhaps best written off as a pretentious bore.

CHAPTER EIGHT

The Trilogy
(D'un Château l'autre, Nord, Rigodon)

During the years of ostracism, it was commonly held that Céline was played out, that *Voyage* and *Mort à crédit* were interesting phenomena, but that of course no one who had such a despairing and negative attitude could really hope to continue developing creatively. (Moreover, the relative failure of *Féerie I* and *II* seemed to confirm this.) Indeed, I've found that a surprising number of my French friends, when told that I'm working on Céline, have said (roughly), 'Oh Céline? Of course I've read the early novels and remarkable they were. But surely he then became a collaborator and never wrote anything else of value?' That attitude is now changing and the fact that the late Céline is becoming available, not only in cheap paperback, but also in the Pléïade series, is introducing him to a new generation of readers. There are plenty of examples of this kind of thing in literary history after all. Generations of schoolchildren have been told that late Corneille is no good, that poor Flaubert made a dreadful mistake in trying to write *Bouvard et Pécuchet*. . . .

That Céline's talent was not exhausted after *Mort à crédit* is shown first by *Guignol's Band I* and *II*—when they are looked at as a whole—by parts of *Féerie I*, and definitely by the trilogy *D'un Château l'autre* (1957), *Nord* (1960) and *Rigodon* (1969).[1] Céline finished *Rigodon* on the morning of the day on which he died—1 July 1961, and although there were two versions of the text, the second being a revised version, great problems of deciphering the manuscript delayed publication for eight years. Had he lived, there might have been further modifications, but we do possess a complete text which he regarded as such.

[1] Trilogy published by Gallimard, Paris, in the years indicated, and subsequently (1974) in the Pléïade series of the same publisher (ed. H. Godard).

These three works are not novels in the strict sense. Like *Féerie I* and *II* they are more precisely to be described as *'chroniques'*. They are first-person narratives, the narrator being Céline, not Bardamu, not Ferdinand. They deal with the experiences of the author, his wife Lucette (called Lili throughout), his cat Bébert, and their friend the actor, Le Vigan (called La Vigue throughout) during 1944 and 1945 in Germany. However, they are *narratives*, unlike the loose meditation, *Féerie I*, and unlike the single long hallucinatory fantasy, *Féerie II*. They do contain a great deal of incident, and they have also a chronological development from July 1944 to March 1945. If I add that they do *not* adhere to the strict facts about these months (as far as these can be established), that the chronology is not a straight linear pattern from the beginning of *D'un Château l'autre* to the end of *Rigodon*, that many of the incidents are recounted in Céline's impressionistic hallucinatory manner (here at its best and most appropriate), and that clearly we are *not* being given a piece of straight autobiography but, rather, a very carefully planned and modulated narrative based on general experience, it may be reasonable none the less to regard these works as novels. There is about them an atmosphere which is far removed from what one would find in a series of volumes entitled something like 'Germany in defeat: memories of 1944–5'. They give a powerful impression of verisimilitude— except in the deliberately fantastic passages—yet the reader is constantly aware that he is reading a kind of fiction and not a piece of autobiography, an imaginative re-creation of experience and not a set of historically checked memoirs.

There is a case for regarding these three 'novels' as the supreme artistic achievement of Céline. They are certainly as good as anything he wrote and leave an unforgettable impression of the dramatic months before the collapse of Nazi Germany, and also (a major theme, this) of the way in which the individual is reduced to all kinds of humiliating sycophancy when struggling for mere survival.

The actual movements of Céline during this period were as follows. July 1944 marked his departure from Paris (with his wife Lucette, Le Vigan and Bébert), and a short stay in Baden-Baden. There followed a journey to Berlin and then establishment for some months at Kränzlin, near Neu-Ruppin, Brandenburg, north-west of Berlin, where they were not interned, but under a kind of obligatory residence. With the retirement of the Vichy government to Sigmaringen (near Ulm) and the formation of a French enclave, Céline obtained permission to move there, arriving in November 1944. He remained a doctor to the French colony until March 1945, when, having received from the German authorities the necessary exit permit, he set off (with Lucette and Bébert, but without Le Vigan) on what was to be a three-week journey northwards, reaching Copenhagen on 27 March on the last Swedish Red Cross train out of Germany, shortly before the end of the war in Europe.

If we look at the trilogy we find that events are not narrated in the same order. In *D'un Château l'autre*, after an introductory section set in post-war Meudon, we have a coverage of the period in Sigmaringen (including, towards the end, a long journey to Prussia and back). In *Nord* we are taken back to an earlier stage in his wanderings—first the stay in Baden-Baden, then the stay in Kränzlin (called Zornhof in the book), terminating with permission being granted to go to Rostock and Warnemünde on the Baltic coast. *Rigodon* gives us first the journey to Warnemünde (it proved impossible to get to Denmark that way), and then the long journey south via Berlin and Ulm to Sigmaringen. There is only the briefest of stays there, before the final return northwards through Hamburg to Flensburg and Copenhagen. A further indication of Céline's deliberate desire to confuse the chronology is to be found in *Rigodon* (p. 800), where, during this brief stay in Sigmaringen, he says that he had been there six months earlier, *before* 'cette escapade, Brandenbourg et zigzag. . . .'

Accordingly we can see that the related events in the trilogy coincide with the actual events, more or less, but that the chronology is different. *D'un Château l'autre* should strictly be an insert halfway through *Rigodon*. Those parts of the novels which can be checked by other sources show, as by now we would expect, a mixture of accuracy and fantasy. The Sigmaringen sequences, for example, contain very interesting specific references to public figures like Pétain, Laval, De Brinon and others, which are very much in accordance with what is known of them.[2] Yet some of

---

[2] Céline considered that he knew a lot about the French colony in Sigmaringen. In a letter of 1958 to Galtier-Boissière, editor of *Crapouillot* (published in *Cahiers de l'Herne*, p. 193), he wrote 'Il vous faudra un jour faire un numéro de Sigmaringen. Il y a beaucoup de rescapés à Paris. Quand ce sera prêt, vous viendrez me voir, et je vous dirai *ce qui est vrai* et *ce qui n'est pas vrai*. Je possède médecin, buveur d'eau, non fumeur, une mémoire atroce.'

('You ought to bring out a number on Sigmaringen one day. There are in Paris

the actual incidents recounted in connection with these characters are almost certainly inventions. As for *Nord*, the fact that the first edition had to be withdrawn as a result of a law-suit and the names of the characters in 'Zornhof' changed, suggests that he'd stuck to some kind of recognizable truth there too.

The way to describe these works, then, is to say that they are firmly based on real experience but that the author adds to this factual basis a great deal of fictional embroidery and fantasy: one might almost say that he uses the same technique as does Rabelais in the Pichrocholine war in *Gargantua*. The result is over 1,000 pages of powerful and highly imaginative narrative from which the reader receives information about the adventures and tribulations of Céline and also gains a vivid impression of the extraordinary atmosphere prevailing in Germany during the final desperate months of the war, with the unsuccessful attempt to assassinate Hitler, the comic opera being enacted in Sigmaringen, the massive Allied bombardments, and the ultimate awareness of the Allied armies closing in from both West and East.

I'm going to talk about these three 'novels' as forming one continuous narrative. It does not matter that they do not form a chronological sequence, because they do certainly have unity of purpose. The tone is naturally going to vary a good deal within each novel, and there are a number of themes which carry right the way through. Perhaps it's best to begin with a word about them.

There is first of all an attitude of amused contempt for the Germans, and an unconcealed hostility to all that represents authority in Nazi terms. Céline may have been in favour of a Franco-German alliance in 1937-8, but once war had come in 1939 his standpoint changed. As has been seen, he at once volunteered for service in the armed forces, was rejected on medical grounds, but became a ship's doctor and his ship was torpedoed in the Mediterranean by a German submarine.

There are also substantial passages of 'black' comedy concerning all those who, despite the horrors and privations of war, manage to live in untroubled gastronomic comfort. The leaders on both sides of the conflict are never going to run short of food,

plenty who escaped from there. When it's ready, you'll come and see me, and I'll tell you *what is true* and *what is not true*. As a doctor, a drinker of water and a non-smoker, I possess a devastating memory.')

nor do the prosperous inhabitants of the Park Hotel in Baden-Baden (*Nord*) (see above, p. 113), nor the inhabitants of the Château in Sigmaringen (*D'un Château l'autre*), nor the 'aristocracy' of Zornhof (*Nord*).

The third continuing theme, present from the start, is, of course, that of the collapse of Germany—*Götterdämmerung* indeed! Céline, if we are to believe Rebatet (see above, p. 178) had already foreseen this by the autumn of 1940, and he had already practised in *Féerie I* and *II* the linguistic manner appropriate for descriptions of the horror of aerial bombardments. By the end of *Rigodon* he has completed what the German, Karl Epting, described as 'l'image la plus grandiose de la chute allemande qui ait jamais paru'[3] ('the most grandiose vision of the fall of Germany that has ever appeared'), and nowhere does the hallucinatory apocalyptic manner find more apt subject matter than this. The impressions of the German collapse are conveyed not only by descriptions of bombardments and their effects, but also by indications of the mood of the German people, of the signs of disregard for law and order, of the presence of great masses of hopeless wandering refugees from the East, and of the material difficulties of existence at this critical time.

Perhaps the most important and most sustained theme is that of what one might call (borrowing from the end of *Mort à crédit*) the 'Oui mon oncle' feeling in Céline. Just as the young Ferdinand in that novel decided early in the face of his over-angry father that the best course was to forestall wrath by apologizing in advance even when innocent, and just as the same Ferdinand at the end of the novel opposes the phrases 'oui mon oncle' and 'non mon oncle' to all the suggestions of Edouard, so here in the trilogy Céline and Lucette (who barely speaks directly throughout) who are totally *victims* throughout the 1000-odd pages of narrative, having no control over events, consistently bend and obey. What else can they do? They are deferential to *all*, because *all* are potentially dangerous to them. Their sole aim is *survival*—survival being represented by the reaching of Denmark—because they consider themselves innocent. They mean to live if they can, if only, we feel in Céline's case, to be able to proclaim that innocence to the victorious part of the French population post-war. And so Céline depicts himself throughout these three novels as cunning, deferential to all, winning the half-trust of those in control—from the Vichy puppets in Sigmaringen to their German SS masters, and including on the one hand the most fanatical of French *miliciens* to the bitterly hostile French deportees in Zornhof on the other. Céline agrees politely with all—to their faces—but does not spare them behind their backs. This sounds both mean and hypocritical, but the point being made all along is the monstrous way in which human beings can be forced into such a position by the elementary urge to keep alive, and win through the period of lunacy which is war, to a state of some security. This idea is only an extension of what has been a permanent view from Céline about the ordinary underprivileged human being—almost all the desires of the poor, he says, are punishable by prison sentences—and the difference in the trilogy is merely that he finds *himself* in precisely this situation of powerlessness. And surely he is right? Give a man a uniform, or a minor bureaucratic post (especially a counter position behind a glass partition), and the chances are that he will love exercising his authority against the humble, the ignorant, those who don't speak his language. . . . (Ever heard a post-office clerk in France trying hard not to help an Algerian to send a money order?) De Tocqueville in his *Ancien Régime* has a couple of sentences which catch the mood of the victim in such circumstances, sentences which show the same kind of understanding of what it is like to be impotent in the face of injustice as is so constantly displayed by Céline. De Tocqueville is here describing the feelings of the peasant in eighteenth-century France, subject first to the feudal exactions of the aristocracy and then on top of that to the similar financial demands of the church:

> Quoi qu'il fasse, il rencontre partout sur son chemin ces voisins incommodes, pour troubler son plaisir, gêner son travail, manger ses produits; et, quand il a fini avec ceux-ci, d'autres, vêtus de noir, se présentent, qui lui prennent le plus clair de sa récolte. Figurez-vous la condition, les besoins, le caractère, les passions de cet homme, et calculez, si vous le pouvez, les trésors de haine et d'envie qui se sont amassés dans son coeur.[4]

> (Whatever he does, everywhere on his way he encounters these troublesome neighbours, who disturb his pleasure, hinder his work, eat his produce; and, when he has finished with them, another lot, dressed in black, come along and take from him the greater part of his harvest. Just imagine the condition, the needs, the character, the

[4] De Tocqueville, *L'Ancien Régime*, Livre II, Ch. 1.

passions of the man, and calculate if you can, the treasures of hatred and envy that have been stored up in his heart.)

'Trésors de haine'—yes, Céline knows how to evoke them, and knew it from *Semmelweis* onwards. Never mind whether Céline had the right to feel innocent in the trilogy: the important point is that he felt so with passion and pulls us to his side. Emotion, conveyed via the spoken language, that is his artistic aim, and if he brings that off, then he has succeeded as an artist.

Let us now have a look at the trilogy, treating it as a whole, and taking it in order of publication. *D'un Château l'autre* (henceforward abbreviated to *Château*), opens with some seventy pages (pp. 3–68) in the manner roughly speaking of *Féerie I*. It has been fashionable to say that here we have Céline going over his grievances again, pouring out scorn and hatred on all and sundry. Well, yes, he does do that. But he does a lot more too, which in the calm reflection of half a generation later seems very reasonable. Take page 12, for instance, where he develops a denunciation of week-end frenzy on the roads out of Paris, or page 19, where he pours scorn on drug firms which inundate doctors with samples of new remedies—here (as from time to time in *Bagatelles*) he rounds on what we have now cosily come to describe as the 'consumer society' in a manner which all right-minded people would approve. So even during his most caustic pieces of complaint and self-justification his mordant humour does not desert him. Here he is on the subject of 'rejuvenating' products:

'Une ampoule avant chaque repas!... vous passez Roméo de choc! la "Relativité en ampoules!... je vous la donne! vous vous rebuvez le Temps, ainsi dire!... les rides!... les mélancolies... les aigreurs! les bouffées de chaleur..." (...) "Madeleine Renaud, Minou, (...) Mauriac, enfin, enfin, enfant de choeur!... nous emmerdant plus! ... tous ses refoulements exposés! une ampoule avant chaque repas! garanti par les Assurances!..." '[5]

('One capsule before each meal!... You become a dynamic Romeo! ... "Relativity in capsules!... I give it to you! you drink yourself back in time, as it were!... the wrinkles!... depressions!... indigestions! hot flushes!..." (...) "Madeleine Renaud, Minou, (...) Mauriac, at last, at long last, a choir-boy!... boring us no more! all his repressions exposed! a capsule before each meal! guaranteed by the (=) Health Service!..." ')

[5] *Château*, p. 20; Minou is a reference to Minou Drouet, child poet of the fifties.

There is a little touch of inimitable genius in the repetition of
'enfin' surrounded by its commas—what an infinity of long
suffered boredom it suggests. . . .

It is wise not to write off the opening seventy pages of this
book, despite what some critics have said. On page 68, however,
the work takes off in a new direction, and (although every now
and again in all three novels, we return momentarily to Céline's
present preoccupation as he writes), we are about to be launched
upon the real subject. It is all triggered off by the onset of illness.
Céline goes down from his house in Meudon one evening in
March toward the banks of Seine to treat an elderly patient,
Madame Niçois. From her windows he sees moored to the quay
an ancient *bateau-mouche* of the type that conveyed tourists up
and down the Seine during his childhood at the beginning of the
century. He goes to investigate and meets an old friend, the
actor Le Vigan, dressed like a gaucho, whom he believes to be in
the Argentine. The *bateau-mouche* with its name *La Publique*
visible in large letters, belongs to Charon, and all its passengers
are dead: Le Vigan is a member of the crew. Their conversation
is full of the inconsequential semi-realism of a dream, and
eventually they quarrel violently—as many years before, says
Céline, in Sigmaringen. Lili, Céline's wife, anxious about him,
comes and takes him home. He has to take to his bed, and stay
there for days, and during his illness he reflects further on the
present and the past before deciding finally to evoke the days in
Germany with Le Vigan at Sigmaringen. On page 102 this all
begins, and the rest of the novel is concerned with the extraordinary milieu of the Vichy government in exile in this
picturesque little town on the upper Danube, overlooked by
the fantastic architectural confusion of the Hohenzollern castle
in which Pétain and his ministers were housed.

The account of Sigmaringen (which Céline spells 'S*i*egmaringen'
throughout) extends over 160 pages (to p. 272), is followed by a
chapter dealing with a journey to Prussia and back (pp. 272–99)
linking with the opening hundred pages. The Sigmaringen
section is at once sinister, comic and pathetic. Sinister when it
deals with the local SS commander von Raumnitz and his
beautiful sadistic levantine wife Aïcha, sinister too in all its
awareness of the coming fate of the French colony as the Allied
armies advance ever nearer. Comic in its description of the
absurdities of some of the Vichy ministers—the admiral Corpé-

chot, for instance, who firmly believes in the imminence of an attack on the French enclave by Russian midget submarines coming up the Danube—and in that of some of the more eccentric refugees from France who have no idea of what awaits them; pathetic in its treatment of the humbler refugees, victims of stupidity very often, girls made pregnant by German soldiers and chased away by their families, a couple of elderly musicians, M. and Mme Delaunys, who had performed at a concert in the German Embassy in Paris, and many others.

Céline is established not in the Château itself, but in a small hotel bedroom nearby, where he has to receive all his patients. Von Raumnitz and his wife have a spacious suite on the floor above and Céline gets to know him quite well through having to give him medical treatment. His whole relationship with von Raumnitz is an illustration of the theme of 'survival'. He never contradicts this all-powerful unscrupulous man who could at any moment have him arrested, tortured, deported, imprisoned, shot. ' "J'écoute, Commandant! Je vous écoute! . . . oh certes, vous avez bien raison!" ' (p. 201) (' "I'm listening, Major! I'm listening! . . . oh certainly, you're absolutely right!" '), is an oft-repeated example of his style of response. But he can some-times risk a slightly macabre joking reply which foreshadows the German defeat which they both expect. Von Raumnitz maintains that all the French inhabitants of the Château are a load of traitors and that if he were to do his duty he'd arrest the lot—and Céline too:

—. . . ils méritent! . . . tous, Docteur! et vous avec! . . . et Luchaire! et votre juif Brinon! et tous les autres juifs du Château: un ghetto, ce Château! . . . vous le savez?
—Certainement, je le sais, Commandant!
—Vous avez l'air de vous en fiche! mais ils vous rateront pas les juifs!
—Vous non plus . . . ils vous rateront pas, Commandant! (p. 201)

('. . . they deserve it! . . . all of them, Doctor! . . . and you too! . . . and Luchaire! and your Jew Brinon! and all the other Jews in the castle: it's a ghetto that castle! . . . you know that?'
'Indeed I know it, Major!'
'You don't seem to care about it much! But the Jews won't fail to get you!'
'Nor you . . . they won't fail to get you, Major!')

Perhaps the most renowned passages of the book are those

directly concerned with the two most controversial political
figures of the Vichy government—Pétain and Laval. Whatever
may be said about these two disastrous figures in French history
(and Céline clearly thought them totally insignificant puppets),
they both had a particular human quality which can command
some admiration—courage. Pétain represents some of the worst
characteristics of the French temperament. He helps to counter
the belief that soldiers make worthy political leaders. The
twentieth-century scene surely provides ample evidence on this:
Eisenhower, Franco, those disgusting Greek colonels, Ghadafi,
and that odious lot in Chile: what a collection! No one like an
army officer given political power to have supreme contempt for
the people he governs. And Pétain was no exception. *But* (and
there's no point in denying this), in 1940 he did seem a kind of
saving father-figure to the majority of Frenchmen. If you could
believe in military honour, and, poor fools, an extraordinary
number of people in 1940 confronted by Nazi Germany still did
believe in it, you could easily persuade yourself that the victor of
Verdun could talk to the victorious German army leaders. If
you believed that, you were wrong. The history of the four years
is categorical. Pétain was a political ignoramus, who understood
neither the French nor the Germans. But at least his rigid, elementary, blinkered military past gave him a kind of prestige that most
Frenchmen in 1940 found reassuring. By 1943 it was different:
but in 1940, at surrender, a Gallup poll would have given Pétain
a majority that no subsequent head of state in France has ever
attained. And even now, there are, deep in the provinces of
France, enough people of that generation still around who would
vote for him again were he alive. . . .

Céline is caustic enough about Pétain at times, and indeed
about the whole Vichy set-up. He does not like military leaders
much, *et pour cause*. But in a quite remarkable passage in *Château*
(pp. 122–35) he pays homage—the term is not excessive—to the
personal courage of Pétain during an air-raid on Sigmaringen.
During a formal walk along the banks of the Danube the Vichy
ministers with Pétain at their head are caught in an Allied air-raid.
They take refuge for a while under the arch of a bridge, the
ministers urinating out of fright—'je connaissais tous leurs
prostates . . . certains avaient de gros besoins . . .' ('I knew all
their prostates . . . some of them had to urinate a lot') comments
the medical officer Céline, and it is Pétain who restores dignity

by giving the order 'En avant' and leading the whole cortège
back to Sigmaringen in impassive military fashion:

> La décision à Pétain qu'a fait sortir tout le monde de sous l'arche!
> . . . comme c'est le caractère à Pétain qui fit remonter l'armée en
> ligne au moment de 17 . . . je peux parler de lui bien librement, il
> m'exécrait . . . je vois encore les balles tout autour . . . la berge, le
> halage, criblés! . . . surtout autour de Pétain! . . . il voyait, s'il
> entendait pas! . . . tout le parcours jusqu'au pont-levis! . . . giclées
> sur giclées! . . . ah, pas un mot! . . . ni lui, ni Debeney . . . parfaite-
> ment dignes . . . et le plus drôle: pas un seul touché! . . . (p. 135)

> (Pétain's decision it was that got everybody out from under the
> arch! . . . just as it was Pétain's character that made the army go
> back up into the line in 1917 . . . I can speak freely about him, he
> detested me . . . I can see the bullets all around . . . the river bank,
> the towpath, riddled! . . . especially around Pétain! . . . he could
> see, even if he couldn't hear! . . . the whole route back to the draw-
> bridge! . . . spurt after spurt! . . . ah! not a word! . . . neither from
> him nor from Debeney . . . perfectly dignified . . . and the funniest
> part of it: not a single person hit! . . .)

For Laval Céline had different feelings: more sympathy fot the
man than he could ever have for Pétain, but the quite detached
portrait of him (especially pp. 235–46) is a mixture of irony and
respect. In his case, too, courage is given its due, as when an
ugly confrontation between an excited crowd at the station and
a detachment of the SA is averted by calm intervention by Laval
(pp. 167–71).

Sigmaringen is a kind of comic opera setting, and apart from
the occasional air-raid the war seems strangely far away for the
time being, despite the troop movements through the station and
the realization that the Allied armies are in Strasbourg. Only the
food shortages and lack of heating affect the day-to-day lives of
the inhabitants. But towards the end of the book Céline accom-
panies a French delegation on a long journey to Prussia to attend
the funeral of a Vichy minister, Bichelonne, who had died in
hospital there, and this journey by special train across Germany,
gives us the first real pictures of the plight of the German cities—
Berlin

> . . . on doit passer par un faubourg . . . enfin des décombres, des
> éboulis . . . un autre éboulis . . . et un autre! . . . c'est Berlin peut-
> être? oui! . . . on aurait jamais cru . . . tout de même, c'est écrit! . . .
> et une flèche! . . . Berlin! (pp. 281–2)

(. . . must be going through a suburb . . . then some ruins, piles of stones . . . another pile of stones . . . and another! perhaps it's Berlin? Yes! . . . couldn't have believed it . . . none the less, there it is written up! . . . and an arrow! Berlin!)

and Ulm:

> . . . un écriteau: ULM . . . c'est tout! . . . tout des hangars crevés autour! . . . tout des ferrailles distordues . . . des sortes de grimaces de maisons . . . et des géants pans de murs ci . . . là . . . en énormes déséquilibres qu'attendent que vous passiez dessous . . . (p. 285)

> (. . . a notice: ULM . . . that's all! . . . flattened sheds around everywhere! . . . mass of twisted metal . . . houses as it were grimacing . . . and gigantic bits of wall here . . . there . . . in enormous disequilibrium waiting for you to pass beneath them.)

Most of the French colony in Sigmaringen ended up in prison or in exile after the war. For Céline it was 'd'un château l'autre'—from the Hohenzollern castle in Sigmaringen to the Vesterfangel prison in Copenhagen. And in the concluding section of the book (pp. 291–9) he looks out from his Meudon house to the military fortress of the Mont-Valérien, full of sinister memories from the time of the *Affaire Dreyfus* onwards, and thinks what a nice quiet job it would be to be its governor:

> . . . de quel calme il jouit pour travailler le Gouverneur du Mont-Valérien! j'aperçois très bien son hôtel, avec ma longue-vue, cette vraiment splendide résidence, gréco-romantique . . . juste ce qu'il me faudrait! . . . (p. 293)

> (. . . what calm he enjoys to work in the Governor of Mount Valerien! I can see his residence very well with my telescope, this really splendid Graeco-romantic abode . . . just what I'd need! . . .)

However, he must return to the reality of his life as a doctor. He thinks of Madame Niçois, the elderly patient whom he went to visit on the day when his own feverish illness began—the day of Le Vigan and the *bateau-mouche*. She has been in hospital, has been discharged as a hopeless terminal cancer case. He must go and visit her daily.

The 432 pages of *Nord* constitute perhaps the most absorbing part of the trilogy. Taking us through a whole series of events and adventures the book leaves an overall impression of a vividly recollected nightmare, of an existence for Céline and Lili over a period of months during which every instant requires

watchfulness, resignation and a will to survive. Céline's 'hallucinatory' manner is much in evidence, but never sustained over long
sections (unlike *Féerie II*), and with it there goes a sharp sense of
humour and a savage awareness of man's cruelty to man. If the
circumstances were not so miserable and depressing, *Nord* would
undoubtedly be a very funny book indeed: as it is there are many
passages where the sense of absurdity is stronger than the sense
of menace and danger, and Céline succeeds in controlling the
balance with consummate skill.

There is in *Nord* a great deal more about the Germans than
in *Château*, where the main subject for comic depiction was the
Vichy set-up in Sigmaringen. Céline regards them throughout
with the utmost distrust, stemming in part from his extreme
Frenchness, but even more from the experience of helplessness
that any relatively suspect foreigner must have felt in wartime
Nazi Germany. Anyone, for any trifling reason, might denounce
you to the authorities, with all the consequent trouble and danger
that might ensue, and therefore he adopts in all circumstances
throughout the book the servile defensive pose seen already in
Château, *vis-à-vis* von Raumnitz and Laval.

There are only three short introductory pages in *Nord* before
we are launched into the setting of the luxurious Simplon Hotel,
Baden-Baden, in July 1944, at the moment of the attempt to
assassinate Hitler. The thirty pages of this section have similarities
with those on Sigmaringen in *Château*. The satirical verve of
Céline is here exercised on the subject of those whose comfort
and ease has not been affected by the war—the privileged very
rich (see above, p. 113). That most of them have started to hedge
their bets by turning against Hitler and moving even in favour of
the Allies is no great surprise. When it becomes known that the
plot against Hitler has failed, the whole lot of them are promptly
turned out of the hotel, Céline, Lili and Le Vigan being despatched
to Berlin, Céline being told that a certain Dr Harras will take
charge of them.

Their stay in Berlin (pp. 331–400) shows first their helplessness
in the face of bureaucracy, the devastation that has already
occurred in Berlin and the great sense of insecurity that they feel
as unwanted suspect foreigners. Céline hesitates before making
contact with Harras, whom he knows to be the head of the
'ordre des médecins du Reich', a powerful figure in the Nazi
regime—and a member of the SS. A very compromising contact

. . . They are obliged, however, to disregard that, and Harras does indeed make plans for them.

They are taken off by him to the village of Zornhof, some seventy miles north-west of Berlin, where they remain for some months and for the whole of the rest of the book (pp. 401–707). The life they lead in Zornhof is a hard one: they are objects of suspicion and even of hatred to some members of this extraordinary community and they need at all times to be vigilant and circumspect. But they are protected by Harras from afar, and by skill and good sense they manage to survive. The war is ever present in everyone's mind now, since Allied aircraft are constantly passing overhead on their way to bomb Berlin and other cities of the Reich, and there is also the realization that eastwards over the limitless plain that stretches all the way to the Urals, the Russian armies are approaching. The inhabitants of Zornhof are a most extraordinary mixture, and it is this which gives rise to the undoubted comic content of the work. There is first the aristocratic family von Leiden. The head of the family is the elderly Rittmeister von Leiden who is a Prussian aristocrat of a traditional kind, cultured, French-speaking, but now more than half off his head and displaying an interest only in three little Ukrainian refugee girls of ten to twelve years of age whose task is to flagellate him. Harmless and kindly except to his dog, Iago, whom he treats with the utmost cruelty, he has a sister, Marie-Thérèse von Leiden, sixty years of age, educated in Lausanne, who is kind to the Célines, but he also has a son who is a legless cripple and whose hatred for them is openly and violently expressed.[6] The cripple's wife, Inge, daughter of the Countess Thor von Thorfels, owner of vast estates in East Prussia, is an equivocal, over-sexed creature who is not to be trusted an inch. Then there are the Kretzers, husband and wife, who run the estate and whose concealed hostility is obvious, and Kracht, an elderly SS member and Harras's contact in Zornhof, not ill-disposed and bribable. Beyond these principal inhabitants there is a remarkable mixed community in Zornhof—the villagers themselves (secretive and distrustful), a contingent of conscientious objectors (silent, well-nourished and employed on the manufacture of coffins), two French deportees of extreme nastiness, and, not far away, a large group of evacuated prostitutes from Berlin. In this exotic and dangerous milieu the Célines have to

[6] He has much of the temperament of Jules in *Féerie*.

fend for themselves as best they can, and they do so with considerable sycophantic skill. And we are continually made aware of the monotonous bleakness of this endless north Prussian plain, still and comfortless, of the noisy presence of hundreds of raucous geese (pp. 409 and 545), of the continual throbbing of the engines of Allied aircraft on their way to and from Berlin (pp. 679–89). A nightmare landscape, in fact, peopled by an eccentric and menacing selection of human beings, forms the subject of this whole long section of the book. There is no 'plot' to *Nord* in the ordinary sense of the word, but there is a continual stream of incident, comic, alarming, macabre, grotesque, punctuated by visits of Harras who speaks freely to Céline and does not hide his views about the imminent collapse of the German resistance.

At the end of the work the Zornhof community is broken up. Rittmeister von Leiden dies, his crippled son is murdered, the Berlin prostitutes are despatched to Hamburg to await the arrival of the Allied armies, Countess von Leiden, Countess von Thorfels, Inge and the Kretzers are sent off by Harras eastwards, ostensibly to the von Thorfels' domain near Königsberg but in fact to almost certain capture by the advancing Russians. Céline and Lili are allowed to make a short journey to the Baltic coast. As the eastward-bound group leaves in a cart drawn by eight cows, *Nord* ends on an argument between Harras and an even more important medical functionary, Werner Göring, about the exact route taken by Napoleon's armies in their retreat from Moscow. Defeat for Nazi Germany is inevitable, and merely a matter of time.

Rigodon opens with the customary introduction in post-war Meudon. This time it is Céline pursued by journalists wanting an interview, harassed by attacks from ex-collaborators and from the extreme left, aware of the need to continue his work, and now convinced of the ultimate fate of the white man. What will the history books say of us in A.D. 3000? 'Les hommes blancs avaient inventé la bombe atomique, peu après ils ont disparu' (p. 729).[7] This thought is further developed. The white man was destroyed in the twentieth century partly by war, but also by alcoholism, cars, over-eating. Some would add, also through religion and other ersatz fanaticisms. France is a country without any future,

[7] See above, p. 114.

containing merely a few undertakers charged with conducting
its obsequies. The future lies with the coloured races; the Chinese
will soon be in Brest—and the sooner the better! After these
declarations (which we shall see are repeated at the end of the
work) Céline takes up again the theme of himself as an entertainer
—seen already in *Guignol's Band II* and in *Féerie I* (see above, pp.
190 and 204):

> . . . moi chroniqueur des Grands Guignols, je peux très honnête-
> ment vous faire voir le très beau spectacle que ce fut, la mise à feu
> des forts bastions . . . les contorsions et mimiques . . . (p. 732)

> (. . . as Grand-Guignol chronicler, I can very honestly show you
> the very fine spectacle which it was, the setting on fire of powerful
> bastions . . . the contortions and mimings . . .)

The rest of *Rigodon* is indeed mainly concerned with the
destruction of the German citadel in those extraordinary weeks
during the summer of 1945.

The link back to the end of *Nord* is made on page 733, and
until very few pages (p. 923) before the end (p. 927) the subject
is the long wandering through Germany undertaken by Céline,
Lucette and (for all except the first stage) their cat, Bébert. First
they leave Zornhof (Kränzlin) for Warnemünde on the Baltic
coast, where they find that there is no chance of crossing to
Denmark. They return via Zornhof (where Bébert and Le Vigan
join them) and proceed via Berlin, Leipzig and Ulm to
Sigmaringen (p. 800). Von Raumnitz is there to meet them: Le
Vigan is sent off to Rome, and Céline, Lili and Bébert are despatched northwards again. Their journey via Hanover, Hamburg
and Flensburg to the apparent safety of Copenhagen takes up the
rest of the book.

The simplest way to describe *Rigodon* is to say that Céline here
brings off what he failed to do in *Féerie II, Normance*. In the earlier
work he was forging a style which was not in full accord with the
truth of the incidents narrated, but which did fit the grandeur of
the collapse of Germany in 1945. Read in isolation, *Rigodon*
impresses less than *Château* or *Nord*—partly because Céline had
no chance to revise and enrich it—but taken as the final section
of the whole trilogy, containing, as it does, many cross references
to the two earlier works, it forms an extremely worthy conclusion.
Once again—as with the two parts of *Guignol's Band*—it is desirable to regard these three novels as an aesthetic unity. *Rigodon*

continues, of course, the main theme of the trilogy, but with special emphasis on the horrors of war and on the power of the instinct of self-preservation. It is a fast-flowing, continuous narrative, having at its centre the journeys of Céline, Lili and Bébert, and with only incidental presentation of other characters.

The first of these episodic characters is encountered at Rostock on the Baltic coast. He is a Greek doctor named Proseidon, qualified in France at Montpellier, with long service in the Soviet Union as a pathologist and as a specialist in leprosy. His wife, also a doctor, escaped from Russia via Romania and he via Poland. His function in the novel is to bring home to Céline the reality of the German situation at this point in 1945. The hospitals of Berlin are over-full: their patients are being evacuated in all directions, including to Rostock which will soon be over-run by the Russian armies. As Proseidon explains, the medical officer in charge at Rostock has a simple Nietzschean method of coping with the influx of invalids: when a train arrives all the passengers are laid out in the snow beside the track. Those who are strong enough limp their way into Rostock; the rest die of exposure. Harras's comment on this (p. 751) is simple and revealing—
' "Oh vous savez il ne peut faire mieux! . . . dans les circon-stances!" ' (' "Well, you know, he can't do better! . . . in the circumstances!" ') These *circonstances* are made clearer and clearer as the Célines continue their journey. On return from Rostock to Zornhof they are despatched to Sigmaringen at the far end of Germany, and on the way there, have to change trains at Berlin Anhalt. The station is in ruins, the express to Ulm absolutely packed with travellers—except for one coach, a sleeper reserved for high officers of the *Wehrmacht*. This coach is suddenly invaded by a mob of infuriated civilians:

J'ai vu bien des choses mais l'Allemagne en furie nihiliste vous oubliez pas . . . tous les mécontents et leurs mômes et les nour-rissons dans les bras à l'assaut du sleeping Wehrmacht (. . .)
    Les officiers comme ils sont, en pyjama, contre toutes ces rom-bières furieuses, qui cassent encore des carreaux, sont forcés de se lever, de sortir, courir rattraper leurs culottes . . . (pp. 759–60)

(I've seen a good few things but Germany in nihilistic fury you don't forget . . . and these discontented people with their kids, and the babes in arms in attack on the army sleeping-car.
    The officers as they are, in pyjamas, against these furious

harridans who are still breaking windows, are obliged to get up and get out, to run and get back their trousers . . .)

A Field-Marshal is evicted from his compartment and ends up travelling amidst the coal in the locomotive tender. The train is attacked by the RAF (pp. 764–7), but even if evicted from the Wehrmacht sleeper *en route*[8] the Célines arrive safely at Ulm, where on the very same day is taking place the official funeral of Rommel, in the presence of Field-Marshal von Rundstedt.[9] The sequence in Ulm (pp. 775–96), including a conversation with von Rundstedt mainly about Bébert, is all pure invention, though it is true that Rommel was buried there on 18 October 1944, and that von Rundstedt was present to deliver the funeral oration.

The separation from Le Vigan at Sigmaringen (p. 803) is in a way a turning-point in the narrative of the trilogy. He has been present from the start of Céline's account of Germany, unimportant in *Château*, very much in the foreground in *Nord*, and is again playing a minor role in most of *Rigodon*. He is one of the few links with the past, with France, with the world of the arts that seemed now so remote and unreal. He is treated throughout by Céline as slightly grotesque, vain, unpredictable and yet not unlikeable: an actor, and as such, never able to come to terms with the reality of his situation, which was that of someone greatly compromised as a collaborator during the Occupation. Little wonder that he declined all comment on Céline's portrait of him in the trilogy. . . .[10]

The journey from Sigmaringen to Flensburg on the Danish frontier is a long nightmare experience, from which can be highlighted a number of remarkable passages, three of which I propose to discuss. After a narrow escape from extermination at Oddort, near Hanover, where the Germans have arranged to concentrate a large number of useless and unwanted persons with the intention of slaughtering the lot by intensive artillery

[8] Céline's comment on this is representative of the attitude he and his wife are forced to take throughout their time in Germany: 'être lépreux a des agréments, vous avez plus à être poli avec personne, on vous fout dehors de partout et vous demandez que ça! . . .' (p. 773) ('there are some pleasant things about being a leper, you don't have to be polite any more to anyone, you get chucked out from everywhere and you don't ask for anything else! . . .')

[9] The circumstances of Rommel's death are of course now well known. Implicated in the plot against Hitler, he was allowed to commit suicide and was given an honourable military funeral.

[10] See *Cahiers de l'Herne*, pp. 424–5.

bombardment, the Célines travel to Hamburg on a train composed
of open waggons loaded with searchlights for defence against
air-raids. But in order to reach this train they have to cross
Hanover on foot, and this gives rise to a remarkable description
(pp. 815–24) of the city in flames after a succession of heavy
air-raids:

> . . . le drôle c'était que sur chaque maison croulée, chaque butte de
> décombres, les flammes vertes roses dansaient en rond . . . vers le
> ciel! . . . il faut dire que ces rues en décombres verts . . . roses,
> rouges . . . flamboyantes, faisaient autrement plus gaies, en vraie
> fêtes, qu'en leur état ordinaire, briques revêches mornes . . . ce
> qu'elles arrivent jamais à être, gaies, si ce n'est pas le Chaos,
> soulèvement, tremblement de la terre, une conflagration que
> l'apocalypse en sort! . . . (pp. 816–17)
>
> (. . . the comic thing was that on each fallen house, each mound of
> wreckage, green, rose-pink flames were dancing in the round . . .
> towards the sky! . . . it must be said that these streets of wreckage,
> green . . . pink, red . . . flaming away, had a much more cheerful
> aspect, really like a festival, than in their ordinary state, sad,
> melancholy bricks . . . something they never manage to be, cheerful,
> but for chaos, upheaval, earthquake, such a conflagration that the
> apocalypse is the consequence! . . .)

We begin to see the sense of the title *Rigodon*. . . .

During the crossing of Hanover, Céline is struck on the head
by a falling brick: the descriptions of chaos and destruction that
follow are in what we have become accustomed since *Voyage* to
call his hallucinatory manner. Céline is careful to give warning to
the reader of the onset of this particular mode and it is wise to
heed these indications. The journey from Hanover, through
Hamburg and across the Kiel canal to Flensburg is a case in
point, since the state of semi-concussion in which the narrator
finds himself—and which is represented in the writing—confers
on the subject matter an aura of fantasy which, paradoxically,
increases and heightens the reality of the experience received by
the reader. Nowhere else in Céline does that perspicacious phrase
by Gide (already quoted) have more aptness—'Ce n'est pas la
réalité que peint Céline; c'est l'hallucination que la réalité
provoque.'[11] The first manifestation of this comes a few miles
north of Hanover. The train stops near an immense heap of

---

[11] *La Nouvelle Revue Française* (April, 1938), (cit. *Cahiers de l'Herne*, p. 469); see
above, p. 90.

twisted metal—100 metres high, says Céline—and on the top of
this 'montagne de ferraille' is perched, upside-down, a huge
six-axled locomotive . . . The passengers, refugees from all over
Europe, speculate on how this could have come about, and the
incident provokes several dense and representative pages of
Céline's late manner at its best (pp. 833–5), in which the sense of
the grotesqueness of war and the helplessness of its victims come
out with full force:

> . . . cette locomotive ventre en l'air! . . . oui! . . . ça aurait pu nous
> arriver, évidemment . . . pas une fois, cent fois! . . . nous et notre
> façon de zigzaguer à travers l'Allemagne . . . tout de même cette
> loco là-haut, si haut? . . . et à l'envers? comme saint Thomas je
> crois que ce que je vois! . . . (. . .) comment ça avait pu se produire?
> . . . une éruption dans cette prairie? une bombe aurait pas suffi à
> projeter et à l'envers un monstre pareil! . . . au haut d'une falaise
> ainsi dire . . . ils discutaient de ça tous . . . je dois dire pas fort,
> plutôt chuchotant . . . par bribes de mots . . . c'était du simili
> allemand . . . ils devaient venir de drôles de pays . . . enfin ils
> n'étaient pas d'accord . . . une explication valait: que c'était un
> dépôt de munitions . . . une autre aussi, bien plausible, que c'était
> un retour d'arme secrète . . . en boomerang, . . . lancée de Peene-
> münde[12] . . . (. . .) en principe c'était pour Londres . . . moi je dois
> dire je voyais pas de raison qu'ils ne recommencent pas . . . qu'ils
> nous envoient pas nous aussi là-haut sur une crête . . . (p. 834)[12]

(this locomotive, belly in the air! . . . yes! . . . could have happened
to us of course . . . not just once, a hundred times! . . . us and our
fashion of zigzagging across Germany . . . all the same. This loco
up there, so high? . . . and upside-down? like St Thomas I believe
only what I see! . . . (. . .) how could it have come about? . . . an
eruption in this meadow? a bomb would never have been enough
to project such a monster and upside down too! . . . on top of a
cliff as it were . . . they were all discussing it . . . I must say not
loudly, more whispering . . . snatches of words . . . it was a kind
of off German . . . they must have come from some funny countries
. . . anyway they weren't agreed . . . one explanation seemed valid:
that it was a munitions dump . . . another, quite plausible, that it
was a misguided secret weapon . . . boomerang . . . launched from
Peenemünde . . . (. . .) meant really for London . . . as for me, I
have to say I couldn't see any reason why they shouldn't start up
again . . . shouldn't send us also up there on top of a crest . . .)

---

[12] It will be remembered that in 1944–5 German propaganda made much of the
'secret weapon' which was to win the war for the Nazis. Peenemünde, an island off
the north German coast, was where the V1 and V2 missiles were developed.

The opening reference to the wanderings in zigzag over Germany gives a further sense to the title *Rigodon*. Shortly after this Céline and Lili encounter a young French girl, Odile Pomaré *agrégée d'Allemand, lectrice* at the University of Breslau, whom Céline sees at once to be suffering from an advanced stage of tuberculosis, and who was despatched from Breslau to Oddort in charge of a group of some fifty defective children. Fortunately for her she never got to Oddort, but by this stage she has lost most of the children (they died of measles? or from something else? the Red Cross at Chemnitz weren't quite sure), and there are only about twenty of them left. At Hamburg these children pass into the care of Céline and his wife. Their expedition into the ruined city in search of food is perhaps the most remarkable passage in the book, and indeed one of Céline's finest pieces of writing. There is first a description of the chaos in the docks:

> pardi, c'est un port! . . . et même: un bassin! un immense . . . avec plein de bateaux . . . mais ces bateaux tous culs en l'air, hélices sorties . . . les nez donc piqués dans la vase . . . je suis pas saoul mais c'est drôle! bouffon! . . . au moins dix navires, et des sérieux, des de quinze mille tonnes au moins . . . (. . .) nous avions vu finir Berlin . . . Ulm . . . Rostock . . . mais Hambourg c'était fini . . . pas que la ville, les docks et la population . . . (p. 846)

> (Good God, it's a port! . . . and indeed: a dock, a huge one . . . full of ships too . . . but these ships all had their arses in the air, propellers exposed . . . noses therefore stuck in the mud . . . I'm not drunk but it's comic! absurd! . . . at least ten ships, and proper ones, of 15 thousand tons at least . . . (. . .) we had seen Berlin finishing . . . Ulm . . . Rostock . . . but Hamburg was finished . . . not only the town, the docks and the inhabitants . . .)

Céline and Lili, with the cat Bébert (very important in this incident), together with an elderly Italian immigrant worker, penetrate the deserted and desolate city that was Hamburg:

> Tas de décombres et morceaux de boutiques . . . et plein de pavés par monticules, en sortes de buttes . . . tramways en dessus, les uns dans les autres, debout et de travers, à califourchon . . . plus rien à reconnaître . . . surtout en plus des fumées, je vous ai dit, si épaisses, crasseuses, noires et jaunes . . . (. . .) pas rencontré un seul vivant . . . je dois dire . . . ils sont partis où? . . . aussi sous des tas de pavés? pourtant c'était du monde Hambourg! . . . (p. 862)

(Piles of wreckage and bits of shops . . . full of heaps of paving-stones, kinds of mounds . . . tramcars on top, all mixed up together, upright, across, astride . . . nothing at all recognizable . . . besides above all masses of smoke, as I've told you, so thick, filthy, black and yellow . . . (. . .) didn't meet a living soul . . . I must say . . . they've gone where? . . . are they also beneath the heaps of paving-stones? Still Hamburg had a big population! . . .)

As they proceed through the ruins of the city, amidst the smoke and fire of the previous night's air-raid, along streets where the tar on the road-surface is still hot and soft from the heat of the incendiary bombs, they suddenly come to a monstrous heap of twisted wreckage (three or four times as high as Notre Dame says Céline, with pardonable epic exaggeration), shaped like an enormous bell, floored with slippery mud, seamed with narrow cracks, through one of which disappears Bébert, followed by all the children, with Céline, Lili and Felipe bringing up the rear. In the open there were dead bodies, a few, mostly odd limbs, especially feet, embedded in the warm tar, but inside this huge grotto there is a strong smell of death, of decomposition. And there is also, intact, a grocer's shop—'une épicerie! . . . comme plaquée contre le fond, prise dans la paroi . . . je dis: épicerie, vous me comprenez: Kolonialwaren . . .' (pp. 866–7) ('a grocer's shop! . . . as though stuck against the back, caught in the wall . . . I say: grocer's shop, you understand me: Kolonialwaren . . .'). Inside they find not only all the food they need, but also the grocer himself, dead, killed by a bomb-splinter:

> . . . là . . . le cadavre . . . je dirais un mort de cinq à six jours . . . il fait froid, il a pas beaucoup fermenté, tout de même il sent . . . je m'approche . . . c'est un commerçant à sa caisse . . . assis . . . la tête, le buste croulés en avant . . . (. . .) mais ce qui m'intéresse: de quoi il est mort? . . . oh, d'un éclat! les boyaux lui sortent par une plaie d'à peu près la hanche au nombril . . . éventré, en somme . . . les intestins et tout l'épiploon sur les genoux . . . (pp. 867–68)

> (there! . . . the corpse . . . I'd say dead five or six days . . . it's cold, he hasn't decomposed much, but he smells all the same . . . I go up to him, it's a tradesman at his cash-desk . . . seated . . . head, bust fallen forwards . . . (. . .) but what interests me: what did he die of? . . . Oh, a splinter! his guts have come out through a wound from his hip to his navel or thereabouts . . . eviscerated in fact . . . intestines and the whole epiploon on his knees . . .)

There are some thirty pages (pp. 846–75) devoted to the evocation of Hamburg: they are worth reading if you want to know what the result of mass bombardment (pre-Hiroshima, of course) is like.

Almost surprisingly there is some kind of a train—open waggons—going northwards and the same group climb aboard. They are halted by a heavy air-raid just short of the bridge that carried the line over the Kiel canal: this once more produces some nine pages (pp. 877–86) from which comes this representative extract containing the title-word of the novel:

> Je vous disais ce pont tremblotait, gigotait même! . . . pourtant pas un pont fragile, une géante armature de poutres et d'arcs . . . vous auriez dit impossible . . . si! et rien qu'aux souffles des explosions . . . le genre de rigodon que c'était! et nous à nous amuser à regarder l'éclosion des mines! . . . violettes! rouges! . . . jaunes! . . . au fond du gouffre . . . sûr, dans le canal! les sous-marins devaient écoper! vous parlez de remous d'air . . . de quoi bien valser nous aussi! . . . (p. 882)

> (I told you the bridge was quivering, jigging up and down even! . . . yet not a fragile bridge, a huge assemblage of girders and arches . . . you'd have thought it impossible . . . yes! and merely from the air displaced by the explosions . . . what a rigadoon it was! and there we were enjoying watching the blossoming of the mines! . . . violet, red . . . yellow! . . . down at the bottom of the gulf . . . of course, in the canal! the submarines must have been catching it! talk about currents in the air . . . enough to make us waltz too! . . .)

The train eventually passes on and reaches the frontier station of Flensburg. After much tension and uncertainty about the chances of being allowed over the frontier into Denmark, Céline and his wife are allowed on board a Swedish Red Cross train which is repatriating Swedish women and children from Germany, after having declared that the group of children they have with them are Swedish—after all, says Céline, they might have been— and the Swedish Red Cross officer who lets them on the train seems to understand the situation too. So the long journey from Montmartre to safety seems to be ending. The smooth and kindly comfort of the special train gliding through the undamaged Danish countryside, across the Great Belt by ferry, landing at Korsör—' "je ferai visiter" ' (' "I'll take you round" ') says Céline (p. 904)—is in tremendous contrast with the nightmare experience of the three weeks since leaving Sigmaringen. Food there is, in plenty, but they are—except for Bébert—almost too exhausted to eat: they are given overcoats to put over the ragged clothes they are wearing: they doze gently during most of the three hours' journey to Copenhagen. If we had no knowledge of what was to follow—the imprisonment, the six years' exile, the long execration—then the end of *Rigodon* would seem mysterious. But for someone who has read *Féerie I* or who knows even the bare facts about the existence of Céline from 1945 to 1951, then the last twenty pages of the book (pp. 906–27) are very clear. Relief there is, of course, at having escaped the perils of bombed Germany, and a sense of amazement at the near normality of life in Copenhagen: they are given ration-cards and are told at the same time that fish, including smoked salmon, is unrationed. But they are still wary and afraid. . . . There are surely microphones in their hotel bedroom. . . . Even the waiter who brings them an early unordered breakfast seems suspect. . . . They have survived so far, indeed, but there is trouble ahead yet. On the far side of the square from their hotel is the French Embassy, closed but untouched by the Germans, and to which the French will soon return.

> . . . mais y aurait bien une après-guerre et retour des Français d'ambassade . . . les Danois peuvent être bien fumiers, ils seront jamais aussi infects que ce qui viendra de France, je veux dire pour nous . . . (p. 918)
>
> (. . . but there would soon be the post-war period and the return of the French embassy people . . . the Danes can be shits alright, but they will never be as disgusting as what will come from France, for us, I mean . . .)

In these pages too there are references to the *Vesterfangel* (the prison where he was to spend some fourteen months—December 1945 to February 1947) and to some of his experiences there. So, the end of the *narrative* of *Rigodon* is muted: survival, thanks to the 'oui mon oncle' technique has been achieved, but the loyal reader who knows *Féerie I* realizes that there are six years to go before the relative calm of Meudon is reached.

However, it would be unlike Céline for an enormous work like the trilogy—over 900 pages in the Pléïade edition—to end on such a note. There is indeed a final defiant, dismissive blast, not unexpected for those who have had occasion to read some of his

late correspondence or who heard his broadcast interview (conducted by an extremely pompous and tedious interviewer called
Albert Zbinden) on Radio Lausanne on 25 July 1957,[13] or who
have heard the record 'Louis Ferdinand Céline vous parle'.[14]
Europe is finished: the supremacy of the white races is over.
The future—for a while—lies with the Chinese, who seem, from
all the evidence, to have the energy, the force and the will for
world domination. They are already in Breslau, they'll soon be
in Paris. But there is one great hope for France, one great defensive mechanism that will defeat even the invading Chinese—
alcohol. The closing lines of *Rigodon*—the last he ever wrote—
indicate that this is the new defence on which the rulers of France
now pin their hopes. . . . It is 1961. De Gaulle's Maginot line is
described in these terms:

A Byzance ils s'occupaient du sexe des anges au moment où déjà les
Turcs secouaient les remparts . . . foutaient le feu aux bas quartiers,
comme chez nous maintenant l'Algérie . . . nos Grands-Transitaires
vont pas s'en occuper du sexe des anges! . . . ni du péril jaune!
manger qui les intéresse . . . toujours mieux! . . . et fins assortis . . .
de ces cartes! de ces menus! ils sont ou sont pas les maîtres du
peuple le plus gourmand du monde? et le mieux imbibé? . . . qu'ils
viennent, qu'ils osent les Chinois, ils iront pas plus loin que Cognac!
il finira tout saoul heureux, dans les caves, le fameus péril jaune!
encore Cognac est bien loin . . . milliards par milliards ils auront
déjà eu leur compte en passant par où vous savez . . . Reims . . .
Epernay . . . de ces profondeurs pétillantes que plus rien existe . . .
(pp. 926–7)

(In Byzantium they were discussing the sex of angels at the moment
when the Turks were battering at the ramparts . . . setting fire to
the poor quarters, just like us now with Algeria . . . our Great
Leaders [lit. 'forwarding agents'] aren't going to be worried about
the sex of angels! . . . nor the yellow peril! eating is what interests
them . . . always better! . . . with appropriate wines . . . what menus!
what meals! are they or are they not the masters of the most greedy
people in the world? and the most drink-sodden? . . . let them come,
let them dare, the Chinese, they won't go further than Cognac! the
famous yellow peril will end up completely drunk and happy, in
the cellars! Moreover Cognac is pretty far . . . milliards and milliards
of them will already have had their lot in going where you know . . .

---

[13] Text reproduced in Pléïade, vol. II, pp. 936–45.
[14] Festival FLD 149: text reproduced in: Pléïade, vol. II, pp. 931–6.

Reims ... Epernay ... from those sparkling depths so that nothing will remain ...)

Is it an accident that the first novel, *Voyage*, and the last, *Rigodon*, end on what is syntactically an identical note—'qu'on n'en parle plus' and 'que plus rien existe'? I doubt it.

CHAPTER NINE

Some Last Words

There was undoubtedly a theatrical talent in Céline. His first piece of substantial 'creative' writing was a play probably written about 1925, first called *Périclès* and later *Progrès*.

This little work, only published in 1978, is a fascinating piece of evidence about our author. One of the first attempts by him to display his imaginative sensibility in literary form, it contains a number of themes that he was to develop much more richly later, and in certain respects it calls to mind the early Ionesco and the Genet of *Le Balcon*. (I hasten to add that there is not the slightest suggestion that these authors could have known it.)

Progrès is a mixture of realism and fantasy. It has little of the linguistic inventiveness of the mature Céline (perhaps he found theatrical dialogue too restrictive), but it does already prepare us for substantial sections of *Mort à crédit*, for his frequent allusions to the art of ballet, and for his delight in moving from an earthy and even cynical presentation of the lives of ordinary people to a highly stylized mood of imaginative unreality, including, in this case, a more than irreverent representation of God, on a cloud in heaven, and visibly yawning at the celestial songs of praise.

The only play published in his lifetime, *L'Eglise*, was also written early on, before *Voyage*, and covers some of the same ground as that novel—Africa, America, the Parisian suburbs—besides having Bardamu as its central character. It had an unsuccessful airing by an amateur company in Lyon in 1936, but not until 1973 did it receive a professional production. This was by *Le Théâtre Chantier* directed by François Joxe (who also played Bardamu). This young company made an extremely good job of it and rightly received very favourable notices in the Paris press. The play came through alright. A series of comic scenes set in the League of Nations in Geneva were over-played and under-directed, but those passages of the play where there is genuine Célinian emotion and fantasy emerged as moving and very theatrically viable, notably the splendid final act. But Céline was convinced that the play was no good, and never tried to write another. He was probably right to devote himself to the less constricted art of the novel, but *L'Eglise* is interesting enough for one to feel some regret at his decision. He did, however, maintain an interest in the art of acting, as is seen in his portrait of Le Vigan in *Nord*, and apparently had plenty of histrionic talent himself, as many of the anecdotal testimonies about him show. His love of ballet was undying, and the various scenarii for ballet which he had devised and published at odd times from 1937 onwards were grouped together and published in 1959 (Gallimard) under the title *Ballets sans musique, sans personne, sans rien*. In this volume we see a Céline who has revealed himself often enough in the novels —and surprisingly in the pamphlets too—but whose existence has been rather neglected by those who have written about him.

Books and articles often allude to disgust, despair, nausea, even lunacy, when referring to Céline, but much more rarely to the fact that he had the most intense and sincere views about what constitutes beauty, grace, delicacy, kindness, humanity. That these views are clearly visible in the novels has been suggested throughout this study: the ballet scenarii (especially, perhaps, the one called *Voyou Paul, brave Virginie*) provide extra evidence for those who wish to seek it. Hard to assess as literature—they do not so aspire—they demonstrate none the less a sensitivity and a belief in human achievement that is present throughout the whole artistic creation of Céline. His *apparent* commitment— through crass stupidity, as we have seen him admit—to an extreme right-wing point of view, has caused much arrant nonsense to have been written about him. From the extreme right have come views of him which are to be rejected as praise for the wrong reasons (the exceptions here being Brasillach and Rebatet, both men of distinction and discernment in matters of literary judgement). From the left have come views of almost greater stupidity (beginning with Sartre), motivated by Céline's entirely understandable contempt for the wetness of the French left since—at least—1935, and justified virtuously by the anti-semitic aberrations of 1937-8. Sartre wrote in 1945: 'Voyez Céline: sa vision de l'univers est catastrophique'.[1] Rubbish.

[1] In *Les Temps Modernes* (December, 1945).

Céline's view of the universe is disturbingly true.[2] It is just that
he does not believe that the meek will inherit the earth. He thinks
that the strong will always prevail. That—up-dating him somewhat—Presidents and Vice-Presidents of powerful nations can be
proved guilty of crimes that would put humble people behind
bars for years and get away with it (he was, in his own day, right
about Stalin . . .). That almost all the desires of the underprivileged are punishable by prison sentences. That Soviet
communism is an imposture, designed to mislead the poor, just
like medieval Christianity. That the consumer society of the
twentieth century is an unspeakable horror, designed to provide
a small fraction of humanity with too much food, too much
drink and too many cars, yachts and aeroplanes. That our rulers,
'Les Grands Transitaires', are not saints working for the greatest
good of the greatest number, but are either incompetent, or
self-seeking, or both. That working-class solidarity is sentimental
nonsense, and that the dream of the European proletariat is to
become bourgeois—like in Switzerland. . . . That war is a device of
the rich for making yet more money and thinning out the poor. . . .

All that sounds pretty gloomy. But is it all false? He also
believes that human beings are capable of infinite tenderness and
self-sacrifice. That the diminution of pain and suffering is the
worthiest of human aims. That war is the greatest of human
stupidities. That courage is a virtue. That there is beauty in the
world about us, in the perfection of the body, in the innocence
of childhood. That once man has accepted the first important
truth about himself—the inevitability of death—then, freed from
fear that breeds cruelty and hatred, he can make sense of his
existence. That art is the highest form of human expression, but
that it can only be created by long and painful effort. That
modern society, because of its materialism, is destructive of joy,
and regardless of health. That what we now call the media have
as their purpose the reduction of all to an equal level of ignorance,
credulity and stupidity. That education should be directed to
awakening in the child a sense of beauty and an understanding
of art. That sex is an excellent thing to indulge in, but boring to
describe.[3] That emotion is more important than intelligence, and
fantasy more interesting than fact.

[2] As Bernanos maintained, see above, p. 19.
[3] See for example, *Rigodon*: 'Tout notre théâtre et nos belles-lettres sont au coït et
autour . . . fastidieux rassassages! . . . L'orgasme est peu intéressant, tout le battage

It is as easy to make out a case for regarding Céline as an idealist in a corrupt society, as it is to do the same thing for La Rochefoucauld. But there is nothing of the *grand seigneur* about Céline: while La Rochefoucauld expresses his disillusion and bitterness with aristocratic distinction, Céline voices his rancour with a polemical violence not seen in French since the sixteenth century and an explosion of popular terminology, yet with studied literary effect. Nowhere is this seen to better advantage than in the short attack on Sartre, *A l'Agité du bocal*.[4] This piece was provoked by the allegation made by Sartre in the third number of *Les Temps Modernes* (1 December 1945), that Céline had been *paid* to express support for the socialist theses of the Nazis. Henri Godard's comment on this is that it was:

> L'affirmation d'un fait qu'*aucune preuve* ni *aucun témoignage* n'étayaient et qui, venant en décembre 1945 au moment où commençait l'instruction du dossier de Céline, pouvait avoir des conséquences judiciaires.[5]

> (The affirmation of a fact supported by not *one proof* and by not *one testimony* and which, coming in December 1945 when the examination of Céline's dossier was beginning, could have had legal consequences.)

Moreover, Sartre had repeated the same allegation in the same words in his *Réflexions sur la question juive* (Gallimard, Paris, 1954). (There might have been some excuse for such behaviour in the excited climate of 1945: in 1954 it amounted to cynical *mauvaise foi* of a shocking kind.) Céline never forgot and did not forgive. For him, Sartre, who had initially been influenced by him (witness an epigraph on the title-page of *La Nausée* taken from *L'Eglise*) and who had tried hard, he alleges, to get him to go and see *Les Mouches* which was performed during the German occupation, was best to be described as an intestinal parasite, a tape-worm (*ténia*), who now had the nerve to emerge from his master's

---

des géants de plume et de cinéma, les millions de publicité ont jamais pu mettre en valeur que deux trois petites secousses de croupions . . . le sperme fait son travail bien trop en douce, bien trop intime, tout nous échappe . . .' ('. . . all our theatre and our art-literature are round and about the act of copulation . . . tedious repetition! . . . orgasm is not very interesting, all the noise made by giants of the pen and the cinema, the millions spent on publicity have never been able to give prominence to more than two, three wigglings of backsides . . . sperm does its work much too subtly, much too privately, it all escapes us . . .')

[4] Most accessible in *Cahiers de l'Herne*, pp. 36–8; see bibliographical note.
[5] Pléiade, vol. II, p. 1076.

rectum and presume to attack him. Apparently the image of *ténia* applied to Sartre (apart from the foregoing reason) was inspired by looking at the depiction of a *ténia* in a pre-war edition of the *Petit Larousse Illustré*: it is certainly true that the small drawing there of the head of the parasite bears a striking resemblance to the author of *L'Etre et le néant*. . . . *A l'Agité du bocal* has been republished in *Cahiers de l'Herne* and is therefore available to a wide public. It is a nice illustration of how to deal with Establishment figures who think self-righteousness authorizes one to print lies with impunity.

I have tried not to conceal the weaknesses and the errors of Céline: one could say that the virulence of *A l'Agité du bocal*[6] is a weakness: that is why I mention it at this point. And to the two lists of his beliefs given above, we must add that for a period of time he believed that the Jews were responsible for the Second World War and that the German army was the best guarantee of peace in Europe. We must thank the Nazis for one thing: Dachau and Auschwitz, *Nacht und Nebel*, have alerted most of the world to the horror and absurdity of racialism. *It was not so in the thirties.* Even if, moreover, anti-semitism (as distinct from anti-Zionism) is mercifully on the wane, it is going to take God knows how long for racial prejudice in general to cease. (And, some would say, it has taken Him, since the days of Noah, quite some time to make up His mind too. . . .)

The disruptive, violent, corrosive side of Céline is what makes

---

[6] This short excerpt is typical. (N.B. Céline chooses to call his victim Jean-*Baptiste* Sartre). 'Assassin et génial? Cela s'est vu . . . Après tout . . . C'est peut-être le cas de Sartre? Assassin il est, il voudrait l'être, c'est entendu mais, génial? Petite crotte à mon cul génial? Hum? . . . c'est à voir . . . oui, certes, cela peut éclore . . . se déclarer . . . mais J.-B.S.? Ces yeux d'embryonnaire? ces mesquines épaules? . . . ce gros petit bidon? Ténia bien sûr, ténia d'homme, situé où vous savez . . . et philosophique! . . . c'est bien des choses . . . Il a délivré paraît-il Paris à bicyclette. Il a fait joujou . . . au Théâtre, à la Ville, avec les horreurs de l'époque, la guerre, les supplices, les fers, le feu. Mais les temps évoluent, et le voici qui croît, gonfle énormément J.-B.S.! Il ne se possède plus . . . il ne se connaît plus . . . d'embryon qu'il est il tend à passer créature . . .' ('Assassin and genius? It's been known . . . after all . . . Perhaps it's the case with Sartre? Assassin he is, he'd like to be, agreed, but genius? Small turd in my genius arse? him? remains to be seen . . . yes, certainly that can blossom . . . become manifest . . . but J.-B.S.? Those foetus' eyes? those mean shoulders? that little pot-belly? tape-worm, yes, human tape-worm, situated you know where . . . and philosopher! that's quite a few things . . . It seems that he liberated Paris on a bicycle. He has . . . in the theatre, in Society . . . played about with the war, tortures, prison, fire. But times are changing, and now he's growing, swelling enormously J.-B.S.! He cannot control himself any more . . . doesn't recognize himself any more . . . from the embryo which he is, he's moving towards becoming a creature!')

him a man of our century, just as Villon was a product of the Hundred Years War. But my contention above all is that he was a great artist, shot through with compassion born of indignation. Original as a stylist, he makes most other narrative writers in France since 1932 look like either virtuous commercial hacks or like specialists in intellectual self-abuse. And why? Because of his concentration on the portrayal of emotion. There is not one creative work from his pen where this is not the paramount consideration.

There is in the interview with Albert Zbinden on Radio Lausanne a particularly fatuous question from the interviewer, which, by some quirk of good fortune, elicited for us a late expression of Céline's real criticism of his contemporaries (Pléïade II: 944–5):

ZBINDEN: Quel mot voudriez-vous prononcer, quelle phrase voudriez-vous écrire avant de disparaître?

CÉLINE: 'Ils étaient lourds.' Voilà ce que je pense. Les hommes en général, ils sont horriblement lourds. Ils sont lourds et épais, voilà ce qu'ils sont. Plus que méchants et bêtes en plus . . . mais ils sont surtout lourds et épais. (. . .) Je connais très bien les finesses. Très très bien. Je n'ai pas besoin d'être éduqué. Je le sais. Et je sais également la beauté des femmes, comme celle des animaux. Très bien. Je suis expert en *ceci*. Mais pour être expert en ceci, il faut vraiment s'en occuper. C'est dans son laboratoire intime qu'on s'occupe de ces choses-là. Je le répète, je trouve surtout les hommes énormément lourds. C'est surtout ça que je trouverais: Dieu qu'ils étaient lourds! Voilà tout ce qu'ils me font comme effet. Surtout quand ils s'imaginent être malins . . . C'est encore pire. C'est tout que je vois.[7]

(ZBINDEN: Is there a word you would like to pronounce, a sentence you would like to write before you disappear from the world?

CELINE: 'They were dim [lit. heavy].' That's what I think. Men in general, they are horribly dim. They are dim and thick, that's what they are. More than nasty and stupid as well . . . But above all they're dim and thick. (. . .) I know delicacy very well. Very, very well. I don't need educating in that. I know it. And I also know the beauty of women like that of animals. Very well. I'm an expert in this. But to be an expert in this, one really has got to take trouble about it. It's in one's intimate laboratory that one has to take trouble about these things. I say again, above all I find men enormously dim. This is the phrase I would find above

[7] See Pléïade, vol. II, pp. 944–5.

all: God how dim they were! That's the effect they have on me.
Especially when they think they're clever . . . That's even worse.
That's all I see.)

All sorts of labels have been attached to Céline—anarchist
(most frequently), pacifist, anti-semite, pro-Nazi, utopian socialist,
nihilist are some examples. None of them fit him exactly, and
some of them are plain wrong. What he certainly was in the
broadest sense, was a poet. He was also a witness of our century,
of one of the most violent and troublous periods in human
history—from 1900 to 1960. He has no overt didactic purpose, but
nearly all he wrote forces a reader to look at the world around
him with increased understanding and awareness, and this effect
is produced by an assault upon the reader's emotions in the first
instance—and upon his intellect only consequentially. The
testimony this witness gives is bleak and even frightening for
the most part, but by no means exclusively so. It may well be
that future generations will regard it as a reasonable picture of
an age studded with such figures as Mussolini, Stalin, Hitler,
Franco and Senator McCarthy, of an age when geographical
names such as Paschendaele, Verdun, Auschwitz, Dachau, Katyn,
Algiers, Vietnam, will remind them of man's goodness to man,
of an age whose most remarkable single technological achievement was tried out with such signal success at Hiroshima and
Nagasaki. They will perhaps find it more rewarding than that of
most of his contemporaries.

Bibliography of Translations of Céline's Works

Much of Céline's work has been translated into English over the years. However most of the translations are out of print. It seems worth listing even these, since they will be still available in various public libraries. The three that are still available are at the end of the list and are asterisked.

Voyage   *Journey to the end of the night* trans J. H. P. Marks: Chatto and Windus: London: 1934, and Penguin Books: London: 1966.

Semmelweis   *Mea Culpa and the Life and work of Semmelweis* trans R. A. Parker: Allen and Unwin: London: 1937.

Mort à crédit   *Death on the instalment plan* trans J. H. P. Marks: Chatto and Windus: London: 1938 and 1966.

Guignol's Band I   *Guignol's Band I* trans B. Frechtman and J. T. Niles: Vision Press: London: 1950 and New Directions: New York: 1954.

*D'un Château l'autre   *Castle to Castle* trans R. Manheim: American Penguin: 1976.

*Nord   *North* trans R. Manheim: American Penguin: 1976.

*Rigodon   *Rigadoon* trans R. Manheim: American Penguin: 1975.

Index

This index covers references to: (a) persons and groups of persons;
(b) the various works by Céline which are discussed in the book;
(c) certain publications – newspapers, journals, etc.